D0389241

Against Dharma

VOLUMES IN THE TERRY LECTURES SERIES
AVAILABLE FROM YALE UNIVERSITY PRESS

The Courage to Be Paul Tillich
Psychoanalysis and Religion Erich Fromm
A Common Faith John Dewey
Psychology and Religion Carl G. Jung
Belief in God in an Age of Science John Polkinghorne
One World Now: The Ethics of Globalization Peter Singer
Reason, Faith, and Revolution: Reflections on the God Debate Terry
  Eagleton
Thinking in Circles: An Essay on Ring Composition Mary Douglas
The Religion and Science Debate: Why Does It Continue? Edited by
  Harold W. Attridge
*Natural Reflections: Human Cognition at the Nexus of Science and
  Religion* Barbara Herrnstein Smith
*Absence of Mind: The Dispelling of Inwardness from the Modern Myth
  of the Self* Marilynne Robinson
Islam, Science, and the Challenge of History Ahmad Dallal
*The New Universe and the Human Future: How a Shared Cosmol-
  ogy Could Transform the World* Nancy Ellen Abrams and Joel R.
  Primack
The Scientific Buddha: His Short and Happy Life Donald S. Lopez, Jr.
Life After Faith: The Case for Secular Humanism Philip Kitcher
*Private Doubt, Public Dilemma: Religion and Science since Jefferson
  and Darwin* Keith Thomson

For a full list of titles in print in the Terry Lectures Series, visit
yalebooks.com or yalebooks.co.uk.

Against Dharma

Dissent in the Ancient Indian Sciences
of Sex and Politics

WENDY DONIGER

Yale UNIVERSITY PRESS

New Haven and London

Published with assistance from the Louis Stern Memorial Fund.

Yale University Press books may be purchased in quantity for
educational, business, or promotional use. For information, please
email sales.press@yale.edu (US office) or sales@yaleup.co.uk
(UK office).

Set in Minion type by Newgen North America.
Printed in the United States of America.

Library of Congress Control Number: 2017952014
ISBN 978-0-300-21619-6 (hardcover : alk. paper)

A catalogue record for this book is available from the British
Library.
This paper meets the requirements of ANSI/NISO Z39.48-1992
(Permanence of Paper).

10 9 8 7 6 5 4 3 2 1

Contents

Preface

The roots of this book stretch down to the first stirrings of my academic career more than half a century ago. My interest in Indian erotics goes back to my Harvard PhD dissertation, "Asceticism and Eroticism in the Mythology of Siva," which I worked on with Daniel H. H. Ingalls at Harvard from 1963 to 1968, and published in book form in 1973. And the materials on the violation of dharma circle back to my Oxford University DPhil on "The Origin of Heresy in Hindu Mythology," written from 1968 to 1973 under the erratic but inspiring supervision of R. C. Zaehner at All Souls and published in book form in 1976. Later I translated Manu and the *Kamasutra* and wrote several articles on related subjects, one on the Three Aims as a whole. I also edited, in 1978, a book in which Friedrich Wilhelm published his essay "The Concept of Dharma in Artha and Kama Literature." At the other end of the chronology, chapter 2 of this book grew out of my book *The Mare's Trap: Nature and Culture in the* Kamasutra (2015, published in the United States as *Redeeming the* Kamasutra, 2016).

When I studied the ancient texts about heresy so long ago, I regarded my work as purely an intellectual exercise, but over the years I was always drawn to texts—and, indeed, to living movements—that challenged the dominant paradigm. By the time I was invited to give the Terry Lectures at Yale in 2014, my work had become so tangled with issues of dissent and subversion that my understanding of the importance of the issues at stake in Indian history had deepened considerably. And so, at the end of the lectures and this book, there is an epilogue (or epitaph) on the subversion of science by religion under the present-day government of India. For Prime Minister Narendra Modi's attempts to replace genuine science with ludicrous religious "science" debases not only the work of real scientists working in India today but a strong ancient tradition of scientific opposition to religious dogma, a tradition that we can see at work in the two great texts that are the subject of this book.

Acknowledgments

I owe thanks first and foremost to Yale University for inviting me to give the Terry Lectures in 2014, for the great honor of following in the footsteps of so many scholars whom I admire, including several treasured friends, some now long gone—Paul Ricoeur, Clifford Geertz, James Hillman, Mary Douglas—but others happily still present—Hans Kung, Donald Lopez, and Philip Kitcher. I am grateful, too, for the warm reception I received at Yale during my stay there, particularly from Stanley Insler and Phyllis Granoff, Greg Sterling and John Donatich, and my sympathetic and wise editor, Jean Thomson Black. In revising the lectures for publication, I benefited enormously from two wonderfully detailed and incisive readers' reports, from Patrick Olivelle and Richard Lariviere, who showed me what the book really should be about and how to clarify the arguments and the structure. (Patrick also taught me a tremendous amount about the *Arthashastra* as he shared with me progressive drafts of his translation.) I owe a great debt to Gavin Flood for inviting me to give a series of seminars on this subject at the Oxford Center for Hindu Studies in November 2013, where I benefited particularly from discussions with Richard Gombrich and Alexis Sanderson. I also learned a great deal from a faculty forum of the Department of South Asian Languages and Civilizations at the University of Chicago on December 2, 2014, with particularly valuable feedback from Thibaut d'Hubert, Whitney Cox, and Steven Collins. I am indebted to Eli Franco for inviting me to lecture at the Royal Academy of Sciences, Leipzig, in 2015, and for his erudite advice about Charvakas and Lokayatikas. Arshia Sattar, as always, kept me well supplied with news reports on the latest outrages in Modi's India. Finally, I am grateful to Susan Neiman for inviting me to present a paper, "Why Hindu Nationalists Insist That Ancient Indians Had Nuclear Weapons," at the conference Fetishizing Science at the Einstein Forum in Potsdam, June 9–11, 2016. I am particularly grateful for valuable feedback from Susan Neiman, Peter Galison, Lorraine Daston, Anthony Grafton, Philip Kitcher, Glenn Most, and Katy Park.

I am grateful to Ravi Singh of Speaking Tiger and to Oxford University Press for permission to publish, in chapter 2, several pages based on previously published materials in *On Hinduism* and *The Mare's Trap (Redeeming the Kamasutra).*

Note on the Translations and Transliterations

I have translated into English all the Sanskrit words in this book with the exception of the following essential Sanskrit terms (in addition to the names of some texts and their authors): "dharma" (which is already really an English word, though usually misused) and "adharma" (non-dharma, anti-dharma), "kama" and "artha," *shastra, moksha, purva paksha, acharya, bhakti, sanatana, sadharana,* Charvaka, Lokayata, and Nastika/Astika. These are the stars of this drama, and I think I can trust my intelligent readers to get to know them by their first names. I have not italicized the three basic terms "dharma" (and "adharma"), "kama," and "artha," nor have I used conventional diacritical marks for these or other Sanskrit words (except in citing the works of other scholars and in the notes and bibliography).

All translations of the *Kamasutra* in this book are my own, based on the translation that I did (with Sudhir Kakar) in 2002, and all translations from *The Laws of Manu* are also my own, based on the translation that I did (with Brian K. Smith) in 1991. Besides general rewording, the main change I have made in both cases is to leave "dharma," "artha," and "kama" in Sanskrit rather than translating them into English, as the published translations do. Translations from the *Arthashastra* of Kautilya are also my own, though I have leaned heavily on the published translation by Patrick Olivelle. Translations from other Sanskrit texts are my own unless otherwise indicated.

Timeline

Relevant Events and Historical Developments

c. 1500 BCE   The *Rig Veda* is composed

c. 600–400 BCE   The *Upanishads* are composed

c. 500 BCE   The *Shrauta-sutras* are composed

c. 486 BCE   Gautama Shakyamuni, the Buddha, dies

327–325 BCE   Alexander the Great invades northwest South Asia

c. 324 BCE   Chandragupta founds the Mauryan dynasty

c. 300 BCE–300 CE   *Grihya-sutras*, some *dharma-shastras*, and the *Mahabharata* are composed

c. 265–232 BCE   Ashoka reigns

c. 250 BCE   The Third Buddhist Council takes place at Pataliputra

c. 200 BCE–200 CE   More *dharma-shastras* and the *Ramayana* are composed

c. 185 BCE   The Mauryan dynasty ends

c. 185 BCE–73 BCE   The Shunga dynasty is in power

c. 166 BCE–78 CE   Greeks, Scythians, Bactrians, and Parthians enter India

c. 78–144 CE   The Kushanas are in power

c. 100 CE   "Manu" composes his *dharma-shastra*

c. 112–144 CE   Kanishka rules

c. 150 CE   Rudradaman publishes the first Sanskrit inscription at Junagadh

c. 200 CE   Kautilya composes the *Arthashastra*

c. 300 CE   Vatsyayana Mallanaga composes the *Kamasutra*

c. 320–550 CE   The Gupta Empire is in power

c. 750–1500   Medieval Puranas are composed

c. 788–820   The philosopher Shankara lives

1021   The Ghaznavid (Turkish) Muslim Empire is established

1526   Babur founds the Mughal Empire

1556–1605   Akbar rules

1600   Queen Elizabeth I charters the British East India Company

1828   Rammohun Roy founds the Brahmo Samaj

1858   The British Viceroy officially replaces Mughal rule [and the East India Company]

1947   Indian Independence is achieved; Partition takes place

2014   The Bharatiya Janata Party and Narenda Modi are elected

Against Dharma

1

The Three Human Aims

The Time and Place

Between the fall of the Mauryan Empire in the second century BCE and the beginning of the Gupta Empire in the fourth century CE, India experienced a vivid influx of other cultures.[1] There was constant trade from Greece, Central Asia, West Asia, the ports of the Red Sea, and Southeast Asia.[2] Indians exported their culture to the Mekong Delta, the Malay Peninsula, Sumatra, and Xinjiang; to Afghanistan and Vietnam; to the Gobi Desert. Trade flowed along the mountainous northern routes through Central Asia on the silk route and by sea to the great ports of South India. A book with the delicious title of *The Periplus of the Erythraean Sea*, composed by an unnamed Greek in about 80 CE, gave detailed navigational instructions to those planning to sail to what is now Gujarat, and thence to gain access to the Deccan, where one could buy and export such specialties as ginseng, aromatic oils, myrrh, ivory, agate, carnelian, cotton cloth, silk, Indian muslins, yarn, and long pepper. The Indians, in return, imported fine wines (Italian preferred) and cheap ointments, and, for the king, singing boys, beautiful maidens for the harem, thin clothing of the finest weaves, and the choicest ointments.[3]

There were no great dynasties then; the Scythians and Kushanas (who invaded and ruled India between c. 166 and 78 BCE and between 78 and 150 CE, respectively) were bluffing when they used the titles "King of Kings" and "Son of God," on the precedent of the Indo-Greeks. Small kingdoms now began to dominate the political scene and to have enough of a sense of themselves to be almost constantly at war with one another. The ancient Indian king was called "the one who wants to conquer" (*vijigishu*), which, together with the "circle" theory of politics, according to which the country on our border is our enemy, and our enemy's enemy is our ally, and so forth, made for relentless aggression. Kings killed for thrones; parricide was rampant.

Some European historians have regarded this period as India's Dark Age, dark both because it lacked the security of a decently governed empire (the Kushanas very definitely did not rule the waves) and because the abundant but hard-to-date sources leave historians with very little available light to work with. Some Indian nationalist historians regarded it as the Age of Invasions, the decadent age of non-Indian dynasties when barbarians (*mlecchas*) continually slipped into India.

But it looks to us now rather more like a post- and pre-imperial Age of Diversity, a time of rich cultural integration, a creative chaos that inspired the scholars of the time to bring together all their knowledge, as into a fortified city, to preserve it for whatever posterity there might be. The art and literature of this period are far richer than those of either of the two empires that framed it, the Mauryas and the Guptas. The rule of undistinguished, often non-Indian kings opened up the sub-continent to trade and new ideas.[4] Women, including women from marginal social positions (such as courtesans), patronized Buddhists and Jains. The widespread public recognition of such women both as donors and as renouncers also had an impact on the role of women within Hinduism.

The Kushana centers of Gandhara and Mathura produced Hindu images that served as paradigms for regional workshops for centuries to follow. Yet there were also religious challenges; the Kushana king Kanishka (c. 127–50 CE) encouraged a new wave of Buddhist proselytizing, and the Fourth Buddhist Council was held under his patronage. The gloriously miscellaneous quality of the culture of the time is epitomized in the reliefs on the great Buddhist *stupa* (reliquary mound) at Amaravati, carved during this period in the western Deccan. It depicts scenes of everyday life that defy denomination: musicians, dancers, women leaning over balconies, horses cavorting in the street, elephants running amok, bullocks laboring to pull a heavy (but elegant) carriage, ships with sails and oars. In a nice moment of self-referentiality (or infinite regress), there is a carving depicting masons constructing the *stupa* that depicts a scene of masons constructing the *stupa*.[5]

The Sciences and the *Shastras*

This rich intellectual vortex, including the rising challenge of Buddhism, inspired intellectuals (primarily but not only Brahmins) to circle their wagons in a great ingathering of their own knowledge systems preserved in Sanskrit texts. The two great Sanskrit epics, the *Mahabharata* and the *Ramayana,* were composed during this long period *entre deux empires,* and so were the texts called *shastras.*[6]

Shastra means "discipline," in both senses of the word, "knowledge system" and "command" (the root is actually related to the English "chastise"). It also designates a text that contains such knowledge. So *ashva-shastra* in general means the science of breeding and training horses (*ashva* corresponds to the Latin *equus*), while *the Ashva-shastra* attributed to a particular author is a textbook about the breeding and training of horses.

Ancient Indian sciences lived in the *shastras*. *Shastras* had been composed from about the sixth century CE.[7] They began as sciences that were appendixes to the Vedas, the oldest sacred texts of India, composed in about 1500 BCE. These sciences were called "the limbs of the Vedas" (*vedangas*), intrinsically connected to religion. Grammar (the queen of Indian sciences, as theology was once in Europe) was needed to explain the meanings of complex Vedic texts, mathematics to calculate the intricate proportions of Vedic ritual structures, and astronomy (as well as astrology) to determine the auspicious days for Vedic rituals. The *Kamasutra,* the textbook of sexuality, assumes that both priests and ordinary people use the paradigmatic Sanskrit scientific texts of grammar and astronomy for religious purposes (1.3.5).[8]

But the sciences soon developed secular as well as religious uses and eventually branched into separate schools. The *shastras* covered a number of fields, including—in addition to grammar, mathematics, and astronomy and the care, feeding, and training of horses and elephants—architecture, medicine, and metallurgy. India also had logic and knew how to argue from evidence. I would also contend that the textbooks of politics and erotics, the main subjects of this book, are proof that ancient India had psychology, anthropology, and sociology. As for the sort of science that produces useful tools that work—

that is, technology—India had wonderful telescopes, which eventually did enable its astronomers to predict eclipses. These schools amassed truly encyclopedic knowledge, in a spirit well defined in a famous verse from the *Mahabharata,* the great Sanskrit epic (with over 100,000 verses): "Whatever there is here . . . is also found elsewhere; but what is not here is nowhere" (1.576.32; 18.5.38). This is the *shastras'* totalistic claim, despite the fact that the seemingly exhaustive lists of everything under the sun often insist that they offer only a few representative examples.[9]

The foreign flux on the one hand loosened up and broadened the concept of knowledge, making it more cosmopolitan—with more things to eat, to wear, to think about—and at the same time posed a threat that drove the Brahmins to tighten up some aspects of social control. The formulation of encyclopedic knowledge recognized the diversity of opinion on many subjects; at the same time, some, but not all, of the *shastras* closed down many of the options that Buddhism had opened up for women and the lower castes. Both the diversity encompassed by the *shastras* and their authors' drive to control that diversity are best understood in the context of the turbulent period in which they were composed.

The Three Aims

Near the end of this period, the three great *shastras* devoted to the three human aims (*purusharthas*) took their final form. In order to have a full life, every person (particularly, but not only, a male person) was supposed to achieve a balance between the three elements of this triple path, called the Triad or Trio (*tri-varga*): dharma, artha, and kama.[10] Dharma includes duty, religion, religious merit, morality, social obligations, justice, righteousness, and the law—the good life.[11] Artha is money, political power, profit, and success—the high life. (Artha can also designate gain versus loss; advantage; the meaning of a word; or a goal or aim, as in the three human aims.) Kama represents love, desire, and pleasure, not merely sexual pleasure but more broadly sensual pleasure—music, good food, perfume—the fine life.

For assonance, one might call them piety, profit, and pleasure; society, success, and sex; or duty, domination, and desire. Or perhaps the superego, the ego, and the id.

They have been known as a trio from at least the time of the *Mahabharata*. Near the very end of that long, long poem, the poet cries out: "Artha and kama come from dharma; why is it not practiced?" (12.123.1–19; 18.5.49). Earlier in that text, the god of Dharma incarnate, in disguise, posed a riddle: "Dharma, artha, and kama are opposed to one another; how can these perpetual opposites unite in one place?," to which the answer is "When dharma and a wife submit each to the other, then all three—dharma, artha, and kama—come together" (3.313.102–3). The Triad remained important through the centuries. Yashodhara, the thirteenth-century commentator on the textbook of sexuality, told the following story about it at the very start of his commentary:

> The three aims of a person are three divinities. . . . And there is textual evidence that they are in fact divinities. For the historian tells us: "When King Pururavas went from earth to heaven to see Indra, the king of the gods, he saw Dharma, Artha, and Kama embodied. As he approached them, he ignored the other two but paid homage to Dharma, walking around him in a circle to the right. The

other two, unable to put up with this slight, cursed him. Because Kama had cursed him, Pururavas was separated from his wife, Urvashi, and longed for her in her absence. When he had managed to put that right, then, because Artha had cursed him, he became so excessively greedy that he stole from people of all classes. The Brahmin priests, who were upset because they could no longer perform the sacrifice or other rituals without the money he had stolen from them, took blades of sharp sacrificial grass in their hands and killed him. (1.1.2)

There is a parallel to this story in the Greek myth of Paris, who, forced to choose among three goddesses, chose Aphrodite (= Kama) over Hera and Athene (roughly = Dharma and Artha), who cursed him. Dharma and Kama often appear as mythological characters, though not together in the same story;[12] but Artha, to my knowledge, is seldom if ever personified. Yashodhara refers elsewhere, briefly, to the Pururavas story (which was well known in India as early as c. 1500 BCE)[13] when he remarks that "Artha, when it overrides all else, impedes dharma and kama—as it did for Pururavas" (1.2.41). Indeed, the story tells us how compelling and dangerous artha and kama can be, but also how dharma, especially when defended by Brahmin priests, is the most powerful of all. (It also tells us that Brahmins are capable of violently defending their right to be paid for performing rituals.) Not everyone, however, believed this story or the assumptions about the supremacy of dharma that underlie it. Many people—who included the authors of the oldest texts of the sciences of artha and kama—did not swallow the myth at all.

The Three Texts

The Brahmin imaginary has no canon, but if it did, that canon would be the body of *dharma-shastras,* which, from the third or second century BCE, spelled out the dominant paradigm with regard to women, animals, castes, and much else, the mark at which all subsequent antinomian or resistant strains of Hinduism aimed. In the science of dharma, the *dharma-shastra* attributed to Manu is the most famous. Manu's text consists of 2,685 verses on topics as apparently varied—but actually intimately interrelated in Hindu thought—as the social obligations and duties of the four classes (Brahmins, the class from which priests are drawn, at the top; then the royal/ warrior class; then merchants; and then servants) and hundreds of castes; the proper way for a just king to rule and to punish transgressors in his kingdom; the appropriate social relations between men and women of different classes and of husbands and wives in the privacy of the home; birth, death, and taxes; cosmogony, karma, and rebirth; ritual practices; and such details of everyday life as the penance for sexual improprieties with one's teacher's wife. There are many other dharma texts, with significantly different ideas on many of the subjects that concern us here; some are older, some later than Manu. (The *Arthashastra* and the *Kamasutra* cite predecessors whose works did not survive.) But Manu's text remains the gold standard that most later texts either accepted or rebelled against, and it provides a base against which we may measure the two other texts that are our main concern. Moreover, Manu is the only one of the three authors whose night job was as a mythological figure: Manu is recognized by many texts as the son of the Creator and was (by his own testimony in his *dharma-shastra*) present at the original creation; he is also the ancestor of all humans (who are called *manava,* after him). His authority is therefore of a very different nature from that of our other two authors.

Artha-shastra as a generic term refers to the science of politics, government, and economics, while the *Arthashastra* attributed to Kautilya is a single text, a compendium of advice for a king, combining much technical information on the running of a kingdom with a good deal of thought on the subject of human psychology. (Amartya Sen suggests that its title can be translated as *Economics*,[14] but of course Sen is an economist.) Kautilya's *Arthashastra* is even more outstanding for artha than Manu is for dharma, for where there are many *dharma-shastras,* the *Arthashastra* has no real rivals: there are only a very few other *artha-shastras,* all considerably later and nowhere near as comprehensive.

Kama-shastra is the science of erotics,[15] and the *Kamasutra* of Vatsyayana belongs to the general class of *shastra*s but is called a *sutra,* "a treatise" (*sutra,* literally a "string" of aphorisms, is cognate with the English word "suture"), the older term for a scientific text. The *Kamasutra* is the oldest extant Hindu textbook of erotic love (others came much later, and omitted everything but the sexual core) and one of the oldest in the world. It is not, as most people think, a book about the positions for sexual intercourse.[16] Its seven books cover the art of living—finding a partner, maintaining power in a marriage, committing adultery, living as or with a courtesan, using drugs—and also the positions for sexual intercourse.

These three texts, but particularly the *Arthashastra* and *Kamasutra,* supply the main substance of this book. Manu serves primarily as a baseline from which the other two texts diverge.

Hindus have traditionally tended to group important concepts into triads, with an outlying, contrasting fourth.[17] And so, after a while, some people began to speak of a Quadruple

Set (*chatur-varga*) or Quartet of human aims, with a fourth aim consisting of *moksha* or release (from the eternal cycle of rebirths). In fact, the much-quoted *Mahabharata* verse about totality actually says, "Whatever there is here about dharma, artha, kama, and *moksha* is also found elsewhere; but what is not here is nowhere" (1.576.32; 18.5.38), regarding the Quadruple Set as the equivalent of the sum total of possible knowledge.

But *moksha* does not concern us much, because the *Kamasutra* speaks of it only twice, once when it simply assimilates *moksha* to dharma and once when it describes the courtesan's success in achieving the release (*moksha*) of an unwanted lover (6.3.44), a strikingly profane use of the word. The *Arthashastra,* too, never mentions *moksha* in a religious context, but uses it only to designate the release from marriage—divorce (3.4.27, 30). The unusual use of this highly religious word to designate sexual separations in both texts is surely a bit of blasphemy that the *Kamasutra* picked up from the *Arthashastra*. In any case, *moksha* is not part of the worldly realm of the *shastras*. But it is always there in the background, explicitly at considerable length in Manu (1.114; 2.243; 6.35–37, 40–44, 58, 74–81, 85; 12.83–104) and implicitly in the other two, as a final metaphysical option.

In the broadest sense, the entire Triad is religious, since the Hindu view of the meaning of human life includes within its domain artha and kama as well as dharma. But only dharma (which is often translated as "religion") is truly concerned with religion in the narrower sense of morality, theology, and social ethics. Artha and kama are entirely this-worldly, while dharma, though also primarily this-worldly, always works within the shadow of the other world. (*Moksha* is entirely other-worldly.) And there is another significant distinction: dharma is communal, while kama and artha (and *moksha,* too, for that matter) are individual. Pleasure and desire (kama) are always personal. As for artha, in the *Kamasutra*, artha primarily means the money that individuals (playboys, courtesans, wives and husbands) use for kama, while in the *Arthashastra* the king's concern is primarily with his own artha, his own individual survival and thriving, and only secondarily with the thriving of the community, insofar as that is essential to his own success. Yet dharma is what binds all three texts together.

The History of the Three Texts

The history of the three texts is a labyrinth of mutual influences.

The *Arthashastra* is generally attributed to Kautilya ("Crookedness"),[18] also called Vishnugupta ("Protected by the god Vishnu") and Chanakya ("Chick-pea"), the brilliant chief counselor who helped the Mauryan emperor Chandragupta win and maintain a great empire, beginning in the fourth century BCE. And indeed, there may have been some sort of rudimentary *Arthashastra* at the time of the Mauryas, now lost to us. But the actual text of our *Arthashastra* first began to be compiled in the middle of the first century CE,[19] when someone who called himself Kautilya composed the text for a king and his principal advisors and ministers as a guide in the management of economic and military affairs. It was probably handed down and frequently recopied within court and government archives.

The science of artha probably began as a subcategory of the science of dharma and broke away,[20] as the *shastras* in general broke away from their religious base. In any case, sometime in the second half of the second century CE, someone who called himself Manu composed a *dharma-shastra*. This was neither the first nor the last of this genre, but it was the first to incorporate discussions of governance, royal duties, and law, subjects that actually take up more than a third of the text. For these subjects, Manu borrowed heavily from Kautilya or from an older source of the *Arthashastra* that was originally attached to a dharma text.[21] And then, sometime after the second century CE, another scholar updated Kautilya's text by adding material from Manu and other *dharma-shastras*. Finally, right before the Gupta period (in the fourth century CE), more of the dharma materials, particularly pro-Brahmin materials, may have been added, together with verses at the end of each chapter. This is the *Arthashastra* text that we have, a palimpsest starting from a now lost *Arthashastra,* which fed into a *dharma-shastra* by Manu, which fed, in turn, into a revised *Arthashastra.* By this time, the *Arthashastra* was no longer in the hands of government administrators but rather under the control of Brahmin scholars.

The *Kamasutra* was probably composed sometime in the second half of the third century CE, in North India.[22] Virtually nothing is known about the author, Vatsyayana Mallanaga, other than his name and what little we learn from the text. The *Arthashastra* is about a century older than the *Kamasutra* and gives no evidence of knowledge of any *Kamasutra.* The *Kamasutra* mentions a text about artha, twice explicitly (1.1.7 and 1.2.10) and elsewhere implicitly, but not necessarily Kautilya's: it attributes the text on artha to the mythical Brihaspati, chief counselor to the king of the gods, rather than to the quasihistorical Kautilya.[23] Moreover, the *Kamasutra* regards this artha text primarily as a study of merchants making money and superintendents of commerce and agriculture (1.2.9–10), not as a guide for rapacious kings.[24] In general, while the *Arthashastra* is deeply suspicious of kama in any shape or form, the *Kamasutra* has respect for artha as a goal, especially for courtesans.

So the first version of the *Arthashastra* came first (middle of the first century CE); Manu (second half of the second century CE) borrowed from that version of the *Arthashastra* and then, in turn, influenced the second recension of the *Arthashastra* (early third century CE); and that compendium of *Arthashastra* and Manu influenced the *Kamasutra* (late third century CE).

Ranking the Three Aims

The Three Aims are generally said to be mutually supportive, a unified whole, but this is a pious fiction. Artha and kama are in direct conflict with certain aspects of dharma from the very start. Hierarchical ranking is the most basic and pervasive form in which ancient Hindu texts make sense of the world,[25] and the Three Aims are no exception. All three texts (Manu, the *Arthashastra,* and the *Kamasutra*) rank the Triad in the same way—on the surface, at least. All three texts say that all three aims should be present, and balanced, in a good life. That such a general outlook is not limited to ancient India becomes immediately apparent when we consider, for instance, a statement that the Reverend Martin Luther King Jr. made in Atlanta on August 16, 1967: "What is needed is a realization that power without love is reckless and abusive and that love without power is sentimental and anemic. Power at its best is love implementing the demands of justice. Justice at its best is correcting everything that is against love."[26] Translating the relevant terms into their approximate Indian equivalents yields: "What is needed is a realization that artha without kama is reckless and abusive and that kama without artha is sentimental and anemic. Artha at its best is kama implementing the demands of dharma. Dharma at its best is correcting everything that is against kama." It is therefore hardly surprising that the Indian texts, too, assert this general agreement among the three aims.

More surprising is that, at first glance at least, all three texts rank dharma at the top of the Triad. This view is widespread in ancient India. The *Mahabharata* tells us that the good king held dharma supreme, above kama and artha (1.94.4). The other great Sanskrit epic, the *Ramayana* (c. 200 BCE–200 CE), assumes this ranking when Prince Rama criticizes his father for giving in to his young wife's sexual blackmail and putting her son on the throne, in violation of the dharma of royal succession: "When I reflect on the disaster and my father's change of heart, it seems to me that kama is a more potent force than either artha or dharma" (2.47.8–10). This reversal of the usual order is a powerful way of saying that his father's values were entirely upside down.

Manu at first seems to be quite open-minded about the ranking: "Dharma and artha are said to be better, or kama and artha, or dharma alone, or artha alone here on earth; but the fixed rule is that the Triad is best" (2.224). (Even here, kama gets short shrift, never said to stand on its own.) And elsewhere Manu says, "[The householder] should renounce artha and kama if they should conflict with dharma, and even dharma when it results in future unhappiness or arouses peoples' indignation" (4.176). But at the end, Manu shows his true colors: "Kama is the mark of darkness, artha is said to be the mark of energy, and dharma the mark of lucidity, and each is better than the one before it" (12.38).

Kautilya at first, and on several subsequent occasions, mentions only two aims, dharma and artha, as the goals of knowledge (1.2.9), logical thinking (1.2.11), and the aspirations desired in the crown prince (1.17.33). When he first mentions the Three Aims, he lists them in the usual order, dharma first and kama last (1.4.11). He insists that dharma is the root of artha and kama its fruit (9.7.81). And he seems to rank them in the pious order when he returns to the subject and expands upon it. First he cites the usual politically correct statement about the desirable balance between the aims: "[The king] should enjoy kama as long as it does not conflict with dharma or artha; he should not go without happiness. Or he should enjoy the Three Aims equally, each enhancing the others. For if one, among dharma, artha, and kama, is enjoyed too much, it harms itself as well as the other two" (1.7.3–5). But then he stands up for what he really cares about: artha: "'Artha alone is supreme,' says Kautilya, 'for artha is the root of dharma and kama'" (1.7.6–7). Elsewhere, too, he remarks that artha, dharma, and kama are the Triad, and that "each (in that order) is better to experience than the one after it" (9.7.60–61).

Kautilya returns to the Triad at the very end of the book, this time without giving pride of place to artha: "This text promotes and protects dharma, artha, and kama, and condemns [acts] that oppose dharma (adharma), those that oppose artha (anartha), and hatreds (vidvesha)" (15.1.72).[27] This use of "hatred" as the opposite of kama—in place of the word that we might expect in this sequence, akama, "opposing kama"— is picked up by the Kamasutra, which also, significantly, here ranks artha above dharma, just as the Arthashastra usually does: "The three gains are artha, dharma, and kama, and the three losses are loss of artha (anartha), loss of dharma (adharma), and hatred (vidvesha)" (6.6.5–6). This is an unusual divergence from the expected pattern, and the convergence of the two texts in these two passages strongly suggests that the Kamasutra has gotten it from the Arthashastra.

The Kamasutra also echoes the conventional idea of the equality and mutuality of the Three Aims and, conventionally, gives dharma pride of place. Vatsyayana begins the whole book by invoking dharma, artha, and kama and asserting "the mutual agreement among the three" (1.1.3). When he returns to the subject, at the start of the second chapter, he says: "A man's life span is said to be a full hundred years. By dividing his time, he cultivates the Three Aims in such a way that they enhance rather than interfere with each other" (1.2.1). But then the *Kamasutra* goes on to develop a rather idiosyncratic view of the Triad: "Childhood is the time to acquire knowledge and other kinds of artha, the prime of youth is for kama, and old age is for dharma and *moksha.* Or, because the life span is uncertain, a man pursues these aims as the opportunity arises, but he should remain celibate until he has acquired knowledge. . . . When these Three Aims—dharma, artha, and kama—compete, each is more important than the one before it. But artha, in the form of wealth, is the most important aim for a king—because it is the basis of social life— and for a courtesan" (1.2.2–6, 14–15). The attempt to correlate the Three Aims with three ages is awkward: what does childhood have to do with the serious business of artha? (Yashodhara here lamely suggests, "There is no rule against acquiring something such as land during this period.") And *moksha* is squeezed in, in the slot allotted to the third aim, dharma, though Vatsyayana has explicitly said that there are only three aims and never discusses *moksha* as an aim again. It is striking that the *Kamasutra* here gives pride of place not to its own subject, kama, but to artha, the subject of the *Arthashastra,* a clear carryover from the parent text. And it lists artha first and dharma last in the first of the three verses at the end of the second chapter:

A man who serves artha, kama,
and dharma in this way

wins endless happiness that has no thorns,
in this world and the next. (1.2.39)

But then it goes on to invoke the obligatory balance among all three:

Knowledgeable people undertake a project
that does not make them worry,
"What will happen in the next world?"
Or "Is this a pleasure that will not erode my
    power?"
Undertake any project that might achieve
the three aims of life, or two, or even just one,
but not one that achieves one
at the cost of the other two. (1.2.40–41)

And, like the *Arthashastra*, the *Kamasutra* returns to the Three Aims at the very end of the book:

A man who knows its real meaning
sees dharma, artha, and kama,
his own convictions, and the ways of the world
for what they are, and he is not driven by passion.
A man who knows the real meaning of this text
guards the state of his own dharma, artha, and
    kama
as it operates in the world, and he becomes
a man who has truly conquered his senses.
    (7.2.53, 58)

Again Vatsyayana privileges over kama both dharma—which, as we will see, he has relentlessly ignored throughout his book

—and artha, the subject of the text on which he has based his own text. But this is just window dressing.

Intertextuality

The *Arthashastra* and Manu quote one another, and the *Kamasutra* quotes the *Arthashastra*. We have seen that someone added bits of Manu to the *Arthashastra* (and vice versa) and will soon see that the *Kamasutra* borrowed heavily from the *Arthashastra*. This sort of historical conflation is a common phenomenon among ancient Indian texts. These texts grew up side by side, and they exist together in one world. They are all in conversation.

For example, for Manu, a son gives a man a kind of rebirth on earth and an afterlife (9.106–7, 130, 137–38); for Kautilya, a son is a danger to his father the king and irrelevant to the afterlife, since there is no afterlife; for Vatsyayana, a son is simply irrelevant.[28] (In the world of *moksha*, a son is a problem, a shackle.) Manu is very concerned that the extremely low (Dalit) Chandala caste should have no contact with other Hindus (10.51–55); Kautilya mentions in passing that a non-Chandala is forbidden to use a Chandala well (1.14.10); Vatsyayana never mentions any Dalit castes at all. Manu devotes most of an entire book (6) to telling us how to be an ascetic, how ascetics should behave, and how they should be treated; Kautilya tells a spy how to pretend to be an ascetic; and Vatsyayana tells us to employ an ascetic as a go-between. The three texts are manipulating the same cultural conventions in different ways. This is intertextuality with a vengeance.

But the three texts differ in part because they are directed to different sorts of people in different parts of the same society. Manu is meant primarily for Brahmins, the *Arthashastra* for kings, and the *Kamasutra* for all four classes.[29] The *Kama-sutra* makes this clear: a man "begins the lifestyle of a man-about-town [the *nagaraka,* the protagonist of the *Kamasutra*] using the money that he has inherited, on the one hand, or obtained from gifts, conquest, trade, or wages, on the other, or from both" (1.4.1). And the commentator spells this out: "If he is a Brahmin, he gets his money from gifts; a king or warrior, from conquest; a commoner, from trade; and a servant, from wages earned by working as an artisan, a traveling bard, or something of that sort." But it is not the case that only a puritanical Brahmin knew the dharma texts and only a libertine merchant knew the *Kamasutra.* That might well be the case, but it is equally possible that the same man, of either class, might study dharma with learned men by day and the *Kamasutra* with his mistress by night.

The knowledge of Sanskrit was limited to a very small, highly elite group, consisting primarily of men and among them primarily Brahmins, with a sprinkling of royalty and powerful and wealthy merchants, and they alone would have been able to read these texts in the original. Sanskrit texts therefore had a very limited *direct* effect on the actual lives of most people in ancient India, but the ideas in the texts were diffused far beyond this elite male group. The *Kamasutra* explains this in justifying its assertion that women should become familiar with its contents (against unnamed "scholars" who insist, "Since females cannot grasp texts, it is useless to teach women this text" [1.3.3]):

> Throughout the world, in all subjects, there are only
> a few people who know the text, but the practice is
> within the range of everyone. And a text, however
> far removed, is the ultimate source of the practice.

> "Grammar is a science," people say. Yet the sacrificial priests, who are no grammarians, know how to gloss the words in the sacrificial prayers. "Astronomy is a science," they say. But ordinary people perform the rituals on the days when the skies are auspicious. And people know how to ride horses and elephants without studying the texts about horses and elephants. In the same way, even citizens far away from the king do not step across the moral line that he sets. The case of women learning the *Kamasutra* is like those examples. (1.3.5–10)[30]

The "practice . . . within the range of everyone" amounted to translation from Sanskrit into vernaculars and transmission through word of mouth.[31]

Vatsyayana adds, "And there are also women whose understanding has been sharpened by the text: courtesans deluxe and the daughters of kings and ministers of state"(1.3.11). Indeed, there is a much-retold story in ancient India about a queen who knew more Sanskrit than her king. One day when they were fooling around in the water, she protested, in Sanskrit, "Don't throw water at me!," a sentence in which "Don't" (*ma*) and "water" (*udakais*) combine to form *modakais*. The ignorant king mistook the two-word compound for the word for cookies (*modakais*) and threw a modicum of cookies at her.[32] The ensuing embarrassment inspired him to learn Sanskrit properly.[33]

So we may assume that the ideas of the *Arthashastra* and the *Kamasutra* could have become known far beyond the narrow circle of male Brahmin readers. To what extent these ideas were actually known is more difficult to ascertain.

The Hidden Transcript of Adharma

Many of the ideas in these texts were antinomian or transgressive, challenging the dharma tradition and often amounting to a tacit incitement to adharma (non-dharma, anti-dharma, the opposite of dharma). As the great S[ushil] K[umar] De wisely remarked, "It's worth noting that, generally speaking, while the *dharmashastra* was always anxious to note and reprimand transgression, and enjoined *sadachara* [proper behavior] as determinant of conduct, the idea of sense enjoyment and desire for wealth in accordance with the *shastras* of *artha* and *kama* remained more or less unaffected."[34]

The message of the *Arthashastra* and the *Kamasutra* spread throughout the more general population through the process we have just seen described in the *Kamasutra*. And the transgressive part of that message was embedded in the Sanskrit texts through a process that James C. Scott describes in *Domination and the Arts of Resistance: Hidden Transcripts* (1990). Scott uses the term "public transcript" to describe the open, public interactions between those who dominate—whether in the sphere of politics, economics, culture, or religion—and those whom they dominate. The "hidden transcript," then, is the critical discourse that goes on, offstage, among the oppressed, out of the sight and hearing of their oppressors, hidden beneath the surface of evident public behavior. In *Weapons of the Weak: Everyday Forms of Peasant Resistance* (1985), Scott argues that the everyday resistance of subalterns shows that they have not consented to dominance.

The situation of the ancient scientific texts created and perpetuated by Brahmins in ancient India is more complex, for both the surface text and the hidden transcript are embedded in the same document. Brahmins, after all, perpetuated the texts under the noses of other, more conventional/uptight Brahmins; this was no class struggle. The Brahmin tradition in ancient India was far from monolithic; there were many different sorts of Brahmins, with a wide diversity of intellectual traditions and very different relationships to dharma—indeed, to various sorts of dharma. Kautilya and Vatsyayana, both evidently fairly liberal Brahmins (Kautilya far more legalistic than Vatsyayana), largely ignored or evaded, rather than challenged, the power of the more traditional Brahmins, who often appear in both the *Arthashastra* and the *Kamasutra* as anonymous "scholars" or "teachers" (*acharyas*).[35] This is a term used to designate previous authorities within the tradition that one is writing about and is generally a term of great respect in ancient India. But Kautilya and Vatsyayana almost always cite such "scholars" only in order to disagree with them, often to mock them. In the *Kamasutra,* in particular, the word "scholars" almost always has a pejorative tone, perhaps best translated as "pedants."

The public transcript is the message of dharma, put there by the dominant Brahmins and designed for the control of the other, subaltern classes. But the hidden transcript, the subversion[36] of dharma, was put there not by subalterns but by another branch of those same Brahmins, designed to challenge the stranglehold of dharma on both them and the other classes. They did this, I think, not to fulfill a deep revolutionary agenda or a desire to undermine the powers of other sorts of Brahmins, but simply out of their primary allegiance to their own goals: Kautilya to maintain power, Vatsyayana to facilitate pleasure, in both cases without letting dharma get in their way. Kautilya actually describes this trick of the hidden transcript, though he attributes it not to his own tricky text but to materialists, whom he accuses of using the Vedas as "merely a cover for those who know how the world works" (1.2.5).[37] The message hidden beneath the Vedic/ dharmic cloak in the *Arthashastra* and the *Kamasutra* was available to both Brahmins and subalterns through the usual avenues of practice. My book is about the denial of dharma, the dissent against dharma, and at times the subversion of dharma through the hidden transcript in two great scientific Sanskrit texts.

My argument is that these two texts, ideologically closely related (chapter 2), advocate blatant transgressions against dharma (chapters 3 and 4), though both texts developed mechanisms to allow them to pay superficial lip service to dharma (chapter 5). They are evidence of a steady stream of subversive ideas that were maintained by certain Brahmins in the face of the disapproval of other Brahmins. This undermining of the dominant social and religious order by secular scientific disciplines was continued in a most ingenious and devious way by the creation of a mythology about wicked skeptics and materialists (Charvakas and Lokayatikas), whose words were always cited with shock and disapproval—but always cited, always kept alive in the Hindu tradition (chapter 6). The subsequent history of India, particularly under colonization, has led to the present-day undermining of science by a religious government (chapter 7). We can better understand the subversion of science by religion under the present Indian theocracy by going back to trace the history of the subversion of religion by science, first in the two key texts of politics and erotics and then in the subsequent history of dissension against dharma in India.

2

The Influence of the *Arthashastra* on the *Kamasutra*

The Machiavellian *Kamasutra*

Someone who called himself Kautilya evidently borrowed heavily from Manu in drafting the revised standard edition of the *Arthashastra* (and vice versa). It should therefore not be surprising to learn that the *Kamasutra* borrowed heavily from the *Arthashastra* (though, in this case, the *Arthashastra* did not return the compliment).

Soon after 1905, when the European and American academic world became aware of the existence of the *Arthashastra,* scholars began to comment on its general, particularly formal, resemblance to the *Kamasutra*. In 1920, Moriz Winternitz said that Vatsyayana "can virtually be called the Indian Machiavelli of love."[1] He may have meant that Vatsyayana was "of, relating to, or characteristic of Machiavelli, or of his principles or alleged principles; practicing, or characterized by (esp. political) expediency; unscrupulous, duplicitous; astute, cunning, scheming" (as the *Oxford English Dictionary* defines

"Machiavellian"). Or he may simply have meant that Vatsyayana was like Kautilya, who had already been identified as the
Indian Machiavelli: the standard Sanskrit dictionary of Sir
Monier Monier-Williams, published in 1899, before the *Arthashastra* was known in Europe, refers to the historical Kautilya/
Chanakya, the chief counselor of Chandragupta Maurya, as
"the Machiavelli of India."

The *Arthashastra* is often said to be Machiavellian, and
indeed, both the *Arthashastra* and the *Kamasutra* are "unscrupulous, duplicitous; astute, cunning, scheming." Suspicion,
treachery, and trickery pervade the *Arthashastra,* and some
of this carries over into the *Kamasutra.* But in fact, neither
Vatsyayana nor Kautilya resembles Machiavelli in any significant way, in part because Machiavelli himself is not nearly
as Machiavellian as they are.[2] In 1919, Max Weber remarked,
"Truly radical 'Machiavellianism,' in the popular sense of
that word, is classically expressed in Indian literature in the
Arthashastra of Kautilya . . . : compared to it, Machiavelli's *The
Prince* is harmless."[3] Weber was, as usual, right; Kautilya makes
Machiavelli look like Mother Teresa. I would call Vatsyayana
not Machiavellian but Kautilyan, as Friedrich Wilhelm does
("dieser Kauṭalya der Liebe").[4]

The Indebtedness of the *Kamasutra*
to the *Arthashastra*

In 1926, D. R. Bhandarkar noted that the *Kamasutra* quotes a
number of prose passages from the *Arthashastra*,[5] and in 1959,
S. K. De wrote:

> Of course [Vatsyayana's] attitude, as he says, is not
> immoral, but the morality of the Kāmasūtra is not
> unlike that of the Arthaśāstra; in both cases, hard

and shrewd common sense proceeds on the assumption that everything is fair in love and war. . . .
The indifference to uprightness and insistence on
distrust, as we see, for instance, in [Vatsyayana's]
complacent instruction regarding the ways of de-
ceiving maidens, of making shameless use of other
peoples' wives for profit as well as for pleasure, or in
his teaching of calculated and sordid tricks to the
harlot for winning love and lucre, are comparable
to the facile attitude of Kauṭilya in his inculcating
the benefits of defeating an opponent by guile, in
his recommending unscrupulous methods for getting rid of inconvenient counselors, or in his for-
mulating ingenious means of extorting taxes to fill
the treasury.[6]

De is talking not of direct parallels but of general similarities
in attitude.

Others, however, have suggested that there might be
more specific instances of borrowing. Wilhelm, in 1966, citing De, listed several passages in the *Kamasutra* that were
strikingly similar to passages in the *Arthashastra,* and he remarked: "The style and structure of the *Arthaśāstra* are imi-
tated by the *Kāmasūtra,* but not the other way around, because
the *Kāmasūtra* also uses political terms for its own concerns."[7]
In 1968, Thomas Trautmann argued, "The indebtedness of
Vātsyāyana to the *Arthaśāstra* goes a great deal further than
mere quotation, to the plan of the work and the very style
in which it is written, so that [Vātsyāyana] must clearly have
modeled it on the *Arthaśāstra* more or less as we have it today."
And in 1971 Trautmann went on to say, citing Wilhelm, "The
Kāmasūtra of Vātsyāyana shows great stylistic affinities to the

Arthaśāstra. . . . Though the content is, of course, much different, the *Kāmasūtra* uses enough of the rarer terms of its predecessor that a translator ignores the *Arthaśāstra* at his peril." Moreover, Trautmann thought it probable that the same man, Yashodhara, wrote commentaries on both the *Kamasutra* and the *Arthashastra.*[8] In 1994, Jean Fezas remarked on further structural similarities between the two books, and in 2012, Herman Tieken commented on the parallel structures (divisions in chapters, prose capped by verse, long lists) as well as their shared quality of being "ruthlessly practical."[9]

The *Arthashastra* strongly influenced the worldview of the *Kamasutra.* The *Kamasutra* regards artha as a primary aim, especially as far as courtesans are concerned. Much of the *Kamasutra* is devoted to Kautilyan trickery and deception of one sort or another: the man-about-town tricks the parents of a young girl and also tricks the girl (book 3); the married woman tells lies as she jockeys for power against her co-wives (book 4); the adulterer deceives the woman's husband (book 5); the courtesan lies to get her customers to give her more money (book 6); and various people use drugs to cloud the minds of their sexual objects (book 7). Just as the *Panchatantra,* the book of beast fables, is in many ways a spoof on the *Arthashastra,* so the *Kamasutra* can be read as a light-hearted travesty on selected themes of the *Arthashastra.* I agree with Herman Tieken when he remarks, "I believe that we should reckon with the possibility that the *Kāmasūtra* was intended as a parody of the *Arthaśāstra.* . . . The *Kāmasūtra* . . . makes fun of the *Arthaśāstra* by subjecting love and sex to the same detailed, learned treatment as statecraft."[10]

Having established that the two texts are historically related, let's explore the nature of this influence. What did it mean for an erotic text to be so political? How did the two texts tackle related problems in their two different spheres as they walked the tightrope of affirming and undermining dharma? Noting in passing the ways in which the *Kamasutra* pulls away from the *Arthashastra,* we will conclude with a brief speculation about the consequences that arise when the *Kamasutra* applies to sex the principles of politics, more precisely the politics of the *Arthashastra.*

Prose versus Verse

The *Kamasutra* models both its format and its rhetoric closely on that of the *Arthashastra.* This is immediately apparent: in contrast with Manu, which is in verse throughout (the same simple meter as that of the two great Sanskrit epics, the *Ramayana* and the *Mahabharata*), the *Arthashastra* and the *Kamasutra* are primarily in prose. More precisely, their prose chapters, containing down-to-earth, often undharmic instructions, are capped at the ends by one or two verses that often express dharmic exhortations, contradicting the point of the preceding prose. This ambivalent attitude toward dharma, as well as the use of verses to express the dharmic, often pro-Brahmin, overlay,[11] is a pivotal trait that the two texts have in common. In both cases, an author other than the one who composed the main prose passages probably added the verses later,[12] at the moment when other dharma materials, particularly pro-Brahmin materials, were added. Evidently someone tried to clean up the *Arthashastra* with the verses at the end of each chapter,[13] and the *Kamasutra* followed suit. A zealous copyist might also have inserted the line that often introduces such passages in the *Kamasutra* (but not in the *Arthashastra*): "and there is a verse on this subject."[14] In other basic formal aspects, too, the *Kamasutra* has apparently copied the *Arthashastra.* The formats of the tables of contents in both are very similar, as are the chapters, sections, and subsections, later additions in the *Arthashastra*.[15]

The pro-Brahmin verses and chapter breaks (and indeed, a more general pro-Brahmin overlay) were added to the *Arthashastra* before the *Kamasutra* modeled itself on it; that overlay in the *Arthashastra* may have inspired Vatsyayana to add his own pro-Brahmin verses to his *Kamasutra*. (He may have replicated the points of the *Arthashastra* or drawn on similar sources.) In any case, the pro-Brahmin, pro-dharma verses at the ends of the chapters were not part of the original plan of the *Arthashastra* or the *Kamasutra*.[16]

Striking Points of Agreement

In addition to these overarching stylistic forms that the *Kamasutra* has inherited from the *Arthashastra*, there are numerous specific points of agreement, incidental passages in which the *Arthashastra* has clearly provided the paradigm for the *Kamasutra*. For example, the *Arthashastra* gives elaborate instructions on setting up the royal residence: "On land recommended by architects, he should have a palace constructed with a palisade, a moat, and gates, and inner apartments surrounded by many courtyards. . . . At the back, in a courtyard, the women's quarters, nursery, infirmary, and a yard with trees and water. In an outer courtyard, the residence for young girls and princes. In a courtyard in front, the dressing room, the counsel chamber, the assembly hall, and the schoolrooms for the princes. The palace guard should be stationed in the areas between the courtyards" (1.20.1, 10–13). The "inner apartments" include the harem.

This is also how, *mutatis mutandis,* on a more intimate scale, the *Kamasutra* instructs the man-about-town to set up his pad:

He makes his home in a house near water, with an orchard, separate servant quarters, and two bedrooms. This is how the house is furnished: In the outer bedroom there is a bed, low in the middle and very soft, with pillows on both sides and a white top sheet. (There is also a couch.) At the head of the bed there is a grass mat and an altar, on which are placed the oils and garlands left over from the night, a pot of bees wax, a vial of perfume, some bark from a lemon tree, and betel. On the floor, a spittoon. A lute, hanging from an ivory tusk; a board to draw or paint on, and a box of pencils. Some book or other, and garlands of amaranth flowers. On the floor, not too far away, a round bed with a pillow for the head. A board for dice and a board for gambling. Outside, cages of pet birds. And, set aside, a place for carpentry or woodworking and for other games. In the orchard, a well-padded swing in the shade, and a bench made of baked clay and covered with flowers. (1.4.1–4)

The *Kamasutra* goes into much more detail about the layout of the bedroom, of course, and lacks the detailed description of fortifications that the *Arthashastra* supplies, but the blueprints take the same form in both cases.

The *Arthashastra* advises the king to make use of actors dressed as gods of fire and water to demoralize the enemy during a siege (13.1.3). The *Kamasutra* prescribes similar playacting to a man laying siege, as it were, to a virgin: he should have a friend dress up not as a god but as a fortune teller and describe the "man's future good luck and prosperity" to the girl's mother to earn her favor (3.1.6). The *Kamasutra* clearly picks up from the *Arthashastra* the idea of the constant use of male and female messengers, which in the *Kamasutra* replicates the constant employment of male and female spies in the *Arthashastra*.[17]

The use of black magic (which Manu prohibits [9.290; 11.64, 198]) is strikingly similar in the two texts, each of which discusses it in a very short book at the end of the text, as a kind of last resort. (And each touches on magic in passing in other parts of the text, too, the *Kamasutra* only a few times, the *Arthashastra* a great deal.) The *Arthashastra* permits a man to use love magic on a wife who is averse to kama, or a wife to use it on her husband (4.13.28), while the *Kamasutra* cautions wives not to use it on adulterous husbands (4.1.19–21) but, on the other hand, devotes an entire book (book 7) to the magic that a man can use on women, while the corresponding book of the *Arthashastra* (book 14) is devoted to magic used for various purposes, mostly murder, but never love. Still, the magic techniques overlap in interesting ways. Both the *Arthashastra* (14.3.4–18) and the *Kamasutra* (5.6.24–25, 7.1) offer magic spells to make you invisible, using an ointment that you put on *your* eyes, projecting sightlessness onto the person who looks at you. Both texts are concerned that, when you make yourself invisible, your shadow, too, must be invisible.[18] (The *Arthashastra*, but not the *Kamasutra*, says that you should burn the ingredients for this ointment in a woman's vagina.)

The commentator Yashodhara, in glossing the passage in the *Kamasutra* that recommends, for evening parties, "wine [*maireya*] made from honey, grapes, other fruits, or cane sugar" (1.4.23), cites this sentence from the *Arthashastra* almost verbatim: "*Maireya* is an extract from a decoction of 'ram's horn' bark infused with cane sugar and either combined with a mixture of long pepper and black pepper or mixed with three fruits" (2.25.22).[19] Kautilya here has no interest in dinner parties; he is concerned only with instructing the superintendent of liquor to make sure the stuff is made correctly. But it is surely significant that the commentator on the *Kamasutra* knew that he could find relevant material in the *Arthashastra*.

Marginalized People

A close agreement between the *Arthashastra* and *Kamasutra* (and a sharp difference from Manu) can be seen in their attitudes to what ancient India regarded as marginalized people. The very people that Manu warns us to shun (such as actors and women ascetics) Kautilya recruits as secret agents and Vatsyayana employs as his party crew. To consider just one list among many such, Manu warns us not to eat the food that someone has sneezed on (which makes good sense) but then continues, "nor the food of a slanderer, a liar, or the seller of rituals, nor the food of a tumbler or a weaver, nor the food of an ingrate; nor that of a blacksmith, a strolling actor, a goldsmith, a basket-weaver, or an arms-dealer; nor that of a man who raises dogs, a bootlegger, a washerman, or a dyer" (4.214–16). It is not clear to me why some of these people are socially unacceptable, but Manu's dislike of actors—indeed of all artists—stems both from their ability to make the unreal seem real[20] and from the way that they live, moving from place to place, like the Romani (persecuted as "gypsies"), never part of a settled community. In another context, Manu cites a partially overlapping list of those who will end up in the lowest forms of rebirth: strolling actors, pugilists, wrestlers, dancers, arms dealers, and addicted gamblers and drunks (12.44–45). He also remarks that the rules against speaking with women do not apply to the wives of strolling actors or of men who live off their own wives; for these men have their women embrace other men, concealing themselves while they have them do the act (8.361–63).

These people that Manu abhors are the people that do Kautilya's dirty work, as when, for instance, the king wishes to liberate a prince held hostage:

> Actors, dancers, singers, musicians, those who live by speaking, bards, rope-dancers, and jugglers, who have slipped in earlier, should perform for the enemy. One after another, they should approach the prince and he should establish that they may come and go and stay as long as they like. Then he should get away at night disguised as one of them. This also applies to women who live on their looks, disguised as (the performers') wives. Or he should get out carrying the packages of their musical instruments and food. (7.17.34–39)

The *Arthashastra* also prescribes fines for persons who insult the learning of those who live by speaking and the occupation of artisans and performers (3.18.8). As these are the very people whom Manu regards as incapable of being insulted, libel-proof, a blot on the social landscape, Kautilya's assertion here directly challenges Manu.

The *Kamasutra* reveres such people. Here is how Vatsyayana tells his protagonist to treat actors:

> On a specified day at half moon or full moon, there is always an assembly of invited guests at the temple of the goddess Sarasvati. Visiting players also come and give an audition for them, and on

the second day they are rewarded with a fixed fee.
Then they may give a performance or be dismissed,
according to their reception. In case of a disaster or
an occasion for celebration, they substitute for one
another. They honor and protect visitors who join
them. Those are the customs of theatrical compa-
nies. (1.4.15–17)

Note that these actors are performing at a religious festival, but
their services are not limited to this particular goddess, who
happens to be the patron of music and literature: "The festivals
dedicated to this or that particular deity can be described in
this same way, taking into consideration the different circum-
stances" (1.4.18). Clearly Vatsyayana does not regard actors as
a polluting presence.

Religious mendicants and ascetics, both male and female, are an essential part of this marginal society. Though
Manu had great respect for male renunciants, he grouped
the wives of actors with women ascetics and "menial servant
girls who are used by only one man," as women of so little
reputation that a man might converse with them with no con-
sequence but a small fine (8.363). When speaking about the
conduct of a wife, Vatsyayana sings Manu's song, advising her
never to "have a close relationship with any woman who is a
beggar, a religious mendicant, a Buddhist nun,[21] promiscuous,
a juggler, a fortune-teller, or a magician who uses love-sorcery
worked with roots" (4.1.9). But among the "advisors" whom
courtesans and men-about-town employ in their battles and
truces are beggar women, women of low birth, and women
with shaved heads (i.e., ascetic women) (1.4.6). Vatsyayana
also quotes without disagreement the suggestion of another
scholar (Gonikaputra) that a meeting with an adulterous mar-

ried woman "is easy to arrange in the houses of a girlfriend, a beggar woman, a Buddhist nun, or an ascetic woman" (5.4.43). Women ascetics are an essential part of Vatsyayana's crew of panderers, because women will have better access than men to the women the man-about-town wishes to meet. The use of monks, nuns, and male religious mendicants as spies (*Arthashastra*) or go-betweens (*Kamasutra*) demonstrates, in both texts, a total lack of respect for the possible actual religiosity, or reputation, of such people.

Spying and Seducing

The paranoid psychology of the political text casts its shadow over the erotic text. Eternal vigilance is the price of tyranny— but also the price of adultery. Both the *Arthashastra* and the *Kamasutra* often imagine the possible choices being considered in the mind of someone who might be plotting mischief. The internal debate of potential adulterers, in the *Kamasutra*, in persuading themselves of the moral justice of their actions mirrors the king's self-persuasions and justifications for seducing or secretly doing away with an enemy. This is some of what the would-be adulterer says to himself:

> "This woman has her husband entirely under her control, and he is a great and powerful man who is intimate with my enemy. If she becomes intimate with me, out of her affection for me she will make him reverse his allegiance." Or "That powerful man has turned against me and wishes to harm me; she will bring him back to his former nature." Or "If I make him my friend through her, I will be able to do favors for my friends, or ward off my enemies,

or accomplish some other difficult undertaking." Or "If I become intimate with this woman, and kill her husband, I will get for myself the power of his great wealth, which ought to be mine." Or "There is no danger involved in my having this woman, and there is a chance of wealth. And since I am useless, I have exhausted all means of making a living. Such as I am, I will get a lot of money from her in this way, with very little trouble." Or "This woman is madly in love with me and knows all my weaknesses. If I reject her, she will ruin me by publicly exposing my faults; or she will accuse me of some fault which I do not in fact have, but which will be easy to believe of me and hard to clear myself of, and this will be the ruin of me; or she will cause a break between me and her husband, who is a man with a future and under her control, and she will get him to join my enemies; or she herself will become intimate with them." Or "This woman's husband is the seducer of the women of my harem; I will pay him back for that by seducing *his* wives, too." Or "By the king's command, I will kill his enemy, who is hiding inside." Or "My enemy is united with this woman's husband. Through her, I will get him to drink a potion." For these and similar reasons, one may seduce even the wife of another man. (1.5.8–20; see also 5.1.21–42)

Compare this with one of the many scenarios that the king in the *Arthashastra* imagines to justify the counterintuitive tactic of providing power and success to an enemy—ultimately in order to overpower him with the "silent punishment" (secret murder):

"If my enemy gets power, he will oppress his subjects through verbal and physical abuse and by
confiscating property. Or, if he gets success, hunting, gambling, drinking, and women will make him
careless. When he is weakened by his disaffected
subjects, or careless, I will be able to overpower
him." . . . For reasons such as these, he may help
even an enemy to get power and success. (6.2.38)[22]

The goals are very different, but the diction, the reasoning,
and the total disregard of ethics are the same. The quartet of
vices—hunting, gambling, drinking, and women—recurs in
many of the *shastras,* including Manu.[23]

The *Arthashastra* list of people in the enemy's territory
who are dissatisfied and can therefore be seduced politically
(1.14.2) is the model for the *Kamasutra* lists of women in their
husbands' territory, as it were, who are dissatisfied, or unsatisfied, and so can be seduced sexually (5.1.51–55). Let's look at
those lists. First, the *Arthashastra,* explaining how to win over
angry, frightened, greedy, or proud people in an enemy's territory, begins with a list of angry people:

someone who is cheated out of things he had been
promised; between two people who carry out a craft
or a service equally well, the one who is slighted;
someone passed over for a king's favorite; someone
who has been challenged and then defeated; someone who is furious because he has been exiled;
someone who did not get a position for which he
had incurred expenses; someone who is prevented
from carrying out his own dharma (*sva*-dharma) or
from receiving his inheritance; someone stripped
of honors or office; someone who has become

invisible to respectable people; someone whose
wife has been sexually assaulted; someone put in
prison; someone punished for what someone else
said; someone who has been prevented from doing
something wrong; someone whose entire property
has been confiscated; someone who has been ha-
rassed in prison; and someone whose relative has
been banished. (1.14.2)

Each of these items could be unpacked into the plot of a
soap opera. Then comes the list of frightened people:

someone who has injured himself; someone who
has been offended; someone whose evil acts have
been made public; someone who is alarmed at a
punishment given [to someone else] for a similar
crime; someone whose land has been seized; someone who has surrendered to the army; the head of
an entire department who has suddenly become
wealthy; . . . someone hated by the king; and someone who hates the king. (1.14.3)

And so on, for the lists of proud people and greedy people
(1.14.4–5). At the end, Kautilya advises that each of these people may be incited to sedition "by a bribed assassin working
undercover as an ascetic, bald or with matted hair, to whom
the person to be incited may be devoted" (1.14.6). The *Kamasutra* apes this technique in listing married women "who can
be had without any effort, who can be had merely by making advances," a list that includes "a woman who has been
supplanted by a co-wife for no cause; a woman who hates
her husband; a woman who is hated; a very proud woman
who has an inadequate husband; a woman who is proud of

her skills and distressed by her husband's foolishness, lack of distinction, or greediness; a woman who has been dishonored by her husband when she has done nothing wrong" (5.1.50–54).

Both texts play close attention to people's involuntary gestures and revealing facial expressions as betrayals of hidden political or, as the case may be, sexual emotions. (This art was also developed in the textbook of acting and dancing, the *Natyashastra,* composed during the same general period.) All of this scrutiny and manipulation casts a presumption of dishonesty and betrayal over erotic as well as political relationships.

The *Arthashastra* employs spies to determine the particular character flaw of an official that might cause a particular problem:

> He should have them watched by spies. For an official may cause a loss of revenue—through ignorance, if he doesn't know all the rules and methods; through laziness, if he can't bear the boredom of business; through carelessness, if he is addicted to the objects of the senses . . . ; through fear, if he is nervous about acting against dharma or artha in the clamor of a crowd; through kama, if he is inclined to be kind to people who come to plead their cases, and through anger, if he is inclined to hurt them; through arrogance, if he relies on his learning, wealth, or connection to a court favorite; and through greed, if he alters weights, measures, estimates, and accounts. (2.7.9–10)

It is worth noting not only that dharma, artha, and kama are listed in the conventional order but that, instead of revering these ideals, Kautilya regards them as qualities that a worthy official must *overcome* in order to do his job well.

The *Kamasutra* cleverly adapts this template into a precise and rather cunning psychology for devising approaches to women who are differently resistant to adultery, tailoring each approach to the particular source of resistance (5.1.17–42):

> A man should eliminate, from the very beginning, whichever of these causes for rejection he detects in his own situation. If it is connected with her nobility, he excites more passion. If it is a matter of apparent impossibility, he shows her ways to manage it. If the problem is her respect for him, he becomes very intimate with her. If it stems from her contempt, he demonstrates his extraordinary pride and his erudition. If it comes from his contempt, he prostrates himself before her. If she is afraid, he reassures her. (5.1.43–49)

In yet another pair of closely parallel texts, the *Arthashastra* presents a fourfold typology of repentant traitors: "Those who have left and returned are of four types: one who left and returned for a good reason, and the opposite of this; one who left for a good reason but returned without a good reason, and the opposite of that" (7.6.23). It is but the work of a moment for the *Kamasutra* to convert this into a six-fold typology of lovers who leave a courtesan and then may or may not be taken back:

> If he has gone elsewhere, she must find out about him; he may belong in any of the six possible categories, according to the circumstances: He left her

of his own accord and he left the other woman, too,
of his own accord. He left both her and the other
woman because they got rid of him. He left her of
his own accord and he left the other woman because
she got rid of him. He left her of his own accord and
stayed with the other woman. He left her because
she got rid of him and he left the other woman of
his own accord. He left her because she got rid of
him and he stayed with the other woman. (6.4.3–37)

The simple scheme that provided a useful checklist for a king
dealing with a traitor would have become cumbersome and
impractical if it had ever actually been used by a courtesan
dealing with an errant lover. It serves, rather, as a kind of inspiration for cold-heartedness.

Testing

The influence of the *Arthashastra* on the *Kamasutra* is particularly visible in the techniques of testing people (which Manu
briefly alludes to [7.54]). The *Arthashastra* advises the king to
test his potential counselors of various departments to make
sure they are impervious to the temptations of each of the
Three Aims of life, able to say "No" to dharma, artha, or kama.
He also tells him to test the candidate against a fourth aim, not
moksha but fear (often listed as the fourth emotion, after the
primary triad of desire [kama], anger, and greed) (1.10.3–12).[24]
Those who successfully resist dharma are to be put in charge of
the courts (a scenario to which we will return), or, for resisting
the temptation of artha, the treasury. (Elsewhere, the *Arthashastra* cynically remarks that it is as hard to know if a trea-
surer handling money has not kept any as it is to know if a fish

swimming through water has not swallowed any [2.9.33].) Those who have proved that they have no fear may qualify to become royal bodyguards.

Kautilya's test of kama is relatively straightforward:

> A wandering woman ascetic who has won the queen's confidence and is received with honor in the women's quarters should urge each high official one by one: "The chief queen is in love with you and has found ways to meet with you. There will also be a lot of money for you." If he refuses, he has integrity. That is the secret test for kama. (1.10.7–8)

And any man who has thus been proven impervious to kama is to be made a guard of the harem and women's quarters (1.10.13).

This program of testing then appears in the *Kamasutra* as just a single test for the guards of the harem, but this one test combines the four elements, including fear, that the *Arthashastra* used to test four different sorts of counselors:

> Scholars say: "'Guards stationed in the harem should be proved pure by the trial of kama." Gonikaputra says: "But fear or artha may make them let the women use another man; therefore guards should be proved pure by the trials of kama, fear and artha." Vatsyayana says: Dharma prevents treachery. But a man will abandon even dharma because of fear. Therefore guards should be proved pure by the trial of dharma and fear. (5.6.40–42)

In the end, therefore, and in contradiction of Kautilya (whose opinion Vatsyayana cites here under the rubric of "scholars"),

Vatsyayana decides that imperviousness to kama is not the most important quality for a harem guard, after all; fear and dharma trump kama. But since the *Arthashastra* precedes the *Kamasutra* logically as well as chronologically, when the *Kamasutra* tries to take the *Arthashastra* scheme for testing counselors and adopt it for a scheme to test the guards in the harem, it has to condense it so that each guard is tested in four ways, some of which are totally irrelevant to the qualities of a guard in the harem. On the other hand, again unlike Vatsyayana, Kautilya suggests that the *women* of the harem must themselves be tested for "honesty and dishonesty," lest they prove a danger to the king. For Kautilya is primarily concerned not so much to protect the king's wives (Vatsyayana's worry) as to protect the king *from* his wives (1.17.1):

> Going to the harem, he should meet with the queen after old women have made sure she is unarmed. For Bhadrasena was killed by his brother hiding in the queen's chamber, and Karusha by his son hiding under his mother's bed. The king of Kashi was killed by his queen with puffed grain mixed with poison that she said was honey; Vairantya with an anklet, Sauvira with a girdle-jewel, and Jalutha with a mirror—all smeared with poison. And Viduratha's queen killed him with a weapon she had hidden in her braids. He should therefore avoid these situations. (1.20.14–17)

This passage is one of the few in the *Arthashastra* that veers off into pure mythology, the much-told tale of the "poison-damsel" (*visha-kanya*) whose very touch brings immediate death.[25] There is no direct parallel to this list in the *Kamasutra*, which seldom warns men about physical dangers from women, though it often warns men against the physical harm that they may cause women. But, as we are about to see, the *form* of the warning—the list of mythical and historical characters who were destroyed by kama—does indeed appear in both texts to make a related point: the danger to men posed by their own kama, usually in the form of attacks by the men whom they have cuckolded.

And there is another close parallel that appears in the context of this testing. The *Arthashastra*, speaking of testing the counselors, warns against the danger that one might corrupt the uncorrupted, "like water with poison; for you may never find a cure for a person who has been corrupted" (1.10.18) In the same vein, Kautilya also objects to the suggestion that the crown prince who may be plotting to seize his father's throne should be tempted with the four royal vices or the vices that spring from kama (a quartet that we have seen Kautilya imagine as corrupting the enemy king). One of his ministers suggests: "One of the secret agents should entice him with hunting, gambling, drinking, and women, saying, 'Attack your father and seize the kingdom.' Another secret agent should dissuade him; so say the Ambhiyas." Kautilya says: "It's a big mistake to awaken one who is not awake, for a fresh thing absorbs anything smeared on it. In the same way, a prince, whose mind is newly awake, will believe anything he is told as if it were the teaching of a *shastra*. Therefore, one should teach him what accords with dharma and artha, never anything that is contrary to dharma and artha" (1.17.28–33; see also 1.6.5–6; 8.3.38–66).

This same concern about corrupting the uncorrupted appears when the *Kamasutra* speaks of testing the chastity of wives: "The followers of Babhravya say: 'To find out about his own wives' purity or impurity, a man should test them through charming women who have deeply hidden their own involuntary signals and who will report what other people say." But Vatsyayana says: Because corrupt people can succeed among young women, a man should not set in motion, without a reason, the corruption of a person who is not corrupt" (5.6.43–44).

And so the *Kamasutra* suggests better ways to control women, primarily through knowledge of the *Kamasutra*.

The Need to Control the Senses

The widely shared fear of the four vices that arise from kama is part of a larger concern for self-control. Manu, as we might expect, has a great deal to say about this. He warns the king to make a great effort to avoid the vices that arise from kama and anger,[26] which all end badly. For a king who is addicted to the vices born of kama loses his dharma and artha, but if he is addicted to the vices born of anger he loses his very self (7.45–46).

With regard to the other two texts, one would have thought that concern for the control of the senses would make far more sense in the *Arthashastra* than in the *Kamasutra*, but not so. An emphasis on the need for a man to control not (or not just) his women but his own senses pervades both texts; both Vatsyayana and Kautilya would have loved Nixon and hated Clinton. As Lorraine Daston sharply summarizes the issue:

> Since both artha and (surprisingly for Western readers) kama depend on control, on the postponed gratification that scheming demands, there is after all a natural link with dharma: the person capable of far-sighted calculation, sacrifice of short-term indulgence of the passions for long-term gain, and

understanding of how individuals interact (and
therefore how they can be manipulated) is also
the person with sufficient self-discipline and social
savvy to practice dharma.[27]

The *Arthashastra* sees as more dangerous than any other
threat the enemy within—more precisely, the "six enemies"
within: "Conquering the senses results from training in the
knowledge systems and is to be accomplished by giving up desire [kama], anger, greed, arrogance, pride, and excitement. . . .
This entire text is about the conquest of the senses. A king who
behaves in the opposite way and has no control over his senses
will perish immediately" (1.6.1, 3–4).

Again and again, the *Arthashastra* speaks of the need for
control: "[The king] should conquer his senses by abandoning
the set of six enemies" (1.7.1). Spies, in particular, are advised to
avoid women and liquor, to stay sober and sleep alone (1.16.18–
23), for people reveal secrets through the indiscretions of love
affairs (1.51.11). The *Arthashastra*'s definition of the mastery of
the senses is framed by this concern for control. Kautilya says:
"Conquering the senses means that the senses—ear, skin, eye,
tongue, and nose—do not veer about among sounds, touches,
visible forms, tastes, and smells" (1.6.2). Almost the exact same
wording, and the same concern for control, is used for the opposite purpose in the *Kamasutra*'s definition of kama: "Kama,
in general, consists in engaging the ear, skin, eye, tongue,
and nose each in its own appropriate sensation, all under the
control of the mind and heart driven by the conscious self"
(1.2.11–12). Where the *Arthashastra* does not want the senses
to "veer about" among the objects of the senses, which it enu-
merates, using this passage in the context of an argument that
one should *give up* kama, the *Kamasutra* uses the "appropri-

ate" engagement of the same senses enumerated in the *Artha-shastra* in its argument *for* the enjoyment of kama—under the control of the conscious mind.

The *Arthashastra's* list of kings who were destroyed by treacherous women (with mirrors or lips smeared with poison and so forth) is mythologized in another *Arthashastra* list of kings who were destroyed by the far more dangerous enemies within:

> When the Bhoja king named Dandakya was aroused by a Brahmin's daughter, kama destroyed him, along with his relatives and his kingdom, as it did the demon Karala of Videha, too; and anger destroyed Janamejaya when he attacked Brahmins, and Ta-lajangha when he attacked the Bhrigus; greed de-stroyed Pururavas when he took too much from the four social classes, as it did Ajabindu of the Sau-viras; arrogance destroyed Ravana when he would not return another man's wife, and Duryodhana when he would not return a portion of the king-dom; pride destroyed Dambhodbhava, who treated his people with contempt, and Arjuna of the Hai-hayas; and excitement destroyed the demon Vatapi when he attacked Agastya, and the Vrishni con-federacy when it attacked Vyasa. These and many other kings, who were addicted to the set of six enemies and had not conquered their senses, were destroyed, with their kinsmen and kingdoms. But Rama, the son of Jamadagni, who had renounced the set of six enemies and conquered his senses, en-joyed the earth for a long time, as did Ambarisha, the son of Nabhaga. (1.6.5–12)

Several of these figures are heroes of the Sanskrit epics (Janamejaya, Duryodhana, Vyasa, Rama [not Sita's husband, but
another Rama, "Rama of the Axe"]) or of mythological texts,
some killed in conflict with demons or ogres.

The *Kamasutra* (here quoting unnamed "fatalists" rather
than presenting Vatsyayana's own opinion) uses an abbrevi-
ated version of the very same list (notably including Ravana,
the villain of the *Ramayana*), though it attributes all the disas-
ters to kama alone. It begins with a word-for-word quotation
of the tale of the first unfortunate sinner on the *Arthashastra*'s
list: "When the Bhoja king named Dandakya was aroused by a
Brahmin's daughter, kama destroyed him, along with his relatives and his kingdom. And Indra the king of the gods with
Ahalya, the super-powerful Kichaka with Draupadi, Ravana
with Sita, and many others afterwards were seen to fall into
the thrall of kama and were destroyed" (1.2.34–36). Vatsyayana also remarks that a king "who suppresses the band of six
enemies within him conquers the earth too" (5.5.37), though
this sentiment occurs in a verse at the end of a chapter, where
Vatsyayana usually lodges pious sayings that he has contradicted at numerous points of the preceding chapter and does
not really mean.

Kautilya's and Vatsyayana's shared list of kings who were
destroyed by the "enemies within"—their own passions—may
have been inspired by a similar list offered by Manu, though
the kings on Manu's list were destroyed not by kama but by
lack of *vinaya,* a word that can be translated as "humility" as
well as "discipline" or "good manners." The examples of proud
kings given here suggest that what Manu has in mind is the
need for a king to humble himself before a Brahmin:

> The king should rise early in the morning, attend
> respectfully to learned Brahmins who have grown

old in the study of the three Vedas, and abide by
their advice. He should always serve unpolluted old
priests who know the Veda; for a man who serves
old people is always revered, even by ogres. He
should learn humility from them even if he is always humble, for the king who is humble is never
destroyed. Many kings have been destroyed, together with their entourages, through lack of humility, while even forest-dwellers have won kingdoms
through humility. Vena was destroyed through lack
of humility, and so was king Nahusha, Sudas the
son of Pijavana, Sumukha, and Nimi. (7.37–41)

These are all kings who offended Brahmins and, in most traditional tellings, were destroyed by the curses of Brahmins.[28]
Kautilya and Vatsyayana have removed the Brahmin avengers
from Manu's list and shown the king that he is his own worst
enemy.

Sex in the *Arthashastra* and the *Kamasutra*

The list of kings destroyed by their own lust brings us to our
final concern, sexuality. Manu here provides a very simple
benchmark: he is against it. He says:

It is the very nature of women to corrupt men here
on earth; for that reason, circumspect men do not
get careless and wanton among wanton women.
It is not just an ignorant man, but even a learned
man of the world, too, that a wanton woman can
lead astray when he is in the control of lust and anger. No one should sit in a deserted place with his
mother, sister, or daughter; for the strong cluster

of the sensory powers drags away even a learned
man. (2.213–15)

And so forth and so on, blaming women, of course, but also
blaming men. Beyond that, Manu does not have much to say
about sex, other than to forbid sodomy and bestiality (11.174)
and to advise the reader not to eat the food of "a man whose
wife's lover lives in his house; nor that of those who put up
with such lovers, or who are dominated by their wives in all
things" (4.127).

But this is the area in which the other two texts most
directly converge. For though the *Kamasutra* never discusses
politics explicitly, it has absorbed a great many political attitudes from the *Arthashastra,* while the *Arthashastra* does explicitly address sexual issues at various points. In the *Arthashastra,* sex is merely the background for political power,
whereas, in the *Kamasutra,* political power is merely the
background for sex. Both texts are interested in the manipulation of power; the *Kamasutra* applies to sex the *Arthashastra*
theory of power. The *Kamasutra*'s list of reasons that justify
adultery include many that are far more political than erotic.
Vatsyayana accepts as a sufficient reason for adultery the use
of a woman to protect a king or to kill an enemy—and at the
end of the long list he remarks, "But nothing rash should be
done merely because of passion" (1.5.21).[29] Passion is the one
*un*acceptable reason. The basic distrust of passion is a quality that the *Kamasutra* shares with the *Arthashastra,* and the
other, rather far-fetched, political motives are surely the direct
legacy of Kautilya.

The two texts agree on some sexual issues and disagree
on others. Let us begin with the agreements.

All three texts agree that sex is dangerous on the personal level; the *Arthashastra* and the *Kamasutra* also agree that

it is dangerous on the political level. Kautilya states that the penalty for having sexual intercourse with the queen is being boiled alive (4.13.33). Vatsyayana similarly warns of the dangers of sneaking into the harem—but, unlike Kautilya, he still tells the would-be adulterer how to do it:

> Vatsyayana says: A man-about-town should not enter a harem even if it is easy to get into, because this usually ends in disaster. But if he has considered, with an eye to the rewards, all the factors—if the harem has an exit and is deeply hidden by thick woods, the wall enclosing the harem is long and divided up, the guards are few and careless, and the king is away—and if he has been invited many times, and he has worked out a way over the wall, and the women have shown him the way to do it, he may enter. And within the realm of possibility, he should come out every day. (5.6.10–12)

Elsewhere Vatsyayana cites, with agreement, some anonymous sage voicing warnings about certain forms of kama that are politically dangerous: "The man in power should not enter another man's home [to bed his wife]. 'For when Abhira, the Kotta king, went to another man's home, a washerman employed by the king's brother killed him. And the superintendant of horses killed Jayasena, the king of Varanasi.' So it is said" (5.5.28–29). Since neither Abhira nor Jayasena appears in the extant *Arthashastra*, a literal citation of Kautilya is unlikely, but the *form* is Kautilyan, and Kautilya may in fact be the person Vatsyayana has in mind when he remarks, "So it is said"—though the phrase may also be used to mean, "So they say," in the sense of "Some people believe this, but not I."

Both texts accept the concept of eight forms of legal marriage, as set forth by Manu: they include four conventional rituals with minor variations, followed by four more irregular scenarios. One of the irregular ones is the centaur marriage (mutual consent and sexual union, so named because witnessed only by centaurs [Gandharvas]), the love-match union celebrated in Indian myth and poetry. But the other three amount to rape: the demonic marriage (in which the groom bribes the bride's relatives and carries her off), the ogre's marriage (in which he carries the girl off, disregarding her screams, after he has maimed and murdered her male relatives), and the ghoul's marriage (in which the man secretly has sex with a girl who is asleep, drunk, or out of her mind) (3.27–34). The *Arthashastra* ranks these eight forms of marriage only slightly differently than does Manu, raising the centaur marriage from sixth to fifth (3.2.1–10).

Manu condemns the rape of a virgin (8.364), but Kautilya explicitly condemns rape altogether (3.20.16). And Kautilya suggests, as the other two do not, that a woman abducted (presumably not as part of a marriage) should either hire an assassin to kill the abductor or do it herself by means of poison. He advises the abductee to declare that the abductor had killed her lover (11.1.34–39). If this does not work, Kautilya goes on to suggest, an undercover agent should win the confidence of the abductor by providing him with love-potions, then trick him by substituting poison and run away. "Then secret agents should declare that it was the work of a rival," he says (11.1.40–41). There is no concern for dharma here, to put it mildly, but there is a concern for the rights of the abducted woman, a concern that is evident neither in Manu nor even in Vatsyayana.

The *Kamasutra* limits its discussion of the first four forms of marriage, the conventional forms, to one verse at the start of his discussion of virgins (3.1.19). From then on, however, Vatsyayana concentrates instead on what he calls "devious devices for weddings." It begins with four rather manipulative variations on the centaur marriage, in one of which the man tricks a virgin into running away with him and then performs a wedding ritual of some sort himself before deflowering her. The text then adds three more "devices," beginning with two variants of the ghouls' marriage (dividing the category into one in which the man deflowers the girl when she is drunk and another one in which he deflowers her when she is asleep) and, finally (omitting entirely the demonic marriage, the only one in which money exchanges hands), the ogres' marriage (3.5.1–27). In the *Kamasutra*'s view, apparently, drugging a girl is not as bad as killing her relatives, and nothing is as sordid as buying the girl.[30] Predictably, the *Kamasutra* ranks the basic centaur marriage of mutual desire as best of all (though the *Arthashastra* ranks it fifth and Manu sixth). The *Kamasutra* even explicitly remarks, "Since mutual love is the fruit of wedding rites, therefore even the centaur wedding, though of middling rank, is respected as a means to a good end" (3.5.29). Even Manu grudgingly admits the appeal of the centaur marriage, stating that the best marriage for Brahmins is either of the first two forms of marriage, but that the best "for the other classes is when they desire one another" (3.35). The *Kamasutra*, however, at the very end of this passage, puts in a good word for dharma, in a verse citing the familiar rule for ranking concepts such as the Three Aims:

> With regard to maintaining dharma,
> each form of wedding is better than the one that
>   follows it;
> but each time the preceding one is not possible,
> the following one should be used. (3.5.28)

Yashodhara spells it out: the centaur wedding is better than that of the demons, then the ghouls, and last the ogres. We often see such verses in the *Kamasutra* restoring a dharmic balance that the preceding prose has shattered, and often, as in this case, admitting that dharma is sometimes impossible to fulfill.

Vatsyayana also takes for granted the type of rape that we now call sexual harassment, as he describes men in power who can take whatever women they want:

> A young village headman, or a king's officer, or the son of the superintendent of farming, can win village women just with a word, and then libertines call these women adulteresses. And in the same manner, the man in charge of the cowherds may take the women of the cowherds; the man in charge of threads [presumably the supervisor of women engaged in sewing and weaving] may take widows, women who have no man to protect them, and wandering women ascetics; the city police chief may take the women who roam about begging, for he knows where they are vulnerable, because of his own night roamings; and the man in charge of the market may take the women who buy and sell. (5.5.7–10)

Where Vatsyayana assumes that these men will simply get away with it, as usual, Kautilya would at least punish the "man in charge of threads," the superintendent of yarns, even for much milder sexual offenses: "For looking at the face of a woman [employed in the work of threads] or for speaking with her on other matters, the penalty is the lowest seizure fine" (2.23.14). The punishment is as minimal as the crime, for Kautilya implicitly agrees with Vatsyayana that this sort of thing will in fact happen.

Both the *Arthashastra* and the *Kamasutra* offer detailed, but not identical, lists of the skills of a courtesan (2.27.28; 1.3.15). Both texts speak about the use of male statues as dildos—the *Arthashastra,* specifying that the statues are of divine beings, disapproves of the practice (4.13.41), while the *Kamasutra* does not specify divine beings and thinks that such statues might be useful in the harem (5.6.3). (Manu's prohibition against damaging "images and statues" [9.285] would also presumably apply here.) The *Arthashastra* regards as sexually available a woman whom a man has saved when she has been carried away by a flood, who has been abandoned in the wilderness during a time of famine or left there for dead, or whom the man who claims her has rescued from robbers, from the current of a river, from a famine, from an upheaval in the region, or from a wilderness, or when she had been lost, abandoned, or left for dead (4.12.36–40). Similarly, the *Kamasutra* suggests that a man might pick up a woman during the spectacle of a house on fire, the commotion after a robbery, or the invasion of the countryside by an army (5.4.42). The *Arthashastra* (like Manu) regards as a crime the deflowering of virgins to whom one is not married (4.12.1–9); the *Kamasutra* regards the deflowering of virgins (to whom one may or may not be married) as a psychological opportunity to initiate a young girl into the pleasures of the bedroom (4.2.1–34).

Sometimes, but rarely, the *Arthashastra* is more sexually permissive than the *Kamasutra*. The *Arthashastra* takes for granted the woman with many husbands (3.2.31), who poses a problem even for the *Kamasutra* (1.5.30). But almost always, the *Arthashastra* toes the dharma line on sexuality, often closely following Manu, where the *Kamasutra* diverges wildly from it. Occasionally Kautilya and Vatsyayana lock horns. In one passage, Vatsyayana first defends dharma against its imagined attackers (materialists), then defends artha against its imagined attackers (fatalists), and then—surely the point of the whole exercise—defends kama against its imagined enemies: "People who worry about artha say: 'People should not indulge in kama, for it is an obstacle to both dharma and artha, which are more important, and to other good people. It makes a man associate with worthless people and undertake bad projects; it makes him impure, a man with no future, as well as careless, lightweight, untrustworthy and unacceptable'" (1.2.26–33). These critics of kama then list, in support of their contentions, the series of kings "in the thrall of kama," who were, as we have seen, destroyed. Finally it is Vatsyayana's turn to reply in defense of kama: "Vatsyayana says: Kama is a means of sustaining the body, just like food, and it is the reward for dharma and artha. But people must be aware of the flaws in kama, flaws that are like diseases. For people do not stop preparing the cooking pots because they think, 'There are beggars,' nor do they stop planting barley because they think, 'There are deer'" (1.2.37–38). (We may note in passing that Vatsyayana blithely assumes that people would prefer not to offer food to beggars, though such charity is an essential part of dharmic behavior.)

The people Vatsyayana claims to be quoting—"people who worry too much about artha" [*arthacintakas*], people we might call pragmatists—are "other schools" whom Vatsyayana imagines as objecting to his book about kama. But is Vatsyayana just imagining such people? Is it not more likely that here he is actually referring to the *Arthashastra* and obliquely criticizing Kautilya for worrying too much about artha? Certainly

Kautilya's definition of the shortcomings of kama—"Kama involves disgrace, the loss of property, and association with worthless people: robbers, gamblers, hunters, singers, and musicians" (8.3.15)—seems to be precisely what Vatsyayana quotes the "people who worry about artha" as saying, an opinion to which he strenuously objects: "Kama makes a man associate with worthless people," etc. (1.2.32). Here, where Kautilya sounds an awful lot like Manu (as he occasionally does), Vatsyayana directly opposes him.

Sex and Politics

The Kautilyan base of the *Kamasutra's* portrayal of the relationship between the sexes is expressed by this astounding statement: "They say that sex is a form of quarreling, because the very essence of kama is a contest, and its character is competitive" (2.7.1). (The commentator, Yashodhara, explains the competition: "because the man and the woman each try to achieve their own desires by overcoming the other.") This agonistic view of sex is the essence of the *Kamasutra*. But who are the "They" in "They say"? Kautilya and his colleagues? And does Vatsyayana concur with this opinion? I think he does.

The *Kamasutra*, under the influence of the *Arthashastra*, politicizes sex. Recall how Freud, in *The Interpretation of Dreams*, used the *political* idea of censorship as the basis of his idea of the censoring superego, which repressed sex more than anything else; for Freud, as for the *Kamasutra*, politics set the pattern for sex. It might have worked the other way, too; in other times and places, political texts, particularly military texts (and much of the *Arthashastra* is about war), have drawn on sex for their metaphors. Clive's invasion of India, for instance, has been called a rape.[31] What is striking in the ancient

Indian example is that this does not happen; politics gets into the *Kamasutra*, but sex does not get into the *Arthashastra*.

Why did the *Kamasutra* copy the *Arthashastra* so closely? Perhaps because Vatsyayana found Kautilya a sympatico fellow traveler; perhaps because he felt that the similarity in form would lend the *Kamasutra* some of the gravitas of the *Arthashastra*. Whatever the cause, the concept of a sexual relationship as a war with no Geneva Conventions; a conflict in which the two parties try to deceive and outmaneuver one another; an encounter that requires ambassadors and truces; a battle in which the combatants conceal or display the wounds they receive (from bites, slaps, and scratches [2.4, 5, and 7]) was Kautilya's gift to Vatsyayana.

3

Dharma and Adharma in the *Arthashastra*

Three Aspects of Dharma

At this point it will be useful to make a distinction among three different aspects of dharma. For, just as there were many different sorts of Brahmins in ancient India, so did the many different traditions within Hinduism ascribe very different meanings to dharma. Three of these meanings play particular roles in the *Arthashastra* and the *Kamasutra*.

The texts tell us that dharma is the moral or ethical law, the site of truth and righteousness; this aspect of dharma is often called *sadharana* dharma, the dharma for everyone, and it involves rules (differently construed in different texts) not unlike the Ten Commandments: tell the truth, do not injure anyone, and so forth. Kautilya summarizes *sadharana* dharma in one line of his brief chapter on dharma: "Noninjury [*ahimsa*], truth, purity, lack of envy, lack of cruelty, and patience are [the dharma] for everyone" (1.3.13).[1] But the *Mahabharata* had already deconstructed this aspect of dharma long before any of our *shastras* were composed. "Dharma is subtle," insists the *Mahabharata,* which in practice means that dharma is intrinsically impossible to achieve.[2] Dharma is a question, not an answer. Throughout the *Mahabharata,* the many people who argue against following dharma in a particular circumstance often quote *artha-shastra* (in the sense of the older and more general science of government, not the text we now have). For example, near the beginning of this vast and tragic epic, when the wicked king Duryodhana expresses his wish to take for himself the great wealth of his cousins and his father urges him to heed dharma, Duryodhana cites Brihaspati, the mythical author of the *Arthashastra,* as he protests, "Brihaspati has said that the path of kings is not the path of the rest of the world, and that therefore the king should always think of his own artha, no matter whether it is dharma or adharma" (2.50.15).

Often the *Mahabharata* plays on the moral ambiguity of political dharma. A warrior, attempting to persuade his companions to massacre their opponents in their sleep (he succeeds), cites a verse that he attributes to unnamed ancient authors "who worried about dharma but had realistic goals"[3]— quite possibly the ancestors of our own Kautilya: "The enemy army can/should be attacked when it is exhausted, wounded, eating, without a commander . . . or asleep at dead of night" (10.1.53–55). The ambiguity comes in the gerundive form "to be attacked" (*prahartavyam*), which can be taken either as a simple statement of fact ("is vulnerable to attack") or as an argument for [im]moral action ("should be attacked," so we should abandon our scruples and attack the sleeping enemy). Kautilya, however, does not scruple to give unambiguous and detailed instructions on how to kill a sleeping enemy (12.5.44–48).

Dharma as moral or ethical law may also be characterized as ideal dharma, the dharma of what should be. In contrast, dharma as social law—*sva*-dharma, one's own particular dharma, in relation to the particular dharmas of other people—is the dharma of what is, the status quo that must be maintained. Social dharma concerns ritual, the worship of the gods, the honoring of ascetics, and various interactions with people of all castes and classes. This second aspect of dharma often entails violation of essential points of ethical dharma. The *sva*-dharma caste requirements of a butcher, for instance, not to mention a king, violate the *sadharana* dharma rule against injuring living creatures. To this degree, *sva*-dharma itself is, in a very real sense, subversive of ethical dharma. Yet the *Arthashastra* and the *Kamasutra* go far beyond this common moral impasse to advocate actions—such as murder and adultery—that are subversive of both *sanatana* dharma and most *sva*-dharmas.

A third type of dharma, what we might term theological dharma, involves faith in and respect for the gods. Our three texts pay far less attention to this aspect than to the other two. In order to appreciate what the *Arthashastra* and the *Kamasutra* risked in their challenge to dharma, it is useful to make a distinction between two aspects of religion, orthodoxy (believing the right thing, believing in the gods) and orthopraxy (doing the right thing, maintaining religious rules and rites). The distinction between orthodoxy and orthopraxy corresponds roughly to the distinction between dharma as moral/ ethical/theological law and dharma as social law. Though the categories are rather crude and there were exceptions, Hindus during the period in question were far more orthoprax than orthodox; they cared far more about social dharma, the way people behaved, than about ethical or theological dharma, the way they thought. They cared about revering the Veda as a part of ritual life rather than as a text whose ideas and gods people knew and accepted. People could therefore always *say* things that they did not dare to *do*.

Manu cares about all three aspects of dharma, though particularly the second, social dharma. Kautilya is totally immune to ethics (his cavalier attitude toward dharma as moral law is what led some scholars to call him Machiavellian) and often brutal in his disregard for ascetics and the gods. His subtle manipulation of dharma as social law, however, was far more complex, for he is very careful about caste. Vatsyayana hardly ever even mentions class or caste and doesn't care at all about the gods or any of the elements of moral dharma, but he has his own particular concern for sexual ethics.

These distinctions clarify what the *Arthashastra* and the *Kamasutra* risked in their challenge to dharma. They constantly violate moral dharma and theological dharma, but these aspects of dharma were never really enforced. They also, however, violate social dharma, the *Kamasutra* by facilitating adultery and the *Arthashastra* by corrupting male renunciants and desecrating temples and rituals, as well as by endorsing torture, murder, invasive spying, and the spreading of lies at home and abroad—that is to say, government. This sort of adharma does have serious consequences; the refusal to honor Hindu social law caused many Buddhists to be excommunicated. Our texts go to fairly elaborate lengths to protect themselves from such consequences, usually by providing a superficial coating of sanctimony, often in the form of moral dharma.

Three Levels of Dharma

In addition to these three aspects of dharma, differently enforced, the texts distinguish three levels of culpability—action,

speech, and thought, also differently enforced. Near the end
of his text, Manu generalizes: "The three kinds of [nega-
tive] mental action are thinking too much about things that
belong to others, meditating in one's mind-and-heart about
what is undesirable, and adhering to falsehoods. The four
kinds of [negative] speech acts are verbal abuse, lies, slander
of all sorts, and unbridled chatter. The three kinds of [nega-
tive] bodily action are traditionally said to be taking things
that have not been given, committing injury against the rules,
and having sex with another man's wife" (12.5–7). The com-
mentators helpfully offer examples of what is undesirable to
think about (beginning with killing a Brahmin) and of false-
hood (saying, "There is no world beyond" or "The body is the
soul"—sentiments that are typically attributed to materialists).
Manu specifies reparations for violations of dharma on each
of the three levels.

Speech acts are of special interest to us here, since this is
the realm in which our texts might find themselves in danger.
Speech acts fall within the domain of social dharma; they are
punished more severely than mental acts, though less severely
than physical acts. For instance, Manu asks the king to be lenient about verbal abuse against himself: "A king who wishes
to do what is good for him will always forgive men who insult
him, if they are parties to legal disputes, children, old, or ill. If
[a king] who is insulted by people in distress tolerates it, he is
exalted in heaven as a result, but if his royal power makes him
unable to endure it, he goes to hell as a result" (8.312–13). Of
course, Manu didn't have to spell out for the king the measures
that could be taken for verbal abuse against the ruler, since (as
we learn from the *Arthashastra*) the king could always, unofficially, send one of his secret agents and assassins to "uproot"
such "thorns" by applying what Kautilya euphemistically calls

the "silent punishment." Still, it is interesting that *lèse majesté* does not seem to have been officially regarded as a crime, and this opening does create a theoretical space for dissent.

But the penalty, in Manu, for verbal abuse of a Brahmin by someone of a lower class is much more severe: "If a man of low birth hurls cruel words at a Brahmin, his tongue should be cut out. If he mentions his name or caste maliciously, a red-hot iron nail ten fingers long should be thrust into his mouth. If he is so proud as to instruct Brahmins about their duty, the king should have hot oil poured into his mouth and ears" (8.270–73). Equally severe punishments prevail if a low-caste man offends a higher-caste man even below the rank of Brahmin:

> If a man of the lowest caste injures a man of a higher caste with some particular part of his body, that very part of his body should be cut off; this is Manu's instruction. If a man raises his hand or a stick, he should have his hand cut off; if in anger he strikes with his foot, he should have his foot cut off. If a man of inferior caste tries to sit down on the same seat as a man of superior caste, he should be branded on the hip and banished, or have his buttocks cut off. If in his pride he spits on him, the king should have his two lips cut off; if he urinates on him, the penis; if he farts at him, the anus. If he grabs him by the hair, or by the feet, the beard, the neck, or the testicles, [the king] should unhesitatingly have his hands cut off. (8.279–84)

The *Arthashastra* is more concise, more vivid, and, significantly, far more lenient than Manu as to prosecution for verbal abuse. The *Arthashastra* prescribes—for *all* classes, unlike

Manu, who discriminates sharply between them—fines of three coins, but no physical punishment, for "insults about a person's body, nature, education, occupation, and country, for an insult about the body using words such as 'one-eyed' and 'lame,' if it's true," and the fine is to be doubled if the insult is false (3.18.2), a circumstance that Manu does not take into consideration at all.

But the *Arthashastra* occasionally does take class into account in dealing with slander. When someone of a lower caste insults the character of someone higher, such as by saying, "Foul Brahmin! [*ku-brahmana*]," the fine is incrementally increased depending on the degree of difference between the classes, and when someone higher insults someone lower, it decreases depending upon the degree of difference (3.18.7). Significantly, neither Manu nor Kautilya prescribes any punishment for verbal abuse of the gods. Hindus in this period had nothing like our concept of blasphemy; slandering Brahmins or the Veda would pose serious problems, but not slandering the gods.

Written insults (libel) do not appear in these texts but might have been prosecuted along the lines set out for slander. The *Arthashastra* and the *Kamasutra*, therefore, had to tread lightly, in their critique of social dharma, with regard to what they said about Brahmins and the Brahmin occupation of performing religious rituals. To that extent, at least, words are dangerous, or at least punishable. The *Arthashastra*, in particular, often went out of its way to avoid antagonizing Brahmins.[4] But it did not hesitate to trample on other aspects of dharma, nor did the *Kamasutra*.

With this web of dharma in mind, let us now consider first the *Arthashastra* and then, in chapter 4, the *Kamasutra*—in both cases noting first the superficial nod to ethical dharma and then the more substantial subversion of social dharma.

Anarchy and the Ambivalent Dharma of Kings

Let us look to Manu, as usual, for our benchmark, recalling that Manu and Kautilya borrowed from one another particularly freely in the section on the dharma of kings. Take the question of the divine nature of the king. Manu basically argues that the king is a god, and we should obey him: "Even a boy king should not be treated with disrespect, with the thought, 'He is just a human being'; for this is a great deity standing there in the form of a man" (7.8). Manu fears the violence of anarchy and uses it to justify the violence of kingship: "If the king did not tirelessly inflict punishment on those who should be punished, the stronger would roast the weaker like fish on a spit. The crow would eat the sacrificial cake and the dog would lick the oblation; there would be no ownership in anyone, and everything would be upside down" (7.20–21).

This Hobbesian view of human and animal nature fuels a widespread ancient Indian myth, famously told in the *Mahabharata*: to stem primeval anarchy, the people chose a king (here, and in most tellings, Manu is that king)[5] and promised to pay him a portion of their income in taxes (12.67.16–34). (In another version of this myth in the *Mahabharata*, the Creator creates the Triad of Human Aims in order to stem anarchy [12.59.30–94].) Manu tells the story, too, but, with uncharacteristic modesty, does not name himself as the king:

> When this world was without a king and people ran about in all directions out of fear, the Lord emitted a king in order to guard this entire realm ... taking lasting elements from Indra, the Wind, Yama [god of the dead], the Sun, Fire, Varuna [god of the waters], the Moon, and [Kubera], the lord of wealth.

Because a king is made from particles of these lords
of the gods, he therefore surpasses all living beings
in brilliant energy (7.3–4).

Kautilya makes a very different use of this same myth of
anarchy. First, near the start of the *Arthashastra*, he establishes
the idea that anarchy is a constant danger, warning the king
that a king's failure to punish the wicked would "give rise to
the law of the fish—for if there is no punishment, a strong man
devours a weak man, but if [the weak man] is protected, he will
prevail" (1.4.13–15). The law of "big fish eating little fish," the
equivalent of our "dog eat dog," is the ancient Indian term for
Hobbesian anarchy, and it is one of the primary justifications
for a repressive regime of law and order. Later in the first book,
the *Arthashastra* cynically advises the king to manipulate the
myth of primeval anarchy, instructing his spies to spread the
story among the people to make them fear the king and to shut
down dissent—what Plato would have regarded as telling the
good lie—in order to control the gullible, to make them fear
the king and pay their taxes:

> Once he has set spies on the high officials, he should
> set spies on the people who live in the cities and
> the countryside. Secret agents in pairs should argue
> with one another at pilgrimage places, assemblies,
> congregations, and wherever people gather. One
> should say: "We hear that this king has all the vir-
> tues. But I don't see any virtue in this man whose
> fines and taxes oppress the people who live in the
> cities and the countryside." As the people there ap-
> plaud this, the other spy should reply to them and
> to the first spy: "Oppressed by the law of the fish,

the people made Manu, the son of Vivasvat, king.
They allocated to him as his share one-sixth of the
grain and one-tenth of the merchandise, and gold,
too. That's how kings are paid to protect their subjects. . . . Even forest dwellers, therefore, present
one-sixth of their gleanings, thinking, 'This is the
share for the one who protects us.' . . . Divine punishment strikes those who treat kings with disrespect. Therefore one should not disrespect kings."
In this way he should restrain petty people. And
[the secret agents] can also find out what people are
saying. (1.13.1–7, 9, 11–14)

It is brutally clear from this passage that the king is using the
well-known Hindu myth of kingship for no purpose other
than to suppress dissent among the people, particularly those
who do not wish to pay their taxes.

Returning to Manu, we take up the other side of the tax
agreement: the king's duty to the people. Manu threatens the
king: "Know that a king who disregards the moral boundaries, who is a Nastika (Naysayer) and plunders the property
of Brahmins, who does not protect his subjects but devours
them, sinks down" (8.309). We will return to the Naysayers;
here let us just note that plundering the property of Brahmins
is what is primarily at stake in this passage. But not much is actually *done* to a king who violates dharma in these ways; "sinks
down" may imply a minor downfall in this life or going to hell
after death, and in any case it is too vague to support any legal
measures. Thus Manu makes sure there will be no revolution:
he tells the people that the king is a god and must be obeyed,
presumably no matter how wicked he is, just as he tells the
king that he is vulnerable and must not be wicked, no matter

how powerful he is. He speaks out of both sides of his mouth, depending upon his intended audience. It's all about rumor: tell the good lie to your people, and make sure no one is telling the bad lie against you.

Other texts, too, warn the king that he will get into trouble if he opposes dharma. In the *Ramayana* (7.41), Rama banishes Sita only because the people think and say that she is unchaste, though he himself knows that she is chaste; he fears public opinion. The problem posed by the king's violations of dharma began much earlier, in the Indo-European period, when the king necessarily sinned and became polluted simply by carrying out his royal duties, which inevitably involved the spilling of blood; and so he needed a chaplain to give him constant absolution.[6] The king is required to maintain universal dharma; that is his defining job. But in the course of doing his own particular dharma, his royal *sva*-dharma, he himself may violate *sadharana* dharma in a number of ways. The king must sin, and the priest must keep cleaning him up.

Kautilya warns the king to shun adharma lest he provoke his subjects: "Excesses such as love affairs infuriate his own subjects" (9.7.1).[7] The sentiment imagined in the *Arthashastra*'s test of dharma that we will soon consider, in which someone says, "This king is adharmic. Come on! Let us install in his place some other, dharmic person," is expected to be believed, presumably because people might in fact say such things. And one passage (significantly, in verse) does seem to threaten the adharmic king with revolution:

> Getting rid of good people and taking up bad
> people,
> setting in motion unprecedented and adharmic
> acts of violence, . . .

not punishing those who ought to be punished
and punishing those who ought not to be pun-
    ished . . .
makes the subjects become impoverished, greedy,
    and disaffected. . . .
When they are disaffected, they either go over to
    the enemy
or kill their ruler themselves. (7.5.19, 22, 26–27)

Kautilya's sermons on the need for self-control are primarily addressed to the king. Parroting Manu, Kautilya insists (in one of his verses at the end of the chapter) that the
king's own dharma leads him to heaven when he protects his
subjects according to dharma but to hell when he does not
(3.1.41). He rephrases this threat in another end-of-chapter
verse: "When dharma is infected by adharma, / it destroys the
ruler who overlooks it" (3.16.42). But, aside from occasional,
unexpanded lines like "they . . . kill their ruler themselves," no
popular revolution is ever described, here or elsewhere in ancient Indian literature. There are, instead, many palace coups
and many myths in which the Brahmins magically destroy a
king who treats *them* badly, such as the myth of Vena[8] and the
story of Pururavas and the three divinized Aims. The *Kamasutra* assumes that the king casts a long shadow: "Even citizens
far away from the king do not step across the moral line that
he sets" (1.3.9). Yet the threats about subjects destroying a bad
king made it essential to his public image that the king preserve the myth of his own dharmic behavior.

Defending Dharma

The *Arthashastra* is therefore careful to say a great deal in defense of dharma. When pacifying a conquered territory, the

king "should arrange for the worship of all deities and hermitages and hand over land, wealth, and exemptions to men who are heroes in knowledge, eloquence, and dharma" (13.5.11). This chapter ends with a verse of general advice to the king:

> He should promote dharmic customs
> even if they are not yet practiced or have been
> established by others;
> he should not promote any customs that violate
> dharma,
> and should abolish them if others have established
> them. (13.5.24)

In dealing with the crown prince, Kautilya remarks, "One should teach him what accords with dharma and artha, never anything that is contrary to dharma and artha" (1.17.33). He could no more reveal his actual disregard for dharma than an American president could say that he did not pray or believe in God.

Perhaps to justify the employment of generally censured "esoteric practices" (such as the use of poison, drugs, and black magic), Kautilya introduces that section of his text by saying, "For the sake of protecting the four social classes [the king] should employ esoteric practices against very adharmic people" (14.1.1). (In fact, the *Arthashastra* proposes the use of poison and black magic against everyone, without regard to their dharma or adharma.) Similar dharmic statements are scattered throughout the *Arthashastra*.

But just as it is not at all clear who might enforce the sanctions against an adharmic king, it is not clear that there would be serious consequences if kings went around yelling, "Foul Brahmin!" The punishment for these anti-Brahmin and adharmic royal acts may have been nothing but a fantasy cherished by the Brahmins. Indeed, even the basic assumption that Brahmins rank above Kshatriyas (the class of warriors and kings) may have been a Brahmin self-delusion.[9] Since the layer of the *Arthashastra* added last contained pro-Brahmin materials, the pro-dharma sections (particularly but not only end-of-chapter verses) may have been afterthoughts, added following a conscious decision to clothe the adharmic core of the *Arthashastra* with a dharmic overlay.

The praise of dharma in its ethical sense may well be just window dressing. Yet Kautilya's investment in the system of class and caste, part of the social aspect of dharma, is, I think, genuine: it is central to the maintenance of law and order, which is a basic goal of the *Arthashastra*. And so we are told that performing our own caste dharma gets us to heaven and eternal bliss; when we transgress it, the mixture of castes destroys us (1.3.14–15). Kautilya cites as given truths aphorisms that support the caste system: "A cow that belongs to people who hunt with dogs is milked for the dogs and not for Brahmins" and "A Chandala's [Dalit's] well is fit only for Chandalas to use, and not other people" (1.14.9–10). He also repeats, with minor variations (3.7.21–34), Manu's totally fantasized myth about the origin of the castes from the intermarriage of classes (10.8–20).

Somewhat more puzzling is the *Arthashastra*'s ambivalent attitude toward the gods, toward theological dharma. Kautilya states, "If gods, Brahmins, ascetics, women, children, old people or sick people, with no one to help them, can't come to court themselves, justices should act on their behalf" (3.20.22). Does this mean that Kautilya thought that sometimes gods *could* come to court? (Indeed, in the modern period there have been suits brought on behalf of the god Vishnu, who has been represented in court by his image or, sometimes, by the priests of his temple.)[10] In this same vein, Kautilya advises the king to offer sacrifices on a number of occasions, both public and private, particularly on the eve of a great battle (10.3.32–36).[11] We might write all of this off as public relations: because there was no privacy for the king, the "private" rituals were announced and served to encourage the troops just as the public sacrifices did. Moreover, Kautilya may have been indulging in Pascal's wager: it can't hurt to pray to the gods, just in case they really do exist and have power. But Kautilya's scorn for the gods, evident in numerous other parts of the work, cancels out any possible piety that we might have seen in these passages.

Subverting Dharma

Highly disrespectful attitudes toward social dharma, and toward the gods, persist throughout the presumably old, pre-Manu, adharmic *Arthashastra* material but also sometimes in the generally pro-Brahmin verses added as an afterthought, where we would not expect them.

Amartya Sen regards the *Arthashastra* as "basically a secular treatise."[12] And indeed, the king's education, after a brief nod to the Vedas, was entirely secular and scientific, not religious (1.5). To the extent that adharma would be part of what we would call "secularity," we might ask, Does Kautilya's adharma not only make this text secular but justify Sen's view that it is a bulwark against "religiosity" and one of the pillars of "the reach of public reasoning in India and the diversity of its coverage"?[13] In fact, the evidence for both the adharma and the secularity of the *Arthashastra* is profuse and profound.

The *Arthashastra* doesn't always treat Brahmins with the great respect that Manu demands for them: when a Brahmin commits a crime, the king is instructed to proclaim it, scar him with a mark, and exile him (4.8.19). So Brahmins were not, at least in theory, entirely immune to punishment. The *Arthashastra* warns the king, in replenishing the treasury, not to take the property of Vedic scholars (5.2.6). But in an emergency (and the king, of course, is the judge of that), his officers should take over the property of religious orders or temples, stating that it was lost because the person with whom it had been deposited died or lost it when his house burnt down. (In other words, lying.) The temple superintendent should similarly take the treasures belonging to the temples of the city (5.2.37–38). The religious exemptions (except for Vedic scholars) were therefore fragile, and the king was *told* to lie when he wanted to violate them.

Manu spends pages and pages describing the most important of all Hindu rituals, the offering to the male ancestors (*shraddha*), which is the occasion that establishes who is and who is not able to share in the feast that defines membership in Hindu society (3.124–286). Kautilya, however, subverts this ritual to a scheme to liberate a hostage, substituting, for the consecrated food that is dedicated to the ancestors, drugged food used to overcome the guards: "When there is an offering to the deities or to the ancestors, or a festival, [the hostage] should give the guards poison or drugged food and drink, and flee" (7.17.44).

A truly stunning subversion of social dharma in the *Arthashastra* occurs in one of the tests that the king is told to use to choose his counselors. The test for dharma is a test *against* dharma, a test to make sure that this counselor is impervious to dharma—for, as we have seen, the *Arthashastra* regards each of the Three Aims as a potential flaw in any official. The dharma test requires the chaplain [*purohita*] to pretend to object to an order from the king. The test begins as follows: "The chaplain [allegedly] refuses to put up with being ordered to officiate at a sacrifice of a person at whose sacrifice one is forbidden to officiate." This order violates the law forbidding Brahmins to perform ceremonies for, or teach, people of lower castes, actions for which Manu prescribes terrible punishments (2.112–16) and which Kautilya himself forbids in one of his chapter-end verses (4.7.28). The test then continues:

> The king should then [pretend to] dismiss him. He should send secret agents to tempt each counselor [to be tested] one by one, under oath, saying: "This king is adharmic. Come on! Let's replace him with some other, dharmic person—someone from his family, a prince in disfavor, a member of the royal household, a single-minded man, a neighboring king, or a forest chief. Everyone likes this plan. How about you?" If he turns it down, he is a man of integrity. That is the secret test for dharma. (1.10.2–4)

In other words, Kautilya wants the chaplain—the chief counselor and priest, the person in charge of the dharma of the entire kingdom—to be someone who doesn't care about dharma as much as he cares about his loyalty to the king. This "test" undermines the ability of the most important priest in the country to perform the rituals correctly; there could be no more serious violation of dharma. In general, in the *Arthashastra* the chaplain has almost no powers (1.9.9–10). But Kautilya cautions that other officials, too, might "cause a loss of revenue through fear," if they hesitate to act against dharma or artha (2.7.9–10). He wants officials who are immune to moral principles of any kind.

The *Arthashastra* seriously undermines another aspect of dharma through the widespread use of ascetics, both male and female, as spies and secret agents—or the use of spies who pretend to be ascetics. Political agents communicated with spies by way of drawings, writings, and signs displayed in holy places and temples (1.16.25). Either the king bribed and corrupted genuine renouncers or, by getting his agents to impersonate such people, he sullied the reputations of the real ones.[14] It's not always at all clear which is the case. Male renouncers, yogis, and ascetic magicians were already regarded with ambivalence in ancient India, officially respected while privately feared and often scorned;[15] women renouncers were even more widely distrusted.[16] The *Arthashastra* further sullied their reputation.

Mocking the Gods

All three texts sometimes read as if their authors believe in the gods, though their attitudes toward them differ widely. For instance, on several occasions Manu mentions Indra, the Vedic king of the gods, as a great god, worthy of worship, and tells the king to emulate him (7.3, 7.7, 9.304). The *Arthashastra* has the king's spies mention Indra when they tell the myth of anarchy to get the people to pay their taxes (1.13.1–12). But the *Kamasutra* mentions the tale of Indra's punishment for adultery as a cautionary tale exemplifying a way that the king should *not* behave (1.2.34–36).

In general, the *Arthashastra* and the *Kamasutra* seem to have no sense of divine sanctions for the rules that they break in such a cavalier manner. But where lack of respect for the gods bleeds over into the area of the corruption of sacrifice or temple rituals, the *Arthashastra* comes into direct conflict with social dharma. In one noteworthy passage, spies dress as gods of fire and water during a siege:

> When an aggressive king desires to capture an enemy settlement, he should encourage his own faction and terrify his enemy's faction by proclaiming his omniscience and his connection with gods. . . . This is how he proclaims his connection with gods: he talks with and worships secret agents posing as gods of a fire sanctuary, agents who have entered the hollows of statues of deities in the fire sanctuary through the mouth of an underground tunnel; or he talks with and worships secret agents disguised as Nagas [cobra deities] and Varuna [god of the waters] emerging from water. (13.1.1, 3)

This sort of divine intimacy was enacted on other occasions, too. When besieging an enemy's fort, the king's astrologers were, once again, instructed to "encourage his own faction and terrify his enemy's faction by proclaiming his omniscience and his intimacy with gods" (10.3.33).

To enrich his treasury further, after stealing from the temples, the king could play sacrilegious theological tricks:

> He should have the shrine of a deity or the mysterious place of a magician built at night, and make a living through pilgrimages and fairs. Or he should proclaim that a god has arrived in a tree in a sanctuary grove that bears flowers and fruit out of season. Or he should announce that a dangerous demon in a tree is demanding a human being as a tax, and then have agents working undercover as

ascetics stop the demon from harming the people
of the city and the countryside in exchange for
gold. Or, for a gift of gold, he should show people a
snake with several heads in a well equipped with an
underground tunnel. (5.2.39–42)

And if there is anyone who is not taken in by these tricks, the
king can always fall back upon a theological variant of the
usual "silent punishment": "If there are people who are not
credulous, he should poison them when they are drinking
water or washing, and announce that this was the curse of the
deity. Or he can get a man condemned to death bitten [by a
real snake and blame his death on the deity]" (5.2.44).

Among the many devices to lure an enemy into a se-
cluded place to murder him are several bits of religious theater:

A man with a shaven head or matted hair should
settle in the vicinity of the city, claiming that he
lives in a mountain cave and is four hundred years
old. His many pupils, also with matted hair, should
approach the enemy king, and his counselors, bear-
ing roots and fruits, should urge him to pay honor
to their master.... [The master] then persuades the
enemy king to stay there for seven nights, with his
sons and wives, and while he is there he can be ambushed.... Or someone posing as a matted-haired
yogi should pretend to live underwater, while he
actually surfaces through a concealed tunnel or an
underground chamber built under the bank. Secret agents should gradually make the enemy king
believe that the yogi is Varuna or the king of the
Nagas. [The yogi] then persuades the enemy king

to stay there for seven nights, with his sons and
wives, and while he is there he can be ambushed.
(13.2.1–2, 5, 16, 19)

How could a counselor who believed in the gods encourage
the king to mock them like this? And it gets worse.

The statues of gods came in handy as murder weapons.
First they were to be used merely to demoralize the enemy:
"[Secret agents] should cause blood to flow profusely from
revered statues of deities. Then other agents should say that
the flow of blood from a god predicts defeat in war" (13.2.27–
28). But the statues could also be used actually to kill the enemy king:

> When the enemy king is on a pilgrimage to wor-
> ship a deity, he will stop at many places to honor
> the deity with his devotion. Those are the places
> to trick him. As he enters the house of the deity,
> [the king's agent] should release a device to make a
> concealed wall or a great stone fall on him; or send
> down a shower of stones or weapons from an upper
> chamber; . . . or make the statue, banner, or weap-
> ons of the god fall upon him. (12.5.1–5)

All aspects of dharma melt together in these scenarios,
straight out of *Indiana Jones and the Temple of Doom*,[17] which
offend both belief in the gods and the human customs that
respect them.

4

Adharma and Dharma in the *Kamasutra*

Vatsyayana generally simply ignores social dharma, with what A. B. Keith called "*sang froid.*"[1] And his idea that the pleasures of kama should be taken wherever one can find them, within reason, is very un-Brahminical indeed. Yet he *is* concerned that people control their sexuality, in a way that is very Brahminical; so I think he really does mean much that is expressed in the cautionary, afterthought, backpedaling verses at the ends of the chapters. Though modeled on both the form and the slippery ethics of the *Arthashastra*, the *Kamasutra* still tries in many ways to make sex ethical in the deepest sense while trashing the conventions of Hindu social dharma.

Defending Dharma

At times, Vatsyayana seems to assume a dharmic position. He offers a detailed defense of dharma against the imagined assertions of skeptics or materialists, whom he quotes as saying: "People should not perform dharmic acts, for their results are in the world to come and that is doubtful. Who but a fool would take what is in his own hand and put it in someone else's hand? Better a pigeon today than a peacock tomorrow, and 'Better a copper coin that is certain / than a gold coin that is doubtful'" (1.2.21–24). Vatsyayana then blows these arguments out of the water with an uncharacteristically otherworldly credo:

> Vatsyayana says: People should perform dharmic acts, because the text cannot be doubted; because, sometimes, black magic and curses are seen to bear fruit; because the constellations, moon, sun, stars, and the circle of the planets are seen to act for the sake of the world as if they thought about it first; because social life is marked by the stability of the system of the four classes and four stages of life; and because people are seen to cast away a seed in their hand for the sake of a crop in the future. (1.2.25)

By defending the "stability of the system of the four classes" Vatsyayana may be subtly seeking the support of the religious and secular critics of his work and undermining their criticism of a text dedicated to pleasure.[2] The argument for the regularity of the planets may be meant either to defend astrology, regarded as a part of dharma, or to imply a divine consciousness in the heavenly bodies. The fact that Vatsyayana cites the use of black magic in defense of dharma would certainly not please Manu. On the whole, this is a strange cluster of defenses of dharma, and the whole exercise (along with the defense of artha) is surely nothing but a prelude to Vatsyayana's real concern: the defense of kama.

In listing reasons why a married woman might resist the protagonist's invitation to betray her husband, one of the "scholars" Vatsyayana often cites as predecessors (in this case, Gonikaputra) says, "A woman does not consider dharma or adharma; she just desires. But consideration of some other factor keeps her from making advances. . . . A man, by contrast, considers the stability of dharma and the conventions of noble people and turns back even when he desires. And even when he is pursued he does not give in, because he is aware of these considerations" (5.1.10, 13–14). Mind you, Vatsyayana by no means necessarily agrees with this view, which, in any case, merely tells us what people do, not what they ought to do. But Vatsyayana himself contradicts at least the first sentence when he mentions, as the very last in a long list of the possible reasons for a woman's resistance to committing adultery, her regard for dharma (5.1.42). And he contradicts his own exemplum of the man turning back from adultery because of dharma by describing, throughout the rest of this long section, men who do in fact commit adultery.

In contrast with almost all other *shastras* of this period (including the *Arthashastra*), the *Kamasutra* largely ignores caste and class. There are only a few references to class (*varna*), all peripheral. And there are equally few references to caste (*jati*), embedded in lists, never discussed (3.5.5, 6.1.17, 6.2.51). But we can read, throughout, the unexpressed assumptions about class and caste behind this text. The *Kamasutra* nods to the notion of class as it introduces its section on the women with whom one may and may not have sex: "Kama enjoyed according to the texts, with a woman who is of the man's own class, and who has not been with another man before, is a means of getting sons, a good reputation, and social acceptance. But . . ." (1.5.1). But that "But" introduces a long, long list of other sorts of women that a man may enjoy if he is not particularly concerned about class, sons, reputation, or social acceptance—indeed, it introduces the rest of the text, since this is the attitude of the man-about-town who is its protagonist. Vatsyayana repeats the dharmic part of this idea later, in slightly different words: "In a [virgin] who is of the same class, who has not been with another man before, and who has been taken in accordance with the texts, a man finds dharma, artha, sons, connections, the growth of his faction, and straightforward sexual pleasure" (3.1.1). Again, there is a "But," though this one comes two chapters later: "But a man who has good qualities but no money, or who has indifferent qualities but no opportunities, [etc. etc.] should not court a virgin, because he will not get her" (3.3.1). And so the text goes on to offer other, more viable alternatives.

In book 1, Vatsyayana notes that kama with women of higher classes or with women married to other men is forbidden (1.5.2),[3] but in book 5, married women of all classes are considered fair game. So the issue of class (and legitimate sons) is briefly considered on several occasions—but always quickly rationalized away. And we can see Manu's deeply ingrained hierarchical and hypergamous attitude toward class—the insistence that the man should always be of an equal or higher class than the woman he marries (3.12, 3.43–44, 10.5)—scandalously adapted, indeed satirized, in the *Kamasutra*'s basic and pervasive ranking of sexual partners according to size, with the insistence that the man's genitals should always be equal to or bigger than those of the woman whom he beds (2.1.1–4).

One of the rationalizations for having sex with a woman normally off limits takes class into consideration:

> Gonikaputra says: "Under the pressure of some other reason, a woman who aids his cause may become his lover, even if she is married to another

man. The man may think, 'This is a loose woman.
She has already ruined her virtue with many other
men. Even though she is of a class higher than
mine, I can go to her as I would go to a courtesan,
without offending against dharma. She is a second-
hand woman. Since another man has kept her before me, there is no reason to hesitate about this.'"
. . . For these and similar reasons one may seduce
even the wife of another man. (1.5.4–7, 21)

Here the justification for disregarding dharma either with a
married woman or with a woman of a higher class (or both) is
put in the mouths of two other people—first Gonikaputra and
then a man of a relatively low class—and rationalized.

The relatively rare references to dharma in the *Kamasutra* sometimes occur in surprising contexts. The courtesan, for
instance, wonders, "Will I serve dharma or violate it if I go, on
the sympathetic advice of a friend, to a Brahmin who knows
the Veda, or to a man who is under a vow of chastity or consecrated for a sacrifice, or a man who has taken a vow or who
wears the sign of a religious order, if he has seen me and conceived a passion for me and wants to die?" (6.6.29). She would
violate dharma in one way if she allowed or helped any of these
men to break his vows, but she would violate it in another way
if she let him die through his unsatisfied passion for her. (The
Kamasutra elsewhere remarks that when a man sees that his
desire is progressing from one stage to the next, then, in order
to ward off these fatal blows to his own body, he should even
make advances to other men's wives [5.1.3]. This escape clause
apparently also applies to men under religious vows.)[4] This
unexpected, and unconvincing, concern for Brahmins also occurs elsewhere in the *Kamasutra*. In the midst of a magic spell,
Vatsyayana remarks, "You become famous and live a long life

if you drink the milk of a white cow who has a white calf," and then adds, surprisingly, and as a kind of afterthought, "or if you receive the blessings of respected Brahmins" (7.2.50–51). Vatsyayana also states that top courtesans spend their excess profits in solidly dharmic ways: "building temples, pools, and gardens; setting up raised mounds and fire altars; giving thousands of cows to Brahmins through the mediation of people worthy to receive them; bringing and offering articles of worship to the gods" (6.5.28). Dharma slips in in another unexpected spot in the *Kamasutra*, too. The long list of women a man should not sleep with ends with "a wandering female ascetic, or the wife of a relative, of a friend, of a Brahmin who knows the Veda, or of a king" (1.5.29), though the final one, the king, reminds us that it is the power, rather than the sanctity, of the Vedic Brahmin that might make a man hesitate to seduce his wife.

These scattered positive references to dharma prompted Albrecht Wezler to suggest that "Vatsyayana either wants to take the wind out of the sails of possible critics or, and more probably, reacts to a criticism already directed against one or the other of his predecessors."[5] And S. K. De tactfully remarks, "On the whole, it would seem that Vatsyayana, contrary to accepted ideas but consistently with his knowledge of human nature, was a believer in free love *so far as social conditions permitted it*" (italics added).[6] Or, as Friedrich Wilhelm drily remarks, "Obviously the *Kamasutra* is less in conformity with dharma than it claims to be."[7]

The Myth of Sexual Anarchy

A bit of indirect support for dharma comes from Yashodhara's commentary on the *Kamasutra*, in a myth told to explain why some women are, theoretically at least, sexually off

limits. Just as the *Arthashastra* uses the myth of anarchy to
justify the creation of the repressive rule of kingship, so the
commentator on the *Kamasutra* imagines a time of sexual
anarchy, an archaic promiscuity that is no longer in effect,
to justify the creation (by several mythical authors, including the sage Shvetaketu) of the rules of the *Kamasutra*, lax
though they are:

> Once upon a time, there was so much seduction
> of other men's wives in the world that there was
> a verse about it: "Women are all alike, / just like
> cooked rice. / Therefore a man should not get angry
> with them / or fall in love with them, but just make
> love with them." But [Shvetaketu] forbade this state
> of affairs, and so people said: "[Shvetaketu] forbade
> common people to take other people's wives." Then,
> with his father's permission, Shvetaketu, who had
> amassed great ascetic power, happily composed
> this text, which distinguishes those who are eligible
> or ineligible for sex. (1.1.9)

Primeval promiscuity devalued women until Shvetaketu invented the law against adultery, which puts married women
off limits to other men.

Yashodhara did not invent this story; it was told, at
greater length, in the *Mahabharata*, pointedly reminding the
woman whose husband tells it to her, and any other women
who may have heard (or read) the text, that female promiscuity was an ancient option no longer available to them:

> In the old days, we hear, women took their plea-
> sure wherever they fancied. They betrayed their

husbands, but this was then dharma. Even today, animals, without passion or hatred, follow this ancient dharma that favors women. The great sage Shvetaketu was a hermit, people say. Once, they say, right before the eyes of Shvetaketu and his father, a Brahmin grasped Shvetaketu's mother by the hand and said, "Let's go!" The sage's son became enraged and could not bear to see his mother being taken away by force like that. But when his father saw that Shvetaketu was angry he said, "Do not be angry, my little son. This is the eternal dharma. The women of all classes on earth live without being fenced in; all creatures behave just like cows, my little son, each in its own class." The sage's son could not tolerate that dharma. He made this moral boundary for men and women on earth, for humans, but not for other creatures. And from then on, we hear, this moral boundary has stood: A woman who is unfaithful to her husband commits a mortal sin that brings great misery, an evil equal to killing an embryo. And a man who seduces another man's wife, when she is a woman who keeps her vow to her husband and is thus a virgin obeying a vow of chastity, that man too commits a mortal sin on earth. (1.113.9–20)

What begins as happy sexual freedom for women and then turns into a rape by a violent man, traumatizing a child, somehow leads to a law that punishes willing female adultery and only as an afterthought punishes adulterous men, as uncontrollable male sexuality is projected onto the need to control allegedly oversexed women. Cows here are paradigms not, as is usual, of motherly purity, but of bovine license, the exemplars of primeval female promiscuity. (Perhaps because they are so pure that nothing they do is wrong?) Yet the author keeps insisting that this is all hearsay, as if to make us doubt it. Elsewhere in the *Mahabharata*, a god who is trying to seduce a young girl (and who does eventually take her against her will) answers her dharmic protests by insisting that women are sexually free, and alludes to this ancient tradition, perhaps to the Shvetaketu story: "All women are unfettered, as are men; this is the nature of people. Anything different is known as perverse; you have not committed any act of adharma" (3.291).[8] The myth can therefore be cited in defense of either dharma or promiscuity, depending on which period one takes as paradigmatic, the present or the past.

The sage Shvetaketu is cited in the *Kamasutra* as the sexual authority who first reduces the divine text to its earthly version, in a sense its first human author (1.1.9–10), as well as, here, the author of the law of sexual dharma. Shvetaketu is well known as a hero of the Upanishads, the ancient Sanskrit philosophical texts that make the case for renunciation but also contain a surprising number of vivid sexual descriptions. In those texts, Shvetaketu's father, Uddalaka, teaches him the central doctrines of Indian philosophy and is taught, in the process, some elementary facts about sex.[9] (This includes advice on how a man should perform the sexual act when he doesn't want his wife to become pregnant, as well as a statement advising a man to beat his wife if she resists his sexual advances.[10] Debiprasad Chattopadhyaya claimed that Uddalaka was the first materialist scientist in India.[11]) The bold sexuality of the *Kamasutra* may preserve an Upanishadic tradition that bypassed Manu. S. K. De sees in Shvetaketu "a glimpse of the dim beginnings of the *Kamashastra* within the Vedic schools, the holy Shvetaketu becoming, in course of time, a recognized authority."[12] Or the possible incongruity of an Upanishadic sage cited as an expert sexologist in the *Kamasutra* may have inspired Vatsyayana to allude to, and Yashodhara to tell, this story to explain how Shvetaketu, sexually traumatized as a child, became simultaneously chaste, an enemy of adultery, and an authority on sex.

The paradigm of the Shvetaketu myth reappears in the *Kamasutra* in a passage justifying the very existence of the text. After Vatsyayana defends dharma against imagined materialists and before he defends kama against imagined pragmatists in the camp of artha, he defends artha against imagined fatalists (1.2.26–31). But supplementing this at least superficially balanced triad of attacks and defenses of each of the Three Aims, the *Kamasutra* includes an extra paragraph justifying the existence of *a text* about kama, though Vatsyayana does not deem it necessary to defend the texts of dharma or artha, in part perhaps because their importance is more generally acknowledged and in part because it is his job to defend kama alone against people who might argue as he imagines here:

> Scholars say: "Since even animals manage sex by themselves, and since it goes on all the time, it should not have to be handled with the help of a text." Vatsyayana says: "Because a man and a woman depend upon one another in sex, it requires a method, and this method is learnt from the *Kamasutra*. The mating of animals, by contrast, is not based upon any method, because they are not fenced in, they mate only when the females are in their fertile season and until they achieve their goal, and they act without thinking about it first." (1.2.17–20; see also 3.1.1)

In arguing that women, unlike animals, are "fenced in," Vatsyayana is drawing indirectly upon the myth of Shvetaketu's rule against adultery, the rule that fenced them in, putting an end to their animal promiscuity. To this extent, the argument for the text is also an argument for dharma, for the civilizing of otherwise anarchic, bestial sex.

But in this same passage Vatsyayana manages in passing to dismiss the dharmic assumption that the purpose of the sexual act for humans (in contrast with that for animals) is to produce children (since humans do not, like animals, "mate only when the females are in their fertile season"). Given the enormous emphasis that the dharma texts place on having sex *only* to produce children, and Manu's insistence (at 3.45–46) that a man *must* have sex with his wife in her every fertile season (which the *Arthashastra* echoes, at 1.3.9 and 3.3.44), and never at any other time (which the *Arthashastra* does *not* echo), the *Kamasutra*'s assumption that people differ from animals precisely in their ability to have sex separate from fertility is wildly adharmic and highly scientific.

Subverting Dharma

Thus even in some passages that seem to defend dharma, the *Kamasutra* seriously undermines it. Vatsyayana portrays an idealized vision of the lives of wealthy people who did not necessarily follow the rules of dharma, especially when it got in the way of kama. (In commenting on the statement that the elements of the Triad must not "interfere with each other" [1.2.1], the commentator Yashodhara remarks, "For example, through too much generosity, dharma impedes artha and kama.") At one point, Vatsyayana says: "Since learned men disagree and there are discrepancies in what the dharma texts [the *smirtis*] say, one should act according to the custom of the region and one's own disposition and confidence" (2.9.34). Note Vatsyayana's casual scorn for the texts of dharma and his awareness of their self-contradictions, as well as his preference for individual conscience.

The most dramatic instance of the irrelevance of dharma for the *Kamasutra* comes in the prelude to its *defense* of dharma against imagined materialist attackers. For, before defending dharma, Vatsyayana defines it in terms that damn it with faint praise: "Dharma consists in engaging, as the texts decree, in sacrifice and other such actions that are disengaged from material life, not of this world, with invisible results; and in refraining, as the texts decree, from eating meat and other such actions that are engaged in material life, that are of this world, and have visible results" (1.2.7).

Vatsyayana here totally dismisses the role of dharma in *this* world, a role that, as we have seen, he cites, with approbation, in his defense of dharma just a few lines later—"because social life is marked by the stability of the system of the four classes and four stages of life." The definition of dharma as entirely involved with things *not* of this world leaves out most of social dharma, the dharma about whom we should marry and what we should eat. (Indeed, the meat eating that Vatsyayana here takes as the paradigmatic adharmic, forbidden act, he casually recommends in another context [2.10.8]). Vatsyayana here seems to confuse dharma with theology or to limit it to its third aspect, theological dharma. Yet, in his earlier defense of dharma, his approval of doing something for the sake of what we can't see—sowing seeds for the future—is an affirmation of this very same otherworldly aspect of dharma.

Adultery

It is in the casual references to adultery that pervade the book, as well as the great detail with which Vatsyayana teaches the reader how to manage it, that we can best see the *Kamasutra's* disregard for dharma. (Here is perhaps the place to remark that "adultery" is technically not the right word to convey the ancient Indian concept. The Sanskrit term for it is *para-darika*, "[sex with] another man's wife"; it is something a man does to another man, like the English term "cuckolding." A married man in this culture is never punished for sleeping with a woman who is not his wife—unless she is another man's wife. Yet the married woman is punished for participating in the *para-darika*, which thus applies, in fact, to both participants, just like the English word "adultery.")

Vatsyayana cites an earlier authority on the best opportunities for picking up married women, of which the first is "on the occasion of visiting the gods" and others include a sacrifice, a wedding, or a religious festival. (Secular opportunities involve playing in a park, bathing or swimming, or attending theatrical spectacles. More extreme occasions are offered by the spectacle of a house on fire, the commotion after a robbery, or the invasion of the countryside by an army [5.4.42].) Somehow I don't think Manu would approve of the man in question meeting married women at all, let alone using devotion to the gods as a shill for it, or equating such an occasion with spectator sports such as hanging around watching houses burn down.

Manu assumes that every woman desires every man she sees: "Good looks do not matter to them, nor do they care about youth; 'A man!' they say, and enjoy sex with him, whether he is good-looking or ugly" (9.12–17). The *Kamasutra* takes off from this same assumption but then limits it to *good-looking* men and modifies it with an egalitarian, if cynical, formulation: "A woman desires any attractive man she sees, and, in the same way, a man desires a woman. But, after some consideration, the matter goes no farther" (5.1.8). The text, however, goes on to state that women have less concern for dharma than men have; it assumes that women don't think about anything but men; and it is written in the service of the protagonist, the would-be adulterer, who reasons, If all women are keen to give it away, why shouldn't one of them give it to him?

Most of all, by devoting an entire book (book 5) to minute and psychologically acute instructions to the man who wishes to commit adultery, the *Kamasutra* is boldly undermining the very basis of the social system. The *Arthashastra* regards adultery as a crime (3.3–4), as does Manu (5.161–64; 8.352–78). Manu says, "If a woman who is proud of her relatives or her own qualities deceives her husband with another man, the king should have her eaten by dogs in a place frequented by many people. And he should have the evil man burnt on a red-hot iron bed, and people should pile wood on it, and the evil-doer should be burnt up" (8.371–72). The *Arthashastra* is slightly more lenient: "If the husband forgives her, both [the woman and her lover] should be set free. If she is not forgiven, the woman's ears and nose should be cut off, and her lover should be put to death" (4.12.32–33). So Manu tells the male reader to kill the adulteress, the *Arthashastra* to forgive her (or mutilate her), but the *Kamasutra* to find a way to get her to go to bed with him.

In his discussion of married women "who can be had without any effort, who can be had merely by making advances," Vatsyayana shows how sympathetic he is to women, particularly in what they suffer from husbands who are inadequate and inferior to them in so many ways. The list of such women is long:

> A woman who stands at the door; a woman who looks out from her rooftop-porch onto the main street; a woman who hangs about the house of the young man who is her neighbor; a woman who stares constantly; a woman who, when someone looks at her, looks sideways; a woman who has been supplanted by a co-wife for no cause; a woman who hates her husband; a woman who is hated; a woman who lacks restraint; a woman who has no children; a woman who has always lived in the house of her relatives; a woman whose children have died; a woman who is fond of society; a woman who shows her love; the wife of an actor; a young woman whose husband has died; a poor woman fond of enjoying herself; the wife of the oldest of several brothers; a very proud woman who has an inadequate husband; a woman who is proud of her skills and distressed by her husband's foolishness, lack of distinction, or greediness; a woman who, when she was a virgin, was courted by a man who made a great effort but somehow did not get her and now woos her again; a woman whose intelligence, nature, wisdom, perception, and personality are similar to those of the would-be lover; a woman who is by nature given to taking sides; a woman who has been dishonored by her husband when she has done nothing wrong; a woman who is put down by women whose beauty and so forth are the same as hers; a woman whose husband trav-

els a lot; the wife of a man who is jealous, putrid,
too pure, impotent, a procrastinator, unmanly, a
hunchback, a dwarf, deformed, a jeweler, a villager,
bad-smelling, sick, or old. (5.1.50–54)

Here Vatsyayana reveals a powerful understanding of
why the wives of such husbands do commit adultery, despite
the dangers, why it is important to them. He realizes that it
fulfills them in some important ways that their marriages
do not. And he understands, sympathetically, that this need
often outweighs a woman's fear that, were she to be taken in
adultery, she might be very severely punished for it. In this he
clearly values kama over dharma. (In passing, we might note
that the authors of the *Mahabharata* and the *Ramayana* also
described, in great and sympathetic detail, what the heroines
of these dramas, Draupadi and Sita, suffered at the hands of
their husbands and how bitterly and sharply each of them
complained to their husbands. That Sita was also accused of
adultery, but completely absolved, serves to make all the more
remarkable Vatsyayana's observation that mistreated wives are
inclined to commit adultery and his implicit suggestion that
they are justified in doing so.)

Vatsyayana also empathetically imagines various women's
reasons *not* to commit adultery, and the would-be seducer
takes seriously the woman's misgivings (of which consideration for dharma comes last, as an afterthought), even if only
to disarm her:

Here are the causes of a woman's resistance: love for
her husband, regard for her children, the fact that
she is past her prime, or overwhelmed by unhappiness, or unable to get away; or she gets angry and

thinks, "He is propositioning me in an insulting
way"; or she fears, "He will soon go away. There is
no future in it; his thoughts are attached to someone else"; or she is nervous, thinking, "He does not
conceal his signals"; or she fears, "His advances
are just a tease"; or she is diffident, thinking, "How
glamorous he is"; or she becomes shy when she
thinks, "He is a man-about-town, accomplished in
all the arts"; or she feels, "He has always treated me
just as a friend"; or she cannot bear him, thinking,
"He does not know the right time and place," or she
does not respect him, thinking, "He is an object of
contempt"; or she despises him when she thinks,
"Even though I have given him signals, he does not
understand"; or she feels sympathy for him and
thinks, "I would not want anything unpleasant to
happen to him because of me"; or she becomes de-
pressed when she sees her own shortcomings, or
afraid when she thinks, "If I am discovered, my own
people will throw me out"; or scornful, thinking,
"He has gray hair"; or she worries, "My husband
has employed him to test me"; or she has regard for
dharma. (5.1.23, 25–26, 28–29, 31–35, 37–41)

Vatsyayana here brilliantly imagines the resistance of a woman
who is tempted to commit adultery, with insights that rival
the psychologizing of Leo Tolstoy and Gustave Flaubert. This
discussion is ostensibly intended to teach the male reader of
the text how to manipulate and exploit such women: "A man
should eliminate, from the very beginning, whichever of these
causes for rejection he detects in his own situation" (5.1.43).
But, perhaps inadvertently, it also provides a most perceptive

exposition of the reasons why women hesitate to begin an affair.

Vatsyayana details dozens of complex stratagems by which the man-about-town may seduce married women even under the eyes of a watchful society (5.2.1–26; 5.4.9–10; etc.). But then, at the very end, he pulls back, with verses warning the man not to do it, and to guard his own wife:

> A man who knows texts and considers, from the
>   text,
> the devices whose telltale signs are detailed
> in the discussion of the seduction of other men's
>   wives,
> is never deceived by his own wives.
> But he himself should never seduce other men's
>   wives,
> because these techniques show only one of the two
>   sides of each case,
> because the dangers are clearly visible,
> and because it goes against both dharma and
>   artha.
> This book was undertaken in order
> to guard wives, for the benefit of men;
> its arrangements should not be learned
> in order to corrupt the people. (5.6.46–48)

There is something blatantly hypocritical about this switch-back move.

But at the same time there is other, more subtle evidence that Vatsyayana may be more genuinely conflicted about adultery. Even when the *Kamasutra* tells stories that the go-between is instructed to tell to the target woman in order to persuade her to betray her husband (5.4.14), the actual content of the stories is better designed to warn her off, as the women in the stories invariably suffer and/or come to a bad end. Ahalya is taken as the paradigm of successful adulterery, but she is cursed to become a stone.[13] The stories that Vatsyayana recommends may be intended to raise doubts even while they are expressly said to be intended to quell them.[14] They are taken from an older, moralistic corpus; the verses at the end of each chapter, which often raise doubts about matters that he has recommended in the prose passages, may also be older folk sayings, though added at a later stage. Both contradict the more cynical message of the main text, the "Take it wherever you can get it" message. But which one expresses Vatsyayana's own opinion?

In general, the *Kamasutra* assumes a kind of sexual freedom for women that would have appalled Manu but simply did not interest Kautilya. Vatsyayana tells us that a woman who does not experience the pleasures of love may hate her man and leave him for another (3.2.35; 4.2.31–35). If, as the context suggests, this woman is married, the casual manner in which Vatsyayana suggests that she leave her husband is in sharp contrast to the position assumed by Manu: "A virtuous wife should constantly serve her husband like a god, even if he behaves badly, freely indulges his lust, and is devoid of any good qualities" (5.154). Vatsyayana casually mentions, among the women that one might sleep with (1.5.22), not only "second-hand" women (whom Manu despises as "previously had by another man")[15] but widows, whom Manu positively forbids to remarry,[16] though Kautilya regards them as quite free to remarry (3.2.19–32). The *Kamasutra* says: "A widow who is tormented by the weakness of the senses . . . finds, again, a man who enjoys life and is well endowed with good qualities" (4.2.31–34).

Vatsyayana has virtually no concern for dharma in the abstract, either as social law or as moral law. He doesn't seem to care at all about the danger that a woman creates for herself (or her children, or her lover) by committing adultery, nor does he care about injuring the institution of marriage. He knows that people will commit adultery. He thus implicitly rejects the traditional patriarchal party line that one finds in most Sanskrit texts, a line that punishes very cruelly indeed any woman who sleeps with a man other than her husband.

But Vatsyayana is genuinely concerned about the harm sex can do to women. In a formula familiar from the lists of kings who came to grief through their failure to control their passions, he warns men about this: "One should also avoid, even in the region where it is used, anything that is dangerous. The King of the Cholas killed Chitrasena, a courtesan, by using the 'wedge' during sex. And the Kuntala king Shatakarni Shatavahana killed his queen, Malayavati, by using the 'scissor.' Naradeva, whose hand was deformed, blinded a dancing-girl in one eye by using the 'drill' clumsily" (2.7.28–30). Vatsyayana caps this passage with cautionary verses:

> For, just as a horse in full gallop,
> blinded by the energy of his own speed,
> pays no attention to any post
> or hole or ditch on the path,
> so two lovers blinded by passion,
> in the friction of sexual battle,
> are caught up in their fierce energy
> and pay no attention to danger.
> And so a man who understands the text
> will apply it only after he has come to know
> the delicacy, ferocity, and strength of his young
> woman. (2.7.33–34)

Admittedly, this comes at the end of the chapter, where the pro-dharma afterthoughts are so often lodged. But Vatsyayana here expresses a concern for human welfare and happiness that is at heart deeply ethical.

Homosexuality

The dharma textbooks either ignore or stigmatize homosexual activity. In general it was punished, albeit mildly: Manu prescribes a ritual bath (11.174–75), Kautilya the payment of a small fine (4.13.40). Manu forbids a man to "shed his semen in nonhuman females, in a man, in a menstruating woman, in something other than a vagina, or in water" (11.174). The *Arthashastra* specifies punishments for many men raping a single prostitute; for a man who has sex with a female wandering ascetic, with a prostitute by force, or with a woman in a place other than the vagina; or for ejaculating in a man or in the vagina of an animal (4.13.37–41). The *Kamasutra* ignores some of these acts and regards others as noncriminal, though in bad taste.

The *Kamasutra* does not use the pejorative term *kliba* (the equivalent of "fairy") that most texts of the period use, but speaks instead of a "third nature" (*tritiya prakriti*) or perhaps a "third sexuality" or even a "third gender" in the sense of sexual behavior rather than anatomy. And it departs from the dharmic view of homosexuality in significant ways, principally by not regarding it as a crime at all. In place of the conventional law against sex between men, it describes, in totally nonjudgmental language, two types of men who make their living performing oral sex on other men. One is a crossdressing male, with women's clothing and stereotypical female gender behavior (chatter, grace, emotions, delicacy, timidity, innocence, frailty, and bashfulness) (2.9.1–5). The other is a closeted man who dresses in men's clothing, and whose fellatio technique Vatsyayana describes in considerable sensual detail, in the longest consecutive passage in the text describing any physical act, and with what might even be called gusto (2.9.6–11). This is a remarkably frank analysis of the mentality of the closet, the extended double entendre of an act that is cleverly designed to appear sexually innocent to a man who does not want, or does not want to admit that he wants, a homosexual encounter, but is an explicit invitation to a man who is willing to admit his desire for such an encounter. Nowhere else in the entire corpus of ancient Sanskrit literature is there a positive portrayal of men who have sex with men.

The legitimacy of this person of the "third nature" is supported by a casual remark in the passage describing the four sorts of love and the contexts in which they arise. One of the four types is called "the love that comes from erotic arousal," and it is said to arise from the imagination, not in response to any object of the senses: "It can be recognized in the course of oral sex with a woman or with a person of the third nature, or in various activities such as kissing" (2.1.42). Vatsyayana also lists the third nature among *women* who can be lovers (1.5.27).

One remark, in a passage warning a bridegroom not to be too shy with his shy bride, suggests that some people disapprove of men of the third nature: "[Certain scholars] say, 'If the girl sees that the man has not spoken a word for three nights, like a pillar, she will be discouraged and will despise him, as if he were someone of the third nature'" (3.2.3). At first glance, Vatsyayana seems to be making a negative judgment about men of the third nature after all. But when we look more closely we see that the people who make this judgment are the "scholars" with whom Vatsyayana almost always disagrees, as he does here, for he goes on to remark, "Vatsyayana says: He begins to entice her and win her trust, but he still remains sexually continent. When he entices her he does not force her in any way, for women are like flowers, and need to be enticed very tenderly. If they are taken by force by men who have not yet won their trust they become women who hate sex. Therefore he wins her over with gentle persuasion" (3.2.4–6). This is the sort of man whom the wrong sort of scholar, but not Vatsyayana, might fear that a young bride might stigmatize as someone of the third nature. It is evidence, all the more impressive for being so casual, of the prevalent homophobia of that time and place, and of Vatsyayana's courage in opposing it.

Two verses describe men who engage in oral sex not by profession, like the men of the third nature, but out of affection:

> Even young men, servants
> who wear polished earrings,
> indulge in oral sex
> only with certain men.
> And, in the same way, certain men-about-town
> who care for one another's welfare
> and have established trust
> do this service for one another. (2.9.35–36)

These men, who seem bound to one another by discriminating affection rather than promiscuous passion, are called "men-about-town" (*nagarakas*), the term used to designate the heterosexual heroes of the *Kamasutra*. In striking contrast with men of the third nature, always designated by the pronoun "she," these men are described with nouns and pronouns that unambiguously designate males. This, too, is stunningly adharmic.

What about homoerotic women? Manu mentions them only to make brief references to the punishments for a woman who seduces a virgin, generally cutting off several of her fingers, but occasionally having her whipped, her head shaved, or making her ride on a donkey (8.369–70). Kautilya prescribes a fine for a woman who deflowers a virgin (4.12.20–21), higher if the virgin did not desire her and the other woman acted only to satisfy her own passion. (The punishment is much more severe for a man who deflowers a virgin; his fingers or his whole hand may be chopped off [4.12.1–3]). It is noteworthy that Kautilya acknowledges that women may have desire and passion for other women. Even Vatsyayana does not say this; the women of the harem whom he discusses engage in sexual acts with one another only in the absence of men, not through the kind of personal choice that drives a man of the third nature: "The women of the harem cannot meet men, because they are carefully guarded; and since they have only one husband shared by many women in common, they are not satisfied. Therefore they give pleasure to one another with the following techniques" (5.6.1). The *Kamasutra* makes only one brief reference to women who may have chosen women as sexual partners: the text says that a girl may lose her virginity with a girlfriend or a servant girl (7.1.20).

Vatsyayana is, however, unique in the literature of the period in describing lesbian activity and never mentioning any punishment at all. He does this at the beginning of the chapter about the harem, where the women use dildos, as well as bulbs, roots, or fruits that have the form of the male organ, and statues of men that have distinct sexual characteristics (5.6.2–4). Yashodhara's commentary helpfully suggests the particular vegetables that one might employ: "By imagining a man, [these women] experience a heightened emotion that gives extreme satisfaction. These things have a form just like the male sexual organ: the bulbs of arrow-root, plantain, and so forth; the roots of coconut palms, breadfruit, and so forth; and the fruits of the bottle gourd, cucumber, and so forth." One can imagine little gardens of plantain and cucumber being lovingly cultivated within the inner rooms of the palace, the harem.

Between Dharma and Adharma

The *Kamasutra* aspires to describe all the things that a person could possibly do to have fun in and around bed; many of these acts, such as adultery and homosexuality, violate dharma, but Vatsyayana seems to feel duty-bound to mention them in order to cover the full spectrum of possibilities, as befits a *shastra,* a genre that aspires to totality. And sometimes this inclusiveness leads him to ricochet between dharmic and adharmic agendas.

Take the case of kings. We have seen how Manu and the *Arthashastra* incorporate conflicting ideas about the dharma of kings. The ambivalence of the *Kamasutra* on this issue is even more blatant. At first the *Kamasutra* states (at the beginning of a chapter, in a verse, always inclined to the dharmic side):

> Kings and counselors of state
> do not enter into other men's homes,
> for the whole populace sees what they do
> and imitates it.
> The three worlds watch the sun rise
> and so they too rise;
> then they watch the sun moving
> and they too start to act. (5.5.1–2)

And, at the end of the chapter detailing "devices" for adulterers, again in verse, we read:

> A king who takes pleasure in the welfare of his
>   people
> should absolutely not use these devices. (5.5.37)

But immediately after the first couplet the text adds, in realistic prose: "Therefore, because it is impossible and because they would be blamed, such men do nothing frivolous. But when they cannot help doing it, they employ stratagems" (5.5.3–4). And the entire body of the chapter contains elaborate "stratagems" that a king can use to lure women to him, of which this one is typical: "He has her husband slandered by a spy, saying, 'He is an enemy of the king,' and then seizes the woman as the man's wife, and by this means has her enter the harem" (5.5.27). It continues: "Those are the secret methods. They are generally used by the king's sons." And it concludes:

> These and many other devices
> for seducing other men's wives
> were put into circulation by kings,
> and are employed in region after region.
>   (5.5.35–36)

The tension between dharma as what should be and dharma as what is is stunningly manifest here.

Albrecht Wezler offers valuable insights into Vatsyayana's ambivalence. He speaks of "the apologetic endeavors of Vatsyayana," which reveal "the tension between kama and ideas and ideals which can appropriately be subsumed under the concept of dharma." He goes on to talk about Vatsyayana's

"wavering, inconsistent, nay contradictory" attitude, result-
ing from the tension between "unchecked professionalism, on
the one hand, and submissive acceptance of the criticism of
practices considered strange." And he concludes: "It is rather a
winningly frank admission of existing difficulties and a noteworthy prudent attempt to preserve the scientific standard of
a particular shastra under historical or contemporary conditions not really favorable to it."[17] Chief among these conditions
was the tightening of the web of social dharma in an age of
societal disruptions.

But there is also a level on which Vatsyayana seems to be
expressing his personal distaste for certain actions, regardless
of their dharmic or adharmic status. Sometimes he says that
such things are done (only) in the South (Vatsyayana probably
came from Pataliputra, in the North) (2.5.20–35);[18] sometimes
he says that only country folk do them, never sophisticated
cosmopolitans (2.10.22–26). And sometimes he simply falls
back on a kind of dharma of individualism: listen to your own
conscience, don't just do what the text says, and always have a
care for your partner's individual tastes and physical capacities
(2.6.52; 2.7.25–27, 34–35). It is on this level, outside the scope
of dharma and adharma, that Vatsyayana seems most secular,
and most rational.

5
Glossing Adharma with Dharma

Dharma and Dissent

Although the *Arthashastra* and the *Kamasutra* occasionally defend ethical dharma, their underlying arguments show a stunning disregard for it, as well as for social dharma and theological dharma. At times these texts seem to ricochet between conventional and more or less antinomian ideas. Indologists have often taken at face value the superficial, explicit statements in support of dharma that both texts made[1] but disregarded the texts' deeper implicit violations of dharma, therefore incorrectly assuming either a balance between pro- and anti-dharmic stances or a basically dharmic stance. I intend here to explore the implications of the contradictions between these superficial pro-dharma assertions and actual anti-dharmic attitudes.

The tension between the promotion of dharma and dissent against dharma was exacerbated by various other conflicts within these texts, whose robust intertextuality allowed them to grow over the centuries like intersecting palimpsests and often led to apparent internal dissonance. The influence of Manu on the *Arthashastra* (and of the *Arthashastra* on the *Kamasutra*) can account for some of the conflations of diametrically opposed points of view in both the *Arthashastra* and the *Kamasutra*. Since many ideas taken from Manu were eventually stitched into the *Arthashastra*, some, but not all, of the bits of pro-Brahmin ideology in the *Arthashastra* may be attributed to that revision, and others to the pro-Brahmin overlay that may have occurred in the *Kamasutra* as well as the *Arthashastra*. But it is also likely that these texts incorporated bits of popular antinomianism that seeped into the Brahmin establishment, bringing traces of widespread resistance to the official moral norms.

There are also contradictions within each text that do not derive from textual conflations. We can see this already in Manu, who speaks both in favor of and against eating meat (5.39–41; 5.45–56) (and, more broadly, in favor of both animal sacrifice and animal noninjury [*ahimsa*]), and both in favor of and against both the bride price and levirate marriage (9.64–68; 9.57–63, 120–21, 145–46, 159, 162–63, 167, 190–91). Manu also offers wildly divergent options for many punishments: For a man who sleeps with his guru's wife (the defining sin in Brahmin dharma), for instance, Manu offers two alternative restorations: either the man can castrate himself and walk, holding his testicles in his hand, until he drops dead, or he can drink for several weeks a mixture of the "five products of the cow" (*pancha-gavya*—milk, cow urine, cow dung, yogurt, and clarified butter) (11.104–7). Clearly the first punishment is the extreme, idealized version, which only the most fanatic (either among the miscreants themselves or among the panel of Brahmin judges who often decided the final verdict) were likely to choose over the second punishment, the practical alternative, the compromise position that Manu offers. Manu also lays out quite subjective criteria by which to judge whether an action is permissible or not.[2] By giving such easy alternatives to serious punishments, and finally offering an emergency loophole (*apad*, "disaster") that abrogates all rules, Manu undermines the impossibly strict laws of his system of dharma in order to make it viable. So, too, are some of the contradictions in the *Arthashastra* and *Kamasutra* intrinsic to the ambivalence of the authors' attitudes toward their subject matter: Kautilya is torn between the king's official commitment to dharma and the need for his martial and political supremacy, and Vatsyayana's man-about-town vacillates between doing the right thing for his partner and having his own fun.[3] These two great texts did not passively assimilate the patchwork and sometimes self-contradictory heritage of conflicting historical forces. They used it all in the service of new, conscious agendas, lodging antinomian ideas in the body of normative texts.

The Hays Office / Bookend Ploy

How did Kautilya and Vatsyayana get away with it? They managed to stay inside the Hindu fold by creating a smoke screen, a façade of dharma as ethical law, to mask the fact that they were trampling actual, practical social dharma into the dust. They deployed a veneer of dharma beneath which they lodged a pervasive adharmic agenda, a kind of body armor for the vulnerable body of the text. Amartya Sen speaks of "the respectful gestures" that the *Arthashastra* makes "to religious and social customs" (aka dharma).[4] Both texts make these "respectful gestures" throughout, but they make them particularly at the beginnings and ends of the texts as a whole and at the ends of the chapters. This is the bookend ploy, which rests upon an ancient tradition: the first and last books of the *Rig Veda* are later additions, and the final volume of the *Ramayana* abounds in afterthoughts and attempts to patch up trouble spots in the main text,[5] as the verses of Kautilya and Vatsyayana often do.

Both texts begin with brief invocations. The *Arthashastra* scrupulously follows the Indian custom of invoking a god or gods at the start of a text—but it invokes Shukra and Brihaspati, the chief counselors of the anti-gods and the gods, respectively (1.2.4).[6] These are not gods anyone worships but unprincipled mythological characters, both of them liars and tricksters, and surely the joint invocation of Brihaspati with his demonic counterpart (and Kautilya puts Shukra first, the demon before the deity) casts doubt upon any authority Brihaspati might have had.

The *Kamasutra* fudges the mandatory invocation by invoking the Three Aims in place of the usual deities that other texts invoke. As S. K. De drily remarks of this invocation, "This is only to bring the *śāstra* on a level of equal authoritativeness with other *śāstra*s which make a similar claim: the work does not invoke holy and hoary mythical sages as the *dharmaśāstra* often does."[7] Vatsyayana's bow to dharma, artha, and kama here is a clever way of *not* bowing to a real god by pretending (against ordinary Hindu usage) that the Three Aims are gods. There, too, and at the end of the book, the *Kamasutra* ranks dharma ahead of kama (though it insists that artha is actually most important for a courtesan), but this is just standard operating procedure for *shastras*. So these framing pro-dharma remarks may be largely written off.

Then, however, Vatsyayana relates a myth involving the Creator, Prajapati, placing at the very start of his work one of the very few passages in it that refer to the gods.[8] According to this account, the Creator himself first made a text about the Three Aims in 100,000 chapters, which was then divided into three: a text by Manu (about dharma), one by Brihaspati (about artha), and one, the *Kamasutra*, by Nandi (the bull-headed servant of the god Shiva). The *Kamasutra* here regards Manu not as a human scholar but as a son of the Creator, echoing the myth with which Manu begins his own dharma text; Vatsyayana includes Manu and his text as part of the divine pedigree of the *Kamasutra*. He then goes on to tell us how two sages (Shvetaketu and Babhravya, whom he cites again in the course of his work, unlike Nandi, who never appears again) reduced Nandi's text (originally in a thousand chapters) to its present seven parts, first in 500 chapters and then in 150 (1.1.9–10). After that we learn that seven human authors,[9] whom Vatsyayana cites and argues with throughout his book, made separate books out of each of the seven parts.

This myth is closely based on a myth in the *Mahabharata* (12.59.30–94), not about the *Kamasutra* but about the *Arthashastra,* a myth that Vatsyayana adapted for his own use (yet another instance of the *Kamasutra*'s dependence on the *Arthashastra*). According to the *Mahabharata,* in order to put an end to the primeval period of anarchy, the Creator first made a text about the Three Aims in 100,000 verses, after which Vishalaksha ("Far-Sighted," an epithet of the god Shiva) reduced the book about artha to 10,000 verses, in view of the brevity of human life. Then Bahudantaka ("Many-Toothed," an epithet of the god Indra) reduced it to 5,000 verses, Brihaspati to 3,000 and Shukra to 1,000.

In the *Arthashastra* (1.17.4–43), Shiva's epithet of Vishalaksha becomes the name of a human sage whom Kautilya quotes several times, and Indra's epithet of Bahudantaka the name of another human sage.[10] So Kautilya has humanized the

old myth, euhemerized it. Vatsyayana similarly humanized the
Mahabharata myth in adapting it for the *Kamasutra:* he kept
the Creator as the prime mover, but then he substituted Shiva's
servant, Nandi, for Shiva as the first author of the *Kamasutra,*
left out Indra and Shukra entirely from the authorship of the
Arthashastra, and retained only the name of Brihaspati un-
changed (and in the company not of gods but of quasi-human
sages, leaving open the possibility that this is Brihaspati the
materialist rather than Brihaspati the god). And even this is
little more than a literary flourish. Thus, even in their most
theological moments—the invocations—the authors of our
two *shastras* try to make some sort of human sense out of the
inherited myth.

Both the *Arthashastra* and the *Kamasutra* begin and end
with statements ranking dharma ahead of artha and kama
(statements that both texts contradict in the bodies of the
works). The *Arthashastra* also devotes an entire, if rather short,
chapter to dharma (1.3.1–17; 1.4.16), including *varnashrama*
dharma (the laws for the four classes and the four stages of
life) and *sadharana* dharma (the general moral law that applies to everyone); much of this reads as if it could have been
taken more or less straight out of Manu, simply putting Manu's
verse into prose.

Similarly, at the very end of the *Kamasutra,* Vatsyayana
muzzles the adharmic arguments that have pervaded the text.[11]
He does this with a particularly complex song and dance that
does not explicitly mention dharma:

> The unusual techniques employed to increase
>   passion,
> which have been described as this particular book
>   required,

are strongly restricted right here in this verse,
right after it.
For the statement that "there is a text for this"
does not justify a practice. People should realize
that the contents of the texts apply in general,
but each actual practice is for one particular re-
    gion. (7.2.54–5)[12]

The "unusual techniques" in the immediately preceding section involve such matters as the use of dildos to compensate
for temporary or permanent impotence and the use of magic
concoctions for various purposes, subjects that Vatsyayana
clearly finds distasteful. The second verse here—"For the statement that . . ."—is the only one in the entire *Kamasutra* that
Vatsyayana uses twice; the first time was after his discussion of
oral sex, which he also regards somewhat askance (2.9.41). On
that occasion he added another verse:

Medical science, for example,
recommends cooking even dog meat,
for juice and virility;
but what intelligent person would eat it? (2.9.42)

This is an extraordinarily critical qualification for an author
to make about his own text. S. K. De considers it a statement
"in the true scientific spirit."[13] Manu, who warns that even the
glance of a dog when you are eating pollutes the food (3.239–
41), would certainly agree with Vatsyayana about eating dog
meat. But where Manu is talking about pollution, Vatsyayana
is talking about taste, in both senses of the word.
    In this final bookend, Vatsyayana adds an even more
surprising verse:

> Vatsyayana . . . made this work in chastity and in
>   the highest meditation,
> for the sake of worldly life;
> he did not compose it
> for the sake of passion. (7.2.57)

No one has any idea what sort of life Vatsyayana actually led,[14] but in any case, using his life to defend his text is a very long shot indeed. The book concludes by placing the control of passion within the Triad:

> The man who is well taught and expert in this text
> pays attention to dharma and artha;
> he does not indulge himself too much in passion,
> and so he succeeds when he plays the part of a
>   lover. (7.2.59)

This bookend technique somewhat resembles the method that Hollywood producers adopted to get around the strict moral code (the Motion Picture Production Code) enforced by the Hays Office from 1930 to 1968 forbidding, inter alia, the depiction of the success of a crime such as murder or adultery. In *The Postman Always Rings Twice* (1946, directed by Tay Garnett), for example, Lana Turner and John Garfield seem to succeed in committing both adultery and murder—until, at the very last minute, as they are driving off into what appears to be a beautiful sunset, he loses control of the car (while kissing her) and drives into a tree, gratuitously and meaninglessly killing her (a death for which he is convicted of murder and executed). In *Ocean's Eleven* (1960, directed by Lewis Milestone), Frank Sinatra and the Rat Pack execute a brilliant and entirely successful robbery of the Las Vegas casinos—only to watch, at the last minute, all their money accidentally burn up in an incinerated coffin. Such tacked-on endings allowed Hollywood to violate the production code in the body of the movie. In the *Arthashastra* and *Kamasutra,* bookend verses were similarly tacked on to exculpate the main text.

Blaming Earlier Scholars and Teachers

After invoking, at the start, their mythical ancestors, the two texts go on to invoke human authors of earlier texts on their subjects, as well as earlier schools of thought. These lists of sources—the ancient Indian equivalent of "citations of the literature" in present-day academic dissertations—are sometimes capped by the statement "This is what the scholars/ teachers (*acharyas*) say." (Manu doesn't cite any predecessors, since he claims to have been there on the spot at the beginning of the world, and *had* no predecessors. Instead, he lists his pupils [1.34–35].)[15]

We do not have the full texts from which such passages are cited, but their authors may not be entirely mythical. Evidence for their reality includes the anthological nature of the *Arthashastra* and the *Kamasutra,* their explicit statements of indebtedness to other texts, and the fact that other texts and commentaries, as well as later *artha-shastra*s and *kama-shastra*s, cite some of the same sources.[16] Ironically, the very "masterly completeness" of the *Kamasutra* (and, indeed, of the *Arthashastra*) "must have deprived early treatises of the possibility of survival."[17] There is less evidence, however, that any of these texts said what Kautilya and Vatsyayana say they said.[18] Friedrich Wilhelm suggests, "[The cited authors] may represent authentic views though their style may be fictitious," and their "authentic views are presented in a fictitious style as the statements of legendary teachers."[19] More precisely, in his view, the *Arthashastra*'s citations are often fictional, while the *Kamasutra*'s are usually more trustworthy.[20] In general, Vatsyayana imposes his own style on the inherited material, though in some places he has "so closely followed his originals that they have heavily influenced his style with their own."[21] Yet Vatsyayana disagrees with his predecessors less than Kautilya does, and is less polemical.[22] Vatsyayana often quotes the opinions of individual teachers without refuting them, while in the *Arthashastra* such views are generally contradicted by another individual author and/or by Kautilya himself.[23]

Both the *Arthashastra* and the *Kamasutra* explicitly acknowledge their debt to previous texts on their respective subjects. Kautilya states: "This one *Arthashastra* was made for the most part by gathering together the *artha-shastras* that former teachers composed for winning the earth and keeping it" (1.1.1). He does not name these former teachers here, but he does name them elsewhere, as, for instance, in his arguments about whether or not a king should kill his sons as soon as they are born (1.17.4–43)[24] and what sorts of people are eligible to be ministers of state (1.8.1–29).[25] Thomas Trautmann interprets the opening statement of the *Arthashastra* to mean "that not merely the views of predecessors quoted in the *Arthashastra*, but the bulk of the entire work is to be referred to previous treatises; that the *Arthashastra* (much like the *Kamasutra*) is a compendium of earlier treatises, whether in abridgement or in full."[26] And indeed, that does seem to be what the opening statement *says*. But here the text that so often advocates lying may well be speaking what Richard Nixon used to call "inoperative" truths (nowadays known as "alternative facts").

Vatsyayana, too, begins by invoking his academic ancestors, "the scholars who made known the mutual agreement among the Triad" (1.1.3), and then, after the brief mythological episode about the Creator, he continues in a long paragraph that mentions his human predecessors by name (1.1.10–12). In the course of the work he invokes these authorities, one by one, in a number of conversations, beginning with an argument about what sorts of women are and are not eligible as sexual partners (1.5.22–26) and continuing in a debate about whether or not women have orgasms as men do, presenting the cockamamie theories of Audalaki and Babhravya (such as that women don't have orgasms but have worms inside them that produce an itch that demands to be scratched) before stating, and defending against objections by several unnamed interlocutors, Vatsyayana's own sensible opinion (that they do have orgasms like those of men) (2.1.8–30). Vatsyayana cites one of his predecessors (Suvarnanabha) in a discussion of the more unusual sexual positions (2.6.13–34), pointing out that having sex in the water, which Suvarnanabha recommends, is forbidden by learned men (whom the commentator glosses as the authors of the dharma texts) (2.6.35).

By situating their texts as mere compilations of previous works, Kautilya and Vatsyayana create and then fully utilize a potential space for free discourse and frank commentary, minimizing the danger of personal repercussions.[27] Casting the blame for their adharma, as well as the credit for their dharma, on their predecessors allows Kautilya and Vatsyayana to incriminate them for whatever trouble they themselves might get into, as if to say, "We are not doing anything new, anything naughty, just rearranging the statements of our illustrious and honored predecessors."

The *Purva Paksha* (Opponent's View) as a Straw Man

Ancestors and predecessors also played another, more specific role in facilitating the adharmic discourse of the *Arthashastra* and the *Kamasutra*. For Kautilya and Vatsyayana often used them to smuggle in dangerous opinions through one of the standard conventions of Indian arguments.

Among the many ways in which the *Arthashastra* and the *Kamasutra* are alike (and different from Manu) is their manner of arguing. Manu never actually argues at all: like a parent to a child, he presents primarily "because" statements (explicit dogmas or appeals to authority: do it because I say so) and only occasionally "this is why" arguments (implicit rationalizations or appeals to persuasion).[28] He also sometimes simply juxtaposes conflicting views, without prioritizing them or making any attempt to reconcile them. In the *Kamasutra* and the *Arthashastra*, by contrast, there are actual arguments: a point of view is stated and defended, an opposing view presented—sometimes a series of views—and the author caps it with what he regards as the best argument. In the *Kamasutra*, as Trautmann remarks, "The opinions of earlier anonymous authorities, individual authors and schools are quoted and sometimes rebutted in the *Arthashastra* manner."[29] These authorities are not only the particular predecessors of Vatsyayana and Kautilya but the general group of anonymous "scholars" (*acharyas*) for whom our authors have far less respect.

Amartya Sen sees in this sort of dialogue the beginning of what he calls the argumentative tradition in India, "the long tradition of arguing."[30] Such argument is indeed generally characteristic of the scientific *shastras*. In particular, and essential to my argument, it is the custom in the *shastra* tradition first to cite an opponent's opinion—known as the *purva paksha* ("prior view" or, literally, "preceding wing"), often without explicitly noting that it is, in the author's view, incorrect—and then to state the author's own, correct opinion (which is called the *siddhanta*, the perfected view, the solution). Our two authors put the *purva paksha* tradition to work in the tap dance they do around dharma. The critical citations of the anonymous "teachers" allow Kautilya and Vatsyayana to put in "opponents'" mouths opinions that may not actually have been expressed by anyone but are merely part of a mythical *purva paksha*. This is a possibility that we will see, in chapter 6, at work in later centuries in India, as the *purva paksha* then shaded off into the entirely mythical in the textual traditions of the skeptics and materialists.

The unspecified "scholars/teachers" (*acharyas*) whom both texts mock, as well as particular named scholars whose ideas are cited from time to time as part of the *purva paksha,* only to be rejected, voice sentiments that the texts officially reject but may want to make the reader think about. Both Kautilya and Vatsyayana sometimes quote older scholars or "opposing schools" to state rather extreme ideas that they may really believe themselves but do not want to own as theirs, to get them on the table, and then say, "Oh no, don't do that!" in much the manner that a lawyer might reveal evidence to a jury and then, when reprimanded by the judge, say, "The jury will disregard those remarks." In this way, an author can hide behind a cited and ostensibly rejected viewpoint as behind a duck blind.[31]

The *purva paksha* technique thus serves the *Arthashastra* and the *Kamasutra* as a very useful way of challenging dharma without seeming to challenge it. It is not always easy to tell the two agendas apart—setting up straw men to demolish and using them as stalking horses to say what the author does not dare to say outright—since they both take the same form: ostensible disagreement. And indeed, the two roles are lexically related, according to *Merriam-Webster* online, which gives a double meaning for "straw man": "a weak or imaginary opposition (as an argument or adversary) set up only to be easily confuted, or a person set up to serve as a cover for a usually questionable transaction." In this second sense, an author uses the *purva paksha* to smuggle a "questionable" opinion into readers' minds under cover of an "easily confuted" quotation.

The very format of quotations in Sanskrit facilitates the use of "opponents" to express one's own secret view. For Sanskrit does not mark the beginning of a direct quotation; it simply marks the end of the quotation with the particle *iti*—"thus," as in *"iti Gonikaputra,"* meaning "This is what Gonikaputra says/said." The reader therefore does not know until the end of the quotation whether the author is speaking for himself or quoting someone he may disagree with, so the reader is inclined to accept the quote as the author's words—unless, at the end, he or she is told not to accept it. For instance, we have seen Vatsyayana, who has elsewhere warned married women (in keeping with social dharma) to avoid beggar women and ascetic women, advise the would-be adulterer as follows: "'A meeting [with a married woman] is easy to arrange in the houses of a girlfriend, a beggar woman, a Buddhist nun, or an ascetic woman'—this is what Gonikaputra says" (5.4.43). Vatsyayana goes on to say that it's really best to meet the woman in her own house, but we have already learned of other forbidden—but possible—meeting places, and when we first read about them we thought, for several seconds, that Vatsyayana was telling us that they, too, are "easy to arrange."

These straw men are the central players in the drama of ancient Indian logic, opponents who are set up only to be demolished, rather like those various confused Greeks whom Socrates sets straight in Plato's dialogues. We can trace them back at least to Plato's counterparts in the Upanishads, in the sixth century BCE, when Uddalaka (father of Shvetaketu) and a series of sages express various wrong ideas until they are told the right idea.[32] In the Upanishads, however, the wrong ideas are clearly rejected; the innovation of the *Arthashastra* and the *Kamasutra* was the use of the *purva paksha* to bring in adharmic ideas that are rejected only officially (and perhaps unofficially recommended), as a device that could be used at the very least in the service of open-mindedness and, at the most, for subversion.

The subversive use of the *purva paksha* may have led some members of the scholarly community to distrust the convention. A medical textbook composed during this approximate period, for instance, depicts a series of physicians arguing about the etiology of a disease until the author states his own view:

> Now, as the sages were arguing in this way, Punar-vasu said, "Don't talk like this. It is hard to get to the truth when people take sides. People who utter arguments and counter-arguments as if they were established facts never get to the end of their own side (*paksha*), as if they were going round and round on an oil press. Not until you shake off the torpor of factionalism from what you want to know will true knowledge emerge."[33]

Yet the *purva paksha* remained the primary pattern of logical discourse in ancient India.

We saw the straightforward *purva paksha* mechanism at work when the *Kamasutra* cited, and dismissed, the opinions of earlier authorities on ways to test guards in the harem (5.6.40–42) or on the possibility that women might have the same sort of orgasms as men do (2.1.10–30). Vatsyayana usually cites his opponents with respect, simply adding his own opinion at the end, while Kautilya often makes fun of the people he disagrees with, remarking that the truth is so obvious,

only a fool could disagree, or shouting "No!" before he introduces his own, correct opinion. But Kautilya uses the method
adharmically when he cites, and officially dismisses, the opinions of a series of earlier authorities on the way to deal with a
king's potentially patricidal sons (1.17.4–21). One of these authorities, likening princes to crabs, who "eat their begetters,"
suggests that they be secretly murdered, "before their father
has started to love them." A second, objecting that it is cruel
to kill the innocent and unwise to wipe out the race of kings,
suggests imprisonment. A third objects that the prince will an-
ticipate this move and seize the king; he suggests sending him
to a frontier fort. A fourth says the fort of a neighboring lord,
outside the territory, would be better. A fifth would send him
to his mother's kinsmen. The sixth suggests that he be made
addicted to vices. Kautilya lets the "scholars" quarrel among
themselves and objects only to this last suggestion: "'That is a
living death,' says Kautilya, 'for if the royal family has undis-
ciplined sons, as soon as it is attacked it will fall apart like a
piece of wood eaten by worms'" (1.17.22–23). (The reference to
worms caps all the animal metaphors that the other scholars
have used: besides crabs, they liken the son to a snake, a ram,
a calf—this is a feral world!) And then Kautilya, having put
on the table, in the mouths of other people, a number of truly
diabolical suggestions that may never have occurred to anyone
but him, caps the argument with his own, less violent though
still rather heartless advice: "If he has only one son, and that
son is dear to him, the king should imprison him. If he has
many sons, the king should banish them to the frontier or to
another region" (1.17.41–42). None of the truly appalling methods are actually recommended, but we will not forget them.
They might come in handy some day.

6

Skepticism and Materialism
in Ancient India

Who Were the Lokayatikas and the Charvakas?

I have argued that the *Kamasutra* and the *Arthashastra* often deviated significantly from dharma in ways that amounted to a covert attack. Now I want to argue that this attack was continued in a most ingenious and devious way by the creation of a mythology about wicked skeptics or materialists whose words were always cited with shock and disapproval but always cited, always kept alive.

The Lokayatikas and the Charvakas, materialists and skeptics, are the heirs of the *Arthashastra* and the *Kamasutra*, at least to the extent that the idea of doing whatever you need to do to get what you want (in the *Arthashastra*) and having as much fun as you possibly can (in the *Kamasutra*), with no regard for dharma in either case, was fuel for the Lokayatika/ Charvaka legend. The texts attributed to Lokayatikas (or, later, Charvakas) carry on the materialist and skeptical legacy of the scientific *shastras,* sniping away at dharma. We can identify places where the *Kamasutra* and the *Arthashastra* are skeptical, and then trace such views as they are attributed to the Lokayatikas and the Charvakas. Thus resistance to the dharmic party line continued to be present in ancient and medieval India, producing numerous fissures in the smooth surface of the conventional theocracy. The *Arthashastra* praises the Lokayatikas and the *Kamasutra* criticizes them, but both texts show a striking congruence with the adharmic sentiments that many texts of the period (including the *Kamasutra*) often pejoratively attributed to the Lokayatikas.

The Sanskrit word *Lokayata* is derived from *loka,* "world" or "people," and *Lokayata* (literally, "spread [*ayata*] throughout the world/people") therefore can be translated as "worldliness" or "[the opinion] of the people." Lokayata is, properly, the doctrine; those who subscribe to it are Lokayatikas.[1] The thirteenth-century commentator on the *Kamasutra* (1.2.21) says that Lokayatikas are people whose thinking is limited (*ayata*) to this world (*loka*). Another suggestion derives *Laukayatika* from *ayati,* meaning "the time to come," the future, so that the Lokayatikas are those for whom this world (*loka*) is the (only) future (*ayati*).[2] *Charvakas* can mean "Sweet-Talkers" (from *charu* ["sweet"] and *vaka* ["speaking"]), but they are also sometimes said to be followers of a philosopher named Charvaka. The verb *char* means "to move about" but also "to get around" (that is, "to be promiscuous")[3] and "to be tricky or slippery with words." To further complicate the issue, sometimes the Lokayatikas or the Charvakas were called "Barhaspatyas," from the allegedly lost (and much-cited) text called the "Sutra of Brihaspati,"[4] attributed to Brihaspati. This Brihaspati could have been either the mythical, conniving chief counselor of the king of the gods or a human person whom the *Kamasutra* regards as the original author of the *Arthashastra*. According to the *Mahabharata*, Brihaspati invented the adharmic Lokayatra [*sic*] doctrine.[5]

Lokayata and Lokayatikas in the *Arthashastra* and the *Kamasutra*

Centuries after their own time, the *Arthashastra* and the *Kamasutra* were widely regarded as having an extensive and striking congruence with Lokayata and Charvaka doctrines. A Charvaka in an eleventh-century satirical play called *The Rise of the Moon of Enlightenment* praises the science of politics (that is, the *Arthashastra*),[6] and the philosopher Madhava in the fourteenth century regarded both the *Arthashastra* and the *Kamasutra* as Charvaka texts:[7] "Most people (*loka*), in accordance with the *Arthashastra* and *Kamasutra*, considering *artha* and *kama* the only Human Aims and denying the existence of any object belonging to a future world, follow only the Charvaka doctrine. Therefore another, appropriate, name for the Charvaka doctrine is 'Lokayata.'"[8] We have seen that this statement is largely valid for what the *Arthashastra* and the *Kamasutra* actually advocate, though it is *not* what they *say* they advocate. Madhava was no fool.

One historian of Indian philosophy held that materialism in India was created for practical politicians like Kautilya: "In it they found a doctrine which, by denying the existence of God, after-life, heaven and hell, etc., put out of their way all moral scruples that were hindrances to their actions."[9] Another said that the *Arthashastra* "certainly draws inspiration from the Lokāyata philosophy."[10] Matthew Kapstein regards the *Arthashastra* as the beginning of the Charvaka/Lokayata tradition.[11] Certainly Kautilya explicitly approves

of the philosophy he calls Lokayata. At the very start of the
Arthashastra, right after the table of contents, Kautilya states
that one of the four knowledge systems that enable a person
to know dharma and artha (he omits kama) is critical inquiry
(*anviksha*) (1.2.1). Critical inquiry (he continues) has three
parts, one of which is the Lokayata system,[12] which critically
applies logic to the other three knowledge systems—the Veda
(i.e., theology), economics (cattle rearing, farming, and trade),
and politics (1.2.10). Lokayata (he concludes) applies logic to
the Vedas to distinguish dharma from adharma; to economics to distinguish artha from anartha; and to politics to determine what is good policy and what is bad policy. (Here he
substitutes politics for the expected kama as the third element
in the Triad.) But it is not at all clear that the people who belong to what Kautilya calls the Lokayata school are the same as
the Lokayatikas whom later texts accuse of making violently
adharmic statements. The Lokayata that the *Arthashastra* approves of and recommends may have been an old system of
materialistic or natural philosophy that rejected both a world
beyond and the process of rebirth.[13] This would indeed make it
a school of skeptics and materialists of a sort, a tradition that
lives on in the passages of later Sanskrit texts that describe the
Charvakas, like the Lokayatikas in the *Arthashastra,* as logicians, philosophers who question the validity of any forms of
knowledge. The Lokayata in the *Arthashastra* is not a sect at all
but simply a philosophical school; yet its commitment to logic,
as well as to economics and politics, may have made it already
suspect in the dharmic world. For the Sanskrit word for "logician," *hetuka,* literally "one who has [argues from] causes
(*hetu*)," often takes on, in dharma texts, much of the pejorative
tone of "rationalist," "casuist," "Sophist," or even "Jesuitical"—
someone who uses cold reason and plays tricks with words to

deny the truths of the heart. Kautilya approves of the followers of the Lokayata school, who study the Vedas in order to distinguish dharma from adharma, even though they do so through the morally suspect techniques of logic.

In laying out the knowledge systems as he does, Kautilya rejects two extant views of critical inquiry. First he challenges the assertion of the followers of Manu (presumably the author of the dharma text, not the sage present at the original creation), who drop critical inquiry entirely, regarding it as subsumed under the Veda. Kautilya's rejection of this view is a vote for reason over Veda (more precisely, a vote against people who value the Veda over reason) and a vote against the world of Manu (with whom Kautilya often disagrees).

But then Kautilya criticizes the views of the Barhaspatyas, who omit both the Veda and critical inquiry and argue that the Veda is "merely a cover for those who know how the world works" (1.2.2–4). Here, in the opening frame of the book, Kautilya is still in his pro-dharma mode, and he clearly disapproves of the anti-Vedic Barhaspatyas, even as he approves of the Lokayatikas. Later this distinction between Lokayatikas and Barhaspatyas becomes blurred by people who assert that someone named Brihaspati both founded the Lokayata school (thus merging the Barhaspatyas and the Lokayatikas) and composed the *Arthashastra* (as the *Kamasutra* says he did). The "Brihaspati politics" that a learned Brahmin teaches in the *Mahabharata* (3.33.57)[14] are deeply Kautilyan. But there may well be several different Brihaspatis, one the guru of the gods, one the alleged human author of an *arthashastra,* and one the alleged human founder of a school of skeptics or materialists. There are several quite different descriptions of "the school of Brihaspati," as there are of the Lokayatikas and the Charvakas.

The *Kamasutra,* in dramatic contrast with the *Artha-shastra,* is highly critical of the Lokayatikas, whom it repre-sents as people who attack dharma (2.2.21–24). Vatsyayana presents their text as the opponent's incorrect argument about dharma, the *purva paksha:* don't believe in anything you can't see; don't waste your money on sacrifice in the hope of the existence of a heaven with gods who will receive your offering and give you something in return. By this time, significantly, the depiction of the Lokayatikas had moved from the realm of ethical dharma (in the *Arthashastra,* where they argue about perception and values) to the world of social and theological dharma (in the *Kamasutra,* where they urge people not to per-form actions in accordance with dharma).

The *Kamasutra* lists the Lokayatikas as part of a group of three, of which the other two are fatalists (who attack artha) and pragmatists (who attack kama), not philosophical schools but types of persons. The Lokayatikas here are just people who care only about material wealth and having fun, as we might speak of a person as a Stoic or Epicurean—not meaning some-one who follows the Roman philosophies but just someone who enjoys a good bottle of wine. This is the cluster of beliefs that the Lokayatikas represented in Vatsyayana's day.

Skeptics and Materialists in Ancient India

The English terms "materialist" and "skeptic," as well as, occa-sionally, "hedonist," are often applied to Charvakas or Lokaya-tikas, though the English words only rather grossly represent the Indian arguments and can serve only as rough placehold-ers for the Sanskrit names. Even so, it is best to define them. A "materialist," as defined by the *Oxford English Dictionary,* is someone who believes that nothing exists except matter, or that mental phenomena are nothing more than the operation of material agencies. The looser meaning is also often appropriate for Lokayatikas or Charvakas: those who prefer material possessions to spiritual values. (Indian Marxists, particularly in Kolkata, are fascinated by the Lokayatikas and the Charvakas and write a lot about them. There is also an active website, "Cārvāka 4 India: Defending Secularism and Rational Inquiry.")[15] A "skeptic," again from the *Oxford English Dictionary,* is a person who doubts the possibility of real knowledge of any kind, holding that there are no adequate grounds for certainty as to the truth of any proposition whatever. The broader, looser meaning denotes someone who denies the competence of reason, or the existence of any justification for certitude, outside the limits of experience. And a hedonist is, still according to the *Oxford English Dictionary,* "one who regards pleasure as the chief good."

Skepticism in India certainly predated the first references to Lokayatikas or Charvakas. Skepticism began in the very earliest of the Hindu texts, the *Rig Veda,* in a poem that is known, from its first words, as the "Nasadiya" (or the "There was not" poem; the phrase "nasad/na-asat," "There was not," is the past tense of "na-asti," "There is not."). This short, linguistically straightforward poem, which explicitly lays out an open-ended attitude to the first things, raises unanswerable questions:

> There was neither nonexistence nor existence
>   then;
> there was neither the realm of space nor the sky
>   that is beyond.
> What stirred? Where? In whose protection?
> Was there water, bottomlessly deep?

There was neither death nor immortality then.
There was no distinguishing sign of night nor
    of day.
. . . Who really knows? Who will here proclaim it?
Whence was it produced? Whence is this creation?
The gods came afterward, with the creation of this
    universe.
Who then knows whence it has arisen?
Whence this creation has arisen—
perhaps it formed itself, or perhaps it did not—
the one who looks down on it, in the highest
    heaven, only he knows,
or perhaps he does not know.[16]

There is a charming open-mindedness in this hymn. The last line—"or perhaps he does not know"—seems almost to mock the rhetoric of more typical hymns in the very text in which it occurs. The hymn asks, "Who really knows?"—questioning the very nature, perhaps the very existence, of God. Amartya Sen cites it as a source of Indian skepticism.[17]

D. N. Jha is right to call skepticism an "undercurrent of Indian thought."[18] But it is often very far under. The general sort of antinomian thinking that eventually flowered in the Charvaka citations was probably always there, as there are always people who resist the dominant paradigms. The folklore that left traces in texts as early as the *Rig Veda* and remains a staple of Indian oral traditions to the present is often stunningly antinomian. But even the more specific and more dangerous statements attributed to the Charvakas, violating social rules and rituals and criticizing Brahmins, had begun to appear, somewhat tentatively, in the Vedic corpus. A text from c. 800 BCE tells the story of a lustful and vicious Brahmin who compelled the wives of other men to come to him and submit to him sexually, and then often killed them.[19] This story was then repeated in the *Mahabharata*, centuries later;[20] it became a well-known part of the tradition. Here is evidence that, at a very early date, some people despised Brahmins who abused their power, and kept on despising them, and said so in Sanskrit. (It is also early evidence of complaints, if not protests, against Brahmin sexual abuse, which we have already considered in the myth of primeval sexual anarchy.) This part of the Charvaka critique, at least, is very old indeed.

Lokayatikas, Charvakas, and Nastikas (Naysayers)

The Lokayata and Charvaka traditions have not played the same sort of role in Indian history as the *Arthashastra* and the *Kamasutra*. We do not have Lokayata or Charvaka texts, so they have no place in the continuous fabric of the Sanskrit textual and commentarial tradition. Nor does any extant text advocate their views; they are cited only as negative examples, indeed as cautionary extremes, *reductio ad absurdum* arguments. Yet their ideas do pop up with impressive frequency in major Sanskrit texts as well as in the much broader oral traditions, and therefore, as bogeymen, they remained alive and well in the consciousness of Indians for many centuries. They cannot have posed real subversive threats to the Brahmin establishment—but this can also be said of the *Arthashastra* and the *Kamasutra*. All of this has been happening only in the Indian *imaginaire,* and the Lokayatikas and Charvakas are simply even more *imaginaire* than the kings and playboys that Kautilya and Vatsyayana imagined.

By about the eighth century CE, the terms *Lokayatika* and *Barhaspatya* came to be used interchangeably with the term *Charvaka,* and eventually *Charvaka* took the place of *Lokayatika* as the word most often used for materialists or skeptics. According to the twelfth-century historian Hemacandra, the Barhaspatyas, Charvakas, and Lokayatikas[21] are usually regarded as a single school, the Lokayata.[22] The Charvakas have often formed a kind of internal diaspora, in contrast with true outsiders such as Buddhists and Jains, who were serious competitors (for royal patronage and other support) against sectarian groups like the worshippers of Shiva or Vishnu. *The Rise of the Moon of Enlightenment* treats the Charvaka tradition as "an offshoot of Brahmanism, and not a heresy originating outside of the Brahmanical fold."[23] Like the authors of the *Arthashastra* and the *Kamasutra,* the Charvakas are depicted as Brahmins working against other Brahmins.

But Charvakas were sometimes grouped together not only with Lokayatikas and Barhaspatyas but also with non-Brahmins such as Buddhists and Jains, who shared with them the explicit denial of the Vedas and the authority of Brahmins. It would appear that, in the dark of social dharma, all heretics look alike.[24] One text groups Charvakas with Buddhists, Jains, Greeks, "Skull-Bearers" (highly antisocial worshippers of Shiva), and Tantrics.[25] Does this classificatory flexibility mean that the Charvakas by that time were nothing more than a term in a list, any list?

There is one other commonly used term that greatly contributed to this confusion, as it was often applied to Charvakas, and that is *Nastika,* a term generally, but rather too loosely, translated as "atheist"—that is, one who denies the existence of the gods. The term *Nastika* is traditionally (and probably historically) derived from the phrase "*na asti*" (the same vocabulary that yielded the title of the Vedic Nasadiya hymn); a Nastika is thus one who says "It/he is not," while an

Astika (a pious Hindu) says, "It/he is."[26] A Nastika is, literally, a "naysayer," but that to which he says "Nay" was regarded quite differently at different times. The subject of the copula is omitted, which has left the more precise meaning of the term open to dispute. "It/he" may refer to a god, as in a phrase in the *Rig Veda*, "They say of him [Indra], 'He is not.'"[27] In a passage in the *Katha Upanishad,* however, a few centuries later, the unexpressed subject could refer to the pantheistic, universal world-soul: "How can [it] be comprehended except by one saying, '[It] is'?"[28] According to one Sanskrit dictionary, a Nastika believes that there is no other world, nor any lord.[29]

In Sir Richard Burton's "translation" (really a retelling) of the story of the king and the vampire, when asked to define the term "atheist," the vampire replies:

> Of a truth, it is most difficult to explain. The sages assign to it three or four several meanings: first, one who denies that the gods exist; secondly, one who owns that the gods exist but denies that they busy themselves with human affairs; and thirdly, one who believes in the gods and in their providence, but also believes that they are easily to be set aside. . . . Thus the Vishnu Swamis of the world have invested the subject with some confusion. The simple, that is to say, the mass of mortality, have confounded that confusion by reproachfully applying the word atheist to those whose opinions differ materially from their own.[30]

Despite the Orientalist swipe at the "Vishnu Swamis," Burton's is a far from inaccurate summary of the range of the term *Nastika.*

In an early period, before the time of the *Arthashastra* or the *Kamasutra,* the Nastika may have been an integral part of the agonistic structure of the Vedic sacrifice, someone who confronted the Astika.[31] The doubts expressed in the *Rig Veda* may have been merely part of the verbal contest with the official "reviler," who does not reject sacrifice as a matter of abstract doctrine but merely rejects his opponent's sacrifice.[32] In other words, the Nastika may have been nothing but an imaginary conversation partner, the *purva paksha* in a contest with the triumphant Astika. Later, however, these complementary ritual roles gave way to mutually exclusive doctrines, as precise terms denoting opposition within the sacrificial structure gave way to imprecise pejoratives directed against people who challenged that very structure.[33]

In verses we considered in the context of dharmic and adharmic kings, Manu refers to Nastikas together with revilers of the Brahmins or the Vedas (4.163). He also speaks of "a king who disregards the moral boundaries, who is a Nastika and plunders the property of Brahmins" (8.309) and he says that anyone who "relies on the teachings of logic should be outcast by virtuous people as a Nastika and a reviler of the Veda" (2.11). (Notice the simultaneous attack on logic, the specialty of the Lokayatikas in the *Arthashastra*). Sometimes Nastika arguments against the existence of the gods or heaven could be used to argue that therefore one should not engage in dharma (or at least ritual), which is precisely what the *Kamasutra* says Lokayatikas say; here there would be an offense against social dharma. One text exhorts the king to punish Nastikas and those who have fallen from caste[34] (again a behavioral rather than doctrinal criterion). Madhava described these teachings as "hard to uproot" (*durucchedam*) precisely because most people live by them,[35] perhaps implying that someone had tried to uproot them, with limited success.

Nastikas are often said to include Buddhists, Jains, and Charvakas, people who deny both the Vedas and the universal world-soul of the Upanishads. Other authors observe finer distinctions: Nastikas are of six kinds: Charvakas, Jains, and the adherents of four great Buddhist schools.[36] Yashodhara, glossing a verse in the *Kamasutra* calling for a balance of the Three Aims, takes Nastikas as the prime example of people who disregard dharma (1.2.39). By these evasive criteria, then, it is often difficult, if not impossible, to distinguish Charvakas from Nastikas. But Charvakas are not the same as Nastikas. Charvakas are usually accused not only (like Nastikas) of not believing in gods but of not believing in piety, in the efficacy of religious rules and rites—in a word, in social dharma.

We can distinguish three levels of doctrines attributed to Lokayatikas/Charvakas during this period. Charvaka doctrine Type A is a kind of extreme logical skepticism: we can't know anything for sure. This may be what the wily Kautilya admires in the Lokayata school, which seems to have been part of a significant philosophical tradition. This was nothing but philosophy; these ideas put no one in danger. The Type A Charvaka is a skeptic.

Type B Charvaka doctrine is an extrapolation from the first argument: if we can't know anything for sure, we can't know if there are gods, and so we might as well enjoy ourselves.[37] At this point the Charvakas become conflated with Nastikas, who offended not Brahmins but just gods. The Type B Charvaka is a materialist and hedonist.

The Type C Charvaka goes on to argue that, if there are no gods, there is therefore no afterlife, and therefore no point in sacrifice (to get us to heaven when we die), and therefore no point in Brahmins or the Veda. This sort of Charvaka could have gotten into trouble—but there's no evidence that they ever did. Apparently authors could put into the mouths of the

Lokayatikas and Charvakas just about any adharmic argument they wanted to air, things that no real people probably ever said and that would probably have gotten them killed if acted upon. The Type C Charvaka is a mythical dissident.

These three types of Charvaka arguments pop up in different ways at different times but are often combined in a single accusation. The history of the statements attributed to Charvakas (and, occasionally, Lokayatikas) is a history of dissent against dharma safely attributed to someone other than the speaker.

Charvakas in Epic Texts

An early travesty of Charvaka/Lokayata views without the label appears in the *Ramayana*. Prince Rama is thinking of disobeying his father (who has violated dharma while under the thrall of kama) and taking the throne that his father has given to Rama's younger brother. (Both the king's action, disregarding primogeniture, and Rama's contemplated rebellion, disobeying his father, would be violations of dharma.) At this moment, Rama is addressed by Jabali, a Vedic sage who has been mentioned elsewhere in the *Ramayana* in the company of respected sages who are Rama's teachers.[38] Jabali pretends to urge Rama to ignore family obligations and live for pleasure alone, and by presenting this extreme position of adharma he actually pushes Rama back into the dharmic view. This is what Jabali says:

> I pity those who care most about dharma and artha. They have nothing but misery in this world, and when they die they just disappear. People devote themselves to performing the ritual meal for the

ancestors. But look at the waste of food! For what
can a dead man eat? And if something that one person ate here could fill the body of someone else,
you could simply offer the ritual meal of the ancestors on behalf of a traveler, and he wouldn't need
to pack provisions for the road. Those books that
tell us, "Sacrifice, give, consecrate yourself, practice
asceticism, renounce," were devised by cunning
men just to charm people into paying them. Your
majesty, you must realize that there exists no world
beyond. Face what is in front of your eyes and turn
your back on what cannot be seen. (2.100.12–16)

The ceremony of feeding one's dead ancestors (*shraddha*)
is the defining ritual of Hinduism; to strike at this is to challenge the very heart of social dharma. Jabali is clearly acting
as the devil's advocate to stir Rama into righteous indignation
(which is precisely what happens). Jabali is not identified as
a Lokayatika or a Charvaka, but in some manuscripts of this
passage Rama calls him a Nastika and says that a Nastika is
no different from a Buddhist or a thief, to which Jabali replies,
"I am not a Nastika; I just talked like a Nastika to turn you
back from what you were doing; please forgive me."[39] Though
Jabali concludes his false speech with the defining Nastika line
("There exists no [nasti] world beyond"), most of his argument is what Sanskrit texts always say that the Type C Charvakas say, accusing the Brahmins of plying their trade just for
the money and mocking the idea of feeding ancestors who are
not physically present.[40]

To my knowledge, this passage in the *Ramayana,* almost certainly written earlier than the *Kamasutra,* is the first
instance of such a citation of (unlabeled) Charvaka doctrine

and may be implicitly quoted in all the subsequent citations attributed to Lokayatikas or Charvakas. Yet elsewhere the *Ramayana* seems to regard Lokayatikas simply as logicians, as when Rama challenges his brother Bharata, saying, "I hope you do not associate with Brahmins who are Lokayatikas, dear brother. Their only skill is in bringing misfortune: they are fools who think themselves wise. Although preeminent texts on dharma are ready to hand, those ignorant fellows derive their ideas from logic alone and so propound utter nonsense" (2.94.29). This confusion between skeptics (or even just logicians in general) and Lokayatikas pervades many later texts as well. But it is in the *Kamasutra* that we first encounter people called Lokayatikas who say the specific naughty things that the *Ramayana* attributes to Jabali.

Charvakas cast their shadows in several parts of the twelfth book of the *Mahabharata*. There Charvaka is the name of an ogre (*rakshasa*) who disguises himself as a Brahmin, wearing the garb of a religious mendicant, carrying the trident that identifies worshippers of Shiva. He chastises King Yudhishthira for killing his own kinsmen (which he has indeed done)[41] and says that all the Brahmins have told him to say that the king should kill himself. The Brahmins, furious, say they said nothing of the kind. Then they realize that Charvaka is an ogre and a friend of Duryodhana, the king whom Yudhishthira has just conquered. They kill Charvaka by chanting "Hum!" at him. Yudhishthira later learns that Charvaka had obtained a boon that he could not be killed unless he insulted Brahmins (12.39.22–47), one of the signature habits of the human Charvakas. No other doctrinal issues arise, and the episode seems designed primarily to literally demonize the Charvakas, evidence that they were regarded as a serious threat to human life (and occasionally indistinguishable from followers of the ascetic god Shiva).

This passage was reworked in an eighth-century play, *The Catastrophe of the Braid,* in which an ogre named Charvaka, a friend of Duryodhana, disguises himself as a Brahmin sage and urges Yudhishthira to commit suicide, this time not out of guilt about the general devastation brought by the war but because, Charvaka says (falsely), Yudhishthira's brother Bhima has been killed. (Charvaka also urges Bhima's wife Draupadi to commit suicide, arguing that it is proper for women of her family to follow their husbands in death.) His dastardly plot almost succeeds, but then Bhima himself arrives and Charvaka is taken into custody.[42] The play now adds details about Charvaka's behavior: he refuses to accept Yudhishthira's drinking water because, he says, Yudhishthira must be ritually impure, since men of his family are being killed every day in battle. And he refuses to let a woman fan him, protesting that it is unseemly for a woman to do such a favor for a sage. David Gitomer suggests that the play "parodies a cluster of stereotypical brahman traits: the demand for hospitality, obsession with the purity of his person, and, when these are violated or denied, an easily triggered irascibility." And he asks, "Could it be that expressions of resentment toward the status-obsessed brahmans [were] off-limits for the classical Sanskrit drama?" He suggests that in this indirect satire the author "is taking a tremendous risk in the character of Carvaka."[43] Here is yet another useful displacement that the figure of the Charvaka enables, allowing the author to mock not just the official dogma of Brahmins but their character.

On another occasion in the *Mahabharata,* the god Indra takes the form of a Nastika, reborn as a jackal, to instruct a Brahmin sage. He says: "I used to be a learned logician (*haituka*) who scorned the Veda; I was devoted to critical inquiry (*anviksha*) and logic (*tarka*), which are useless. I based my arguments on reason and slandered Brahmins. I was a

Nastika who doubted everything, a fool. And this is the result: I've become a jackal!" (12.180.6–8, 45–53). It is probably
not irrelevant that the jackal, in the beast fables based on the
Arthashastra, plays the role of the chief counselor, like Kautilya. Elsewhere (12.10.20), Yudhishthira, whose ideas of non-
violence owe much to Buddhism but who is also known as the
dharma king, is accused of having Nastika tendencies.

Finally, there is a strange *Mahabharata* passage in which
King Janaka (well known from both the Upanishads and the
Ramayana) listens to a long sermon from a sage named Panchashikha, who refers to the doctrine of the Nastikas and
teaches the king that there is no soul and no life after death,
together with other arguments often attributed to the Charvakas (12.211.1–48, 212.1–52). But the passage is so corrupt that
scholars argue whether these statements are actually part of
Panchashikha's own argument or simply the *purva paksha*
against which he states his own, correct, philosophical position.[44] Clearly there is much confusion about Charvakas in
these ancient texts.

Charvakas are indirectly demonized by the incarnate
god Krishna in the *Bhagavad Gita* (a philosophical discourse
that is a part of the *Mahabharata*) in a passage that argues that
there are two sorts of people, the godlike and the demonic.
The demonic bear a suspicious resemblance to both Charvakas and Lokayatikas, whose position is often called the demonic doctrine. Krishna says:

> There is no purity in demonic people, no morality,
> no truth. They say, "The universe has no reality, no
> firm basis, no lord; it has not come into existence
> through mutual causation; kama is its only cause—
> what else?" Since they insist upon this doctrine,

their souls are lost and their wits are feeble; and so they commit horrible actions in their wish to harm and destroy the universe. Immersing themselves in insatiable desire, possessed by hypocrisy, pride, and madness, in their delusion they grasp at false conceptions and undertake impure enterprises. They are afflicted by countless worries that end only at doomsday, for their only aim is to enjoy what they desire, since they are convinced that this is all there is. Bound by the fetters of hope, by the hundreds, obsessed by desire and anger, they long to amass great wealth, by whatever foul means, to satisfy their desires. "I got this today! I'll satisfy this whim. This is my money, and this, and this will be mine soon. I killed that man—he was my enemy; and I will kill the others, too. I'm master, here; I'm the one who enjoys this; I'm successful and powerful and happy. I'm rich and superior; who else is there the likes of me? I'll sacrifice, and I'll give to charities, and I will have *fun*." This is what people say when they are deluded by ignorance.[45]

What begins with a logical problem very like those attributed to the skeptical, Type A Charvakas ("The universe has no reality, no firm basis, no lord; it has not come into existence through mutual causation; desire is its only cause—what else?"), or just to common or garden-variety Nastikas, shifts into the "horrible actions" and "impure enterprises" attributed to the (mythical) dissident Charvakas (Type C) and finally degenerates into pure hedonism (Type B Charvakas). "Mutual causation" is a strongly Buddhist phrase, while "amass[ing] great wealth" puts us in the realm of the *Arthashastra* (as does

"I killed that man—he was my enemy"), while "satisfy[ing] their desires" (not to mention the argument that the whole universe is founded on kama) belongs to the world of the *Kamasutra*. Yet there is still a layer of cunning hypocrisy: such people *do* sacrifice and give to charities, but it all means nothing. And so, Krishna warns, all of it gets them into an eternal hell from which there will never be any way out.

Charvakas in the Puranas and in Medieval Plays and Poems

By the time of the Gupta Empire, in the fourth century CE, the sectarian Hindus were fighting among themselves, Hindus against Hindus, though they often linked imaginary Buddhists and Jains (and Charvakas) with their actual Hindu enemies to degrade their real target, the other Hindus. The myths and dharmic disquisitions known as the Puranas, which range in date from the fourth to the sixteenth century CE, narrate a number of episodes in which the gods initiate various heresies in order to corrupt humans or demons whose excessive dharmic virtue makes them a threat to the gods.[46] Often Brihaspati invents the corrupting, materialist ideas,[47] and since he teaches this doctrine to the demons (in order to destroy them), materialism is also often called the demonic doctrine. Other versions of the story specify that Vishnu took the form of the Buddha and invented the evil doctrines of Buddhism; sometimes it is Jainism; sometimes both. But most of these texts incorporate a miscellaneous, kitchen-sink collection of wicked ideas, usually involving denial of the Vedas and the rituals of sacrifice, which often strangely resemble the alleged doctrines of Lokayatikas or Charvakas.

The *Vishnu Purana*, for instance, one of the earliest Puranas (c. fifth century CE), states that Vishnu first converted many demons to Jainism and then made the rest of them Buddhists, teaching them that animal sacrifice was evil; he said, "If the animal slaughtered in the sacrifice is assured of arrival in heaven, why does the sacrificer not kill his own father?"[48] (This is one of the blasphemies that many texts attributed to the Charvakas.) Vishnu is also said to appeal to "words of reason,"[49] probably an allusion to the logical Lokayatikas, a connection that is explicitly developed in other versions of this story in which Vishnu is said to have founded "the Barhaspatya sect and similar sects that seek liberation by eating flesh, drinking wine, and so forth."[50] In a later Purana, Vishnu becomes the Buddha and teaches the Buddhist doctrine of noninjury (*ahimsa*); he also corrupts all the women by saying that caste distinctions are meaningless and that one should cultivate the pleasures of the body.[51] By this time, it seems, any of the generic adharmic ideas of Charvakas and Lokayatikas could be blamed on the Buddhists.

A ninth-century satirical play titled *A Brouhaha about Doctrines*[52] satirizes Charvakas as well as several other groups, including Buddhists and Jains. In the third act, the Charvaka puts forth adharmic, materialist, and hedonist impieties but also ideas about inference. He begins by saying, "I am going to do away with God, set aside the world-to-come, and demolish the validity of the Vedas" (3.80). Later he says: "Asceticism is just a variety of torture; self-restraint is just a way to cheat yourself of pleasures; while sacrificial rituals seem to me just like children's games" (3.87–88). He goes on to liken the concept of god to logical impossibilities like the son of a barren woman, a mirage, and a bow made of hare-horn (3.91), and to laugh at the idea that the Vedas are authoritative (3.189). But then, when his opponent says that inference proves the existence of god, the Charvaka demolishes the validity of inference, as a skeptic would: "Even if clever logicians infer something with great effort, other, extremely competent logicians account for the same thing in another way" (3.109). He therefore appears to combine the characteristics of the materialist Charvakas (Type B) and the skeptic Charvakas (Type A).

The third act had begun, however, with a complaint that a cruel king has been rounding up quasi-Tantric Shaiva mendicants, beating them up, and expelling them for being outside Vedic religion, and that he threatens to kill them or throw them in prison (3.10–14). "We drink booze, eat meat, have women," one of them remarks (3.13)—all actual offenses against social dharma, and not merely talk about such offenses (like those attributed to Type C Charvakas). If this is a reflection of actual historical policy, for which there is scattered evidence,[53] it would mean that such Tantric groups were in fact actively prosecuted, and this play seems to assume that Charvakas, who do nothing but talk, slipped into the reformer's net as well. The *Saura Purana* says that Charvakas (and several other groups, including Tantrics)[54] should not be allowed to enter a kingdom (38.54). The mythology about Tantric groups prevalent in more conventional Hindu texts functioned in some ways that are closely parallel to the mythology of the Charvakas. Whether or not the Tantrics actually did the things they were said to do (drink menstrual blood, have ritual intercourse with their own sisters or with Dalit women, etc.), the belief that they did so was an important part of Indian religious discourse.[55] So, too, whether or not there were Charvakas who said all those wicked things, stories about them saying them became part of the discourse.

The Rise of the Moon of Enlightenment distinguishes the Charvaka from the Lokayatika. The trouble begins when a man named "Great Illusion" (the name that the Puranas often give to the Buddha/Jina figure) praises Nastikas and acclaims

Brihaspati for founding the Charvaka dynasty. The Charvaka
then enters and says:

> The three Vedas are crooks' patter!
> For they make no difference when it comes to
>   reaching heaven.
> Look:
> If those who perform the sacrifice
> find their way to paradise,
> once agent, act, and object are destroyed,
> then plentiful fruit there ought to be
> after the fire has burned up the trees.
> Moreover:
> If he holds that heaven is attained
> by the beast that's sacrificed,
> then why does not the sacrificer
> slaughter as well his own father?
> And also:
> If funeral rites brought contentment
> even to creatures quite dead,
> the oil might well sustain the flame
> of the lamp once it's quenched.[56]

And so forth. The line about funeral rites is a reference to the
ritual of feeding the dead ancestors (*shraddha*). Much of this
is in Jabali's speech in the *Ramayana*. It is boilerplate extreme
Charvaka talk, Type C.

The twelfth-century poem *The Adventures of Nala* attributes to the demon Kali (the genius of the present evil Kali
Age) a mélange of specific heresies: "In the army of Kali, his
generals were Kama, Anger, Greed, Delusion, and others.
A Charvaka in the ranks mocked the gods, citing various

Buddhist doctrines. . . . Some of the gods called Kali's troops
Nastikas; others called them Lokayatikas, still others heretics.
Kali stood there surrounded by evils, . . . but he looked in vain
for heretics, Jains, or Buddhists in the city."[57] Here the defining bad boys, Charvakas/Buddhists, are linked with the most
basic opponents of Brahmins—Kama, Anger, Greed, and Delusion, four of the six "enemies within" that both Kautilya and
Vatsyayana also confront.

In the fourteenth-century philosophical tract *The Anthology of All Philosophies,* the exaggerated and rote form in
which Charvaka doctrine is depicted places it in the company
of other texts that present the potted form of the doctrine,
which is immediately confuted by the Buddhist in the next
chapter.[58] Significantly, although the author, Madhava, quotes
most of the other fifteen traditions that he discusses, he does
not pretend to quote any text that he calls Charvaka or Lokayatika.[59] This strongly suggests that there were no (or were
no longer) Charvaka works available to Madhava.[60] Johannes
Bronkhorst, too, distinguishes between actual Charvakas, logicians, who may once have existed but from whom we have
no texts, and mythical Charvakas to whom various appalling
sentiments are attributed: "Authors after, say, the twelfth century had no direct knowledge of the Cārvāka and their ideas
any more. They felt free to attribute to them all manner of positions which they disapproved of."[61]

And indeed, *The Anthology of All Philosophies* attributes
"all manner of positions" to the quasi-mythical Brihaspati:

> All this has also been said by Brihaspati: "There is
> no heaven, no final liberation, nor any soul in an-
> other world. Nor do the rituals of the four classes
> and four stages of life produce any real effect. The

sacrificial offering into the fire, the three Vedas, the ascetic's trident, and smearing one's self with ashes, were made by the Creator as the livelihood of those who have neither knowledge nor manliness. If an animal killed in the sacrificial rite will go to heaven, why then doesn't the sacrificer kill his own father in that ritual? If the *shraddha* offering to the ancestors satisfies beings who are dead, . . . then here, too, there's no need to make provisions for the road for people who set out on a journey; they can be satisfied on the road by *shraddha* offerings made by people at home. If those in heaven are gratified by our offerings here, then why not give food down here to people who are standing on the roof terrace? While a man lives let him live happily; let him feed on butter even if he gets into debt. When the body has been reduced to ashes, how can it ever return again? If someone who departs from the body goes to another world, why doesn't he come back again, overwhelmed by love for his family? And so it is only as a means of livelihood that Brahmins have established here the ceremonies for the dead; there's no other use for them. The authors of the three Vedas were buffoons, cheats, and night-prowling ogres. . . ." And so in compassion for the many living beings we must take refuge in the Charvaka doctrine. And that's a very enjoyable agenda.[62]

The first half of this passage is strongly reminiscent of the satirical characterization of the Charvakas in *The Rise of the Moon of Enlightenment*.[63] The first line belongs to the Nastikas, and then, after a brief detour into pure hedonism (Charvaka Type B), the passage shifts to the standard recitation of the Charvaka creed (Type C). (It also veers off into a more unusual attack on the Vedas, complaining against "the notorious ritual in which the [king's] wife takes the phallus of the horse," which is indeed a part of the ritual of royal consecration that the Vedic text itself regards as obscene.)[64] Kapstein says that the passage "seems to characterize the Cārvākas at once as skeptics, materialists, and hedonists, and this is quite typical of the manner in which they are described elsewhere. . . . We may ask then: is there really a system to this 'system,' or is it merely a grab-bag category, into which were poured a miscellany of views that orthodoxy found repugnant?"[65] Amartya Sen regards the presentation in *The Anthology of All Philosophies* as "an elaborately sympathetic . . . [and] reasoned defence of atheism and materialism."[66] I think it is, rather, a witty satire on the wicked sayings attributed to the Charvakas.

Madhava also wrote a hagiography titled *Total Victory of Shankara*, as did seven other scholars of the period.[67] In all of them, the great Shaiva philosopher Shankara defeats advocates of all other religious groups, in philosophical contests rather than real martial encounters. In the *Victory of Shankara* of Anandagiri (thirteenth century), Shankara confutes Hindu antinomian groups (the Shaiva "Left-Hand Worshippers"[68] and "Skull-Bearers") as well as Jains, Buddhists, and Charvakas.[69] The version by Madhava, the most recent and most popular[70] of the eight hagiographies, also tells a story relevant to the larger concerns of this book. Sarasvati, the goddess of knowledge, becomes incarnate in a queen who challenges Shankara to compete with her in knowledge of kama. Shankara asks for time out, during which he enters the body of a king with a large harem. He masters the science of kama, delights the women, and returns to defeat the queen—in effect, knowledge itself—in argument.[71] The text demonstrates that even philosophers need to know about kama, but also that "the royal obligations to uphold dharma are perpetually jeopardized by the king's susceptibility to kama. The ascetic, on the other hand, unsullied by kama, is best able to dispense dharma dispassionately."[72]

Buddhist and Jain Satires on Charvakas

Although, as we have seen, Hindu texts often conflated Charvakas or Lokayatikas with Buddhists and/or Jains, the Buddhists and Jains returned the compliment by supplying some of the earliest attacks on Charvakas and Lokayatikas. The views of a legendary king, Paesi (Payasi)—including the "evil view" that there is no other world, nor any fruit of good or evil deeds—are recorded in Jain and Buddhist works in Prakrit and Pali as well as Sanskrit.[73] The *Investigation into the True Teaching*, by a tenth-century Jain, treats Charvakas alongside members of other schools.[74]

The Buddhists regarded Lokayata as the science of false disputation (*vitandashastra*), which the lexicographer Sir Monier Monier-Williams unpacks as "captious objection, fallacious controversy, perverse or frivolous argument . . . idly carping at the arguments or assertions of another without attempting to prove the opposite side of the question."[75] Buddhist texts record, always with disapproval, the teachings of certain proto-skeptics (or proto-materialists), of whom one of the earliest is said to have been Ajita Keshakambali, a senior contemporary of the Buddha (sixth/fifth century BCE).[76] As in the case of all the legendary Charvakas, nothing survives of his own work but citations by his opponents, in this case Buddhists who say that he wore a blanket of filthy, foul-smelling human hair (his name, *Keshakambali,* means "wear-ing a hair blanket"). He is accused of arguing that there is no use in alms or sacrifice or offering, that neither good deeds nor bad deeds bear fruit, that when a person dies his body sim-ply disperses into the elements, and that fools and wise men, good deeds and evil deeds, are annihilated when the body dissolves.[77] D. D. Kosambi regarded Keshakambali as "a thor-oughgoing materialist."[78] He said that the doctrines attributed to Keshakambali "seem to be of a composite character" in that many different ideas have been lumped together and blamed on him.[79] A passage in the Buddhist Pali Canon attributes to Ajita Keshakambali doctrines strongly evocative of Lokayatika or Charvaka doctrine.[80]

Jayarashi's Skepticism

We do have one text, probably composed between 770 and 830 CE,[81] attributed to a Brahmin author who may have been the only survivor of the early philosophical group that the *Arthashastra* called Lokayatikas. This is Jayarashi Bhatta's *The Lion of the Disturbance of Basic Principles.*[82] And indeed, Jayarashi's text barely survived: a single manuscript of the work was discovered in 1926 and published in 1940.

Jayarashi regarded himself as a follower of "Brihaspati, the guru of the gods."[83] He keeps saying that there is no real difference between his opinions and Brihaspati's. Many schol-ars regard his work as the only surviving text of the Lokayata or Charvaka school, but Jayarashi never calls himself a Char-vaka or Lokayatika. Eli Franco admits that he was "not a true heir to the Materialistic philosophy propounded in the text at-tributed to Brihaspati."[84] Ramakrishna Bhattacharya remarks,

"The very mention of Bṛhaspati as the preceptor of the gods and addressing him as Bhagavān ["Lord"], I believe, are further evidence to prove that Jayarāśi was not a Cārvāka/Lokāyata, for no Cārvāka would deign to admit the existence of the gods and their guru and refer to him as a god or a demigod."[85]

Certainly Jayarashi didn't say any of the more outlandish things that the Charvakas were alleged to have said. To the very limited extent that he was a Charvaka at all, he was Type A, a skeptic, indeed a radical skeptic; his is "the only Sanskrit text in which full-fledged skepticism is propounded."[86] He mocks his opponents, not as individuals but as members of opposing traditions, calling the logicians "beasts" and the Vedic scholars "fanatics of the revealed texts."[87] He argues that no school of philosophy can claim its view of reality as knowledge. He denies even that we can depend upon, for evidence, what we see with our own eyes, a criterion that the texts attributed to Charvaka skeptics had accepted. He was certainly not a materialist, but he was an agnostic.[88] Without him, we might have believed that even the skeptics in the logical tradition (Type A) were nothing but a fictional trope, an occasion to imagine how the world would look to us if we didn't believe in anything at all. But at least one person—Jayarashi—actually argued the point, and we have his testimony to his existence.

Did the Charvakas Once Exist, or Were They Always Just a *Purva Paksha?*

Jayarashi poses interesting questions for the history of skepticism in India. His influence on the Jain school of philosophy may have saved him from oblivion when other skeptics sank from sight.[89] But was he the only one? Were there others who were erased, like the Gnostics, best known from Irenaeus's attack on them in his text *Against Heresies,* but then in 1945 substantiated in the Nag Hammadi materials? We cannot know, but there is scattered evidence, mainly in the form of commentaries and quotations in extant philosophical texts, that there may have been other skeptical philosophers in ancient India.[90] It seems unlikely that the attackers of straw men would all have converged on the same straw man had there not been *some* real precedent—which they then proceeded to exaggerate out of all proportion. It is possible that, just as the predecessors of Kautilya and Vatsyayana cited by the *Arthashastra* and the *Kamasutra* vanished, and all we have are the *Arthashastra* and the *Kamasutra,* which replaced the earlier texts, so, too, did the Lokayatikas and the Charvakas once exist in some form. But no statements of indebtedness in other texts, such as supported arguments for the existence of the texts that the *Kamasutra* and the *Arthashastra* cite as predecessors, exist for the Charvakas.

If Jayarashi is the sole survivor of a lost school of Charvaka skepticism, what is the source of the adharmic statements attributed to the Charvaka materialists, of which there is no trace in Jayarashi? Though Charvakas are never mentioned in royal decrees, as Jains and Buddhists are, quite a few inscriptions in South India, from 968 to 1415 CE, do actually mention a Lokayata school of logic, and others mention Charvakas (usually pejoratively).[91] Most of the inscriptions refer merely to bodies of knowledge, though some refer to individuals who defended that knowledge. Some scholars have argued that there must be, or might be, an entire corpus of lost Charvaka texts dating to the Mauryan period, or a collection of aphorisms (*sutras*) attributed not to the divine chief counselor, Brihaspati, but to a human being (named Purandara), and several commentaries on this or some other skeptical text.[92]

Most of the Charvaka fragments are cited in works composed between the eighth and twelfth centuries, the period in which the satirical poems and plays that we have considered were also composed, and they add nothing of great significance to what we know from those works. Kapstein is skeptical (if I may use that word) both about the fragments ("few of which can be taken as reliable witnesses") and about the anthologies of such fragments that have been made, which may "represent no foundational work at all, but rather an imaginative idea of what such a work might have looked like had it ever existed."[93]

Despite all of this, Eli Franco is sanguine about the actual existence of the Charvakas: "Between the sixth and ninth centuries, the Cārvāka/Lokāyata was a fascinating, vibrant, and innovative philosophical tradition, which engaged critically with the major philosophies of its time."[94] And he believes that some of the fragments are "undoubtedly genuine." Even the skeptical Kapstein acknowledges, "There were no doubt real proponents of ways of thought that came to be known as Cārvāka during the formative age of Indian philosophy, and . . . it is possible that the sophisticated skepticism of Jayarāśi Bhaṭṭa represented, or was at least inspired by, such traditions."[95] Yet he simultaneously argues that "it seems equally sure" that the Charvaka system described in one of our main sources for Charvaka philosophy, *The Anthology of All Philosophies,* is "principally a literary construct."[96]

So there may have been Charvakas. But did such people actually hold the beliefs attributed to them? Or, rather, did other people invent a mythology and put in the mouths of (possibly real) Lokayatikas and Charvakas crazy statements that they never made? All we have now is the mythology about them, which has replaced whatever history there may have been.

Charvaka ideas became very real indeed. Kapstein sums up the case well: "The Cārvākas are difficult to refute. Their skepticism requires us to address the foundations of knowledge, their hedonism our fundamental values, and their materialism the entire ethical and soteriological edifice predicated on the notion that our spirits endure. . . . [They are] 'good to think.' They, or their literary image—it hardly matters any longer—shake our complacent assumptions, and encourage us to reason things through."[97] Indian philosophers kept the Charvakas alive because the viewpoints attributed to them, satirically or not, disclosed hidden questions upon which much of the Indian philosophical edifice reposed. Though the Charvakas lacked an ongoing tradition, what the Indians call a *parampara*, "from one to another," they existed as a tradition of thought without a school. Into the vacuum created by their absence, the Brahmin imagination freely rushed with all their own wicked ideas and attributed them to people unable to defend themselves or to contradict the false statements attributed to them.

Two very different sorts of Brahmins might have developed the ideas attributed to the Charvakas. The first group would have been Brahmins who did not agree with such ideas but cited them because they knew that people did think such thoughts and they hoped that by citing them they might absorb the opposition. They could have destroyed all of the genuine Charvaka texts, made up distorted versions of their ideas and introduced those ideas, satirized and warped, into dharma texts in an effort to discredit them. Or they may have cited the statements attributed to the Charvakas to do just what they said they were doing—warning people to stay away from such ideas.[98] But another group of Brahmins, who secretly agreed with the ideas attributed to the Charvakas, may have cited them in their *shastras* in order to enjoy the forbidden pleasures of airing heretical ideas, to keep the fifth column alive and say, secretly, what they wanted to say. No matter what their intentions, the Brahmins who cited the Charvaka ideas did in fact keep them alive. The people who made up the views of the nonexistent Charvakas or quoted the lost Charvakas *became,* in effect, the Charvakas.

By the time of the *Kamasutra* the Charvakas had become a useful figment of the Hindu imagination. That the *Mahabharata* actually called one of the Charvakas an ogre in disguise suggests how much of a myth they were (though it should be noted that Hindu texts also call Buddhists and Jains demons, and we know that they really existed). And once the mythology was in place, anyone could play. It would have been easy for every village rake who thought wicked thoughts about killing his father to blame them on the Charvakas, convenient scapegoats for various sorts of dissidence. It would also have been easy to pick up an existing tradition of Brahmin bashing (in Buddhist texts as well as Hindu folk traditions, perhaps vernacular traditions)[99] and put it into the Sanskrit texts under the cover of attributing it to the Charvakas.

The Later Fate of Indian Skepticism

One extraordinary piece of evidence that people calling themselves Charvakas might actually have existed even as late as the late sixteenth century is the testimony of Abu'l Fazl, the advisor and chronicler of the great Mughal emperor Akbar. When Akbar held his famous interreligious dialogues in Agra, he invited Charvakas along with Sufis, philosophers, orators, jurists, Sunni, Shi'a, Brahmins, Nazarenes, Jews, Zoroastrians, and others.[100] Abu'l Fazl elsewhere testifies that he himself met

many of the "wise people of India," including Muslim groups
(Sunni, Shi'a, and Ismaili, as well as Sufis), Parsis, Hindus
(devotees of Shiva and of Vishnu), Sikhs, Jains, Jews, Jesuits—
and Charvakas. And this is what he said about the Charvakas:

> Cārvāka, after whom this school is named, was a
> Brahmin, unrecognized [by other Brahmins]. The
> Brahmins call his followers *Nāstikas*.[101] They rec-
> ognize no existence apart from the four elements,
> nor any source of perception save through the five
> organs of sense. They do not believe in a God nor in
> immaterial substances. . . . Paradise they regard as
> a state in which man lives as he chooses, free from
> the control of another, and hell the state in which
> he lives subject to another's rule. The whole end
> of man, they say, is comprised in four things: the
> amassing of wealth, women, fame and good deeds.
> They admit only of such sciences as tend to the pro-
> motion of external order, that is, a knowledge of
> just administration and benevolent government.
> They are somewhat analogous to the sophists in
> their views.[102]

The highly rational Abu'l Fazl seems quite favorable to the
views of these Charvakas, who sound somewhat like the Nastikas that the Brahmins wrongly took them to be. Significantly,
Abu'l Fazl goes on to say: "Others have written many works in
reproach [of them], which rather serve as lasting memorials
of their own mis-reading and short-sightedness."[103] (Elsewhere
he remarks that the Brahmins did not appreciate Buddhists,
Jains, or Charvakas.) Thus Abu'l Fazl notes that the Charvakas

were intelligent—and misunderstood—rationalists, but he also attributes to them hedonistic views. It may well be, therefore, that Charvakas of the old, legitimate logical branch, the Jayarashi branch, still existed at the time of Akbar and were still being confused with the nonexistent dissidents excoriated in all the Sanskrit texts. Or Abu'l Fazl may have fallen for the Brahmins' Charvaka fantasy.

Charvakas continued to exist in the Brahmin *imaginaire*. Abraham Roger, in his 1670 publication *La porte ouverte*, says that the Brahmin Padmanabh told him of a group called the "Schaewaeckas" (evidently a rough approximation of "Charvakas"), whom he regarded as a branch of Epicureans and who believed there was no life after this life and mocked as pure foolishness and dreams all that others said about the life of the soul after death.[104] Two hundred years later, Swami Dayanand Saraswati (1824–83), in *The Light of Truth* (*Satyarth Prakash*), in 1875, used the well-worn trope of the Charvakas' ridicule of the premises of ritual sacrifice to the gods. Another century later, in 1967, V. Raghavan's Sanskrit play *Vimukti* included two Charvakas, one a kind of Nastika and the other a connoisseur of sensual pleasures, whom Raghavan used to make fun of progressive causes of which he disapproved, such as women's liberation and divorce.[105]

In sum, at the time of the *Arthashastra*, Lokayatikas were respected logicians; just a century or so later, in the *Kamasutra*, they were despised iconoclasts. Eventually the real logicians largely died out (Jayarashi alone left a text), and logic itself became suspect in religious circles; the name of the Lokayatikas then became a synonym for a far more offensive group of thinkers, usually called Charvakas. These may once have existed as a more reasonable group and then died out, or they may never have existed at all. In either case, by the eighth century they existed only as a mythical sect of extreme antinomians.

Amartya Sen puts much store in the Charvakas as a strong and enduring line of skeptics.[106] The bad news I have for him is that there was *not* a thriving group of Charvakas, as he hopes, but the good news is that there *was* a thriving argument about nonexistent Charvakas that kept alive for many centuries their ideas (or *someone's* ideas) deconstructing dharma. The great Charvaka contribution is to the unquenchable tradition of challenging the dominant paradigm. They were the champions of those people whose *sva*-dharma is adharma. In a very real sense, the Charvakas were the *purva paksha* for rational Hindus throughout Indian history.

7
Epilogue
Dharma and the Subversion of Science

The Afterlife of the *Kamasutra*
and the *Arthashastra*

The ideas advanced by Kautilya and Vatsyayana remained alive in India. Their texts attracted few commentaries,[1] but they are cited quite frequently in a general rather than literal way, often (particularly in the case of the *Arthashastra*) negatively: these texts, which made such brilliant use of the *purva paksha*, sometimes themselves became, rather like the Charvakas, the *purva paksha* quoted in books that disagreed with them. They inaugurated a line of dissent that preserved certain antinomian, adharmic ideas in the face of the growing authority of social dharma, a line continued, in a shadow form, by the Charvaka mythology. This dissension was carried on in Sanskrit texts created and disseminated by Brahmins of a certain persuasion in the face of the greater Sanskrit tradition maintained by other sorts of Brahmins who upheld social dharma. Evidently these texts answered a need for dissension, for protest against the ever-tightening noose of caste dharma, that never died in intellectual circles in India.

There is an honesty and realism in these two texts that endeared them to later generations. Though heavily embroidered with fantastic details, their basic subject matter is the stuff of real life. Their ideas survived in popular traditions— the *Arthashastra* in the animal fables of the *Panchatantra* and the tales of the lion king and his wily jackal counselor, the *Kamasutra* in miniature paintings and the carvings on the temples of Khajuraho and Konarak. Some of their ideas were also maintained in later political and erotic texts derived from them, though there the concepts were toned down and blunted, brought closer to the rules of social dharma[2]—evidence that the tradition *did* in fact find them in violation of dharma. For instance, one of the *Kamasutra*'s justifications for adultery—"My enemy is united with this woman's husband. Through her, I will get him to drink a potion" (1.5.17)— was considerably modified when it appeared several centuries later in *The Secret of Sexual Pleasure:* "This woman's husband is the friend of my enemy, who wishes to kill me. By uniting with her I may be able to break their alliance."[3]

The two texts had rather different histories.

The *Arthashastra*'s ideas about royal dharma (*raja-dharma*) were taken up by the dharma texts, and its ideas about polity went into the later political texts, the "textbooks of polity" (*niti-shastras*). Perhaps this led to a feeling that one no longer needed the *Arthashastra* itself and contributed to its eventual demise as a separate text, just as the *Arthashastra* and the *Kamasutra* themselves eclipsed their predecessors. The *Arthashastra* wasn't suppressed so much as just allowed to fade out of the textual tradition, though its antinomian content may also have discouraged people from keeping it available.

Only a few other *artha-shastras* have survived, all considerably later and nowhere near as comprehensive. Kamandaka's *Essence of Polity* (*Nitisara*, probably from the Gupta period, the fourth or fifth century CE), essentially an abridgment of the *Arthashastra*, concentrates on foreign policy and war, leaving out many subjects that loom large in Kautilya's text. On the other hand, the last great comprehensive Sanskrit political text, Shukra's *Essence of Polity* (*Nitisara*, probably composed between the ninth and thirteenth centuries CE), though shorter than the *Arthashastra*, is wider in scope, concentrating on the moral norms needed to regulate conduct and sharply distinguishing between politics and ethics. The ethical dharma that Kautilya had so studiously kept out of the actual workings of the state now came back with a vengeance.

As for the *Kamasutra*, the later textbooks of eroticism omit everything but the sexual core, particularly the sexual positions, concentrating on just one of the seven books of the *Kamasutra* and generally ignoring all the cultural material.[4] But some of these later texts include a subject that the *Kamasutra* explicitly ruled out: procreation. *The Complete Urbanite* (*Nagara-sarvasva*) and *The Secret of Sexual Pleasure* (*Rati-rahasya*), both composed sometime between 800 and 1300 CE, discuss impregnation and childbearing, and *The Secret of Sexual Pleasure* provides recipes to facilitate conception, delivery, the relief of postnatal discomfort, and even abortion.[5] It was adharmic of the *Kamasutra* to ignore fertility, the only dharmic justification for sex, but it is surely far more adharmic of the *Secret of Sexual Pleasure* to discuss abortion, which Manu regards as one of the gravest sins, tantamount to murder

(4.208, 5.90, 8.317, 11.88, 11.249), and neither the *Arthashastra* nor the *Kamasutra* mentions.

S. K. De insists that "there is reason to believe that the [*Kamasutra*] was in wide and current use and never actually shelved."[6] But after about 1000 CE, later treatises like *The Complete Urbanite* and *The Secret of Sexual Pleasure* seem to have exerted more influence both within and beyond the tradition of erotic textbooks—for example, in literary commentaries written in the thirteenth and fourteenth centuries and in the fifteenth-century *Compendium of Kama* (*Kama-samuha*). One factor contributing to the decrease in popularity of the *Kamasutra* may have been its linguistic style: Vatsyayana's text consists primarily (aside from verses appended at the ends of chapters) of short, often rather gnomic, prose sentences that are sometimes hard to unpack. In contrast, most of the later erotic treatises are composed entirely in quite readable verse.[7] Apparently the later development of the erotic tradition owed more to poetry than to science.

Moreover, the most unusual parts of the *Kamasutra,* the psychological observations and sociological analyses, were absorbed by the tradition of court poetry, which even satirized the *Kamasutra*'s elaborate positions.[8] The *Kamasutra*'s triad of man-about-town, woman, and female go-between became the eternal triangle of later Sanskrit poetry. (The *Arthashastra* also influenced the political cynicism of court poetry.[9]) And the *Kamasutra*'s agonistic and duplicitous view of sex set the stage for much of the mythological substructure of later Indian erotic drama, poetry, and narrative. The subsequent influence of the *Kamasutra* on the eroticism of the *bhakti* tradition accounts in part for the darkness of that tradition, with its emphasis on divine abandonment, betrayal, and even violence.[10]

The *Kamasutra* was cherished not only as a sex manual and a metrosexual handbook but as a literary sourcebook. It survived in aristocratic quarters because of the sophisticated appeal of its portrait of a fantasized world of luxury and the utility of its often ingenious suggestions for the recreations of a man-about-town. Scholars cherished it for its rich detail about upper-class urban life in ancient India, poets for its ideas about the intrigues of romantic love and its imaginative anatomical detail, and religious leaders for its template for the often agonistic love of god.

The survival of the full Sanskrit texts of the *Arthashastra* and the *Kamasutra,* however, depended on the copying of manuscripts. The desire to win religious merit, a principal motive for the copying of dharma texts, was unlikely to have motivated patrons of the *Arthashastra* or the *Kamasutra.* But the texts must have been copied at least every two hundred years or so by someone who valued them, or we would not have them. The wet heat and the white ants destroy any manuscript in India within a few centuries at the most, especially since taboos about the use of animal skins limited the scribes of ancient India to the use of palm leaves, which do not last nearly as long as vellum. To survive over the centuries, a text must have inspired an unbroken line of people willing to pay to have it copied.

Manu was constantly recopied from the ancient period to the present and became well known in Europe after Sir William Jones translated it into English in 1794. By contrast, after about the twelfth century CE, the full Sanskrit texts of the *Arthashastra* and the *Kamasutra* were only sporadically available to the scholarly community. They were relatively neglected by the scribal traditions all those years because they were dangerous texts, adharmic texts. The *Arthashastra* was lost for centuries and rediscovered only in 1905. (Perhaps the same thing happened to the works of the Charvakas, and someone will someday discover a Charvaka text.) Yet those factions of society that supported the subversive agendas of Kautilya and Vatsyayana must have commissioned enough manuscripts for the two Sanskrit texts to survive. And the texts also lived, like most ancient Indian texts, in the oral tradition, as Vatsyayana himself assures us (1.3.5–10.) The *Arthashastra* and the *Kamasutra* were part of a vibrant, rich oral and written tradition from the time of their composition to the present; they continued to be known and discussed because they remained relevant to the great intellectual legacy of India.

The Colonial Impact

The situation for the *Kamasutra* changed when the British colonized India in the eighteenth century.[11] As not only Protestants but Victorian Protestants, the British rejected as filthy paganism the sensuous strain of Hinduism, both the world of kama and much of Hindu theological dharma, with what they saw as kitschy images of gods with far too many arms. It reminded them of Catholicism. They also opposed aspects of Hindu social dharma, such as child marriage and the burning of widows (suttee).[12] But they respected Hindu ethical dharma, including Indian monism and idealism (so appealing to European philosophers from Schlegel to Hegel) and the *Bhagavad Gita* (so appealing to the American Transcendentalists). At the same time, the underside of Victorian prudery, Victorian pornography (among what Stephen Marcus called "The Other Victorians"), also flourished in its Orientalist form, and it was an Englishman, Sir Richard Burton, who brought the *Kama-*

sutra to the attention of Anglophone Indian as well as British readers in 1883, when he published the first English translation of the book. But proper Europeans were scandalized by the *Kamasutra*. To get around the censorship laws, Burton set up an imaginary publishing house, the Kama Shastra Society of London and Benares, with printers said to be in Benares or Cosmopoli. When Richard Schmidt produced his definitive German translation of the *Kamasutra* in 1897, he put "the presumably scandalous passages" in Latin, and another translation into German, this one unexpurgated, led to a lawsuit in Germany as late as 1964.[13]

Many of the English-speaking Hindus who worked for and with the British came to accept the British evaluation of Hinduism, in a kind of Stockholm syndrome. They developed new forms of what came to be called Reform Hinduism, the Hindu Renaissance or the Bengal Renaissance, which valued the philosophical, ascetic aspect of Hinduism and devalued the world of pleasure represented in the *kama-shastras*. They propounded a white-washed brand of Hinduism limited to ethical dharma, particularly *sanatana* dharma ("the eternal dharma"), heavily flavored by Unitarianism. A number of such Hindus, particularly in Calcutta (now Kolkata), went about trying to silence the love songs to the gods, to cover up the erotic sculptures, and to kick the temple dancers out of the temples.

This sanitized *sanatana* strain of Hinduism was just one form among many, and a minor strain at that. It thrived primarily among the middle castes, who aspired to raise their social class by aping Victorians,[14] this whole strategy aping the much older Hindu strategy of lower classes aping Brahmins, in a process that the great sociologist M. N. Srinivas called "Sanskritization."[15] Most Hindus went on telling their stories and dancing their dances and worshipping their many gods. But the middle castes began to enforce this new brand of dharma. In the twentieth century, kama in general fell into still deeper disrepute. The British lion, even after its official death in India in 1947, dealt another blow to Indian freedom of expression through the Film Censor Board (the cousin of the US Hays Office), which, from the early 1950s, implemented a policy that had roots among the British (who had worried more about sedition than about sex). The Film Censor Board cast a shadow that extended over Indian visual arts and literature as well as film. But where the *sanatana* dharma of nineteenth-century Reform Hinduism had opposed abusive aspects of Hindu social dharma, including those affecting women, this new version enforced social dharma rules repressing women. In the 1960s in Bangalore, Bombay, Delhi, and several other Indian cities, vigilante groups like the Sri Ram Sena ('The Army of Lord Rama") routinely beat up young couples seen together in public and women who visited pubs, and also vandalized shops that sold Valentine's Day cards.

Indian intellectuals generally deplored this prudery and blamed it both on the British, who largely deserved it, and on the Muslims, who generally did not.[16] (Muslims of the Lodi dynasty in the sixteenth century commissioned one of the last great works of Sanskrit eroticism, the *Ananga Ranga*,[17] and the Mughals who succeeded them particularly appreciated the *Kamasutra* and produced lavishly illustrated editions.) V. S. Naipaul, in his book *Half a Life,* offers his own, rather jaded version of the anti-Muslim accusation as applied to the *Kamasutra:* "In our culture there is no seduction. Our marriages are arranged. There is no art of sex. Some of the boys here talk to me of the *Kama Sutra.* Nobody talked about that at home. It was an upper-caste text, but I don't believe my poor father, Brahmin though he is, ever looked at a copy. That philosophical-practical way of dealing with sex belongs to our past, and that world was ravaged and destroyed by the Muslims."[18] And then (the argument continues) came the British missionaries, adding insult to injury. Thus many Hindus blamed India's sexual conservatism on "an unholy combination of imposed Muslim religiosity and imported British 'Victorianism.'"[19] But these psychic wounds actually date, as Pankaj Mishra has noted, not from the period of Muslim rule, in which Hinduism thrived under the new stimulus, but "to the Indian elite's humiliating encounter with the geopolitical and cultural dominance first of Europe and then of America."[20]

The Modern Period

An adolescent girl in Vikram Chandra's story "Kama" (1997) says, "Sister Carmina didn't want to tell us. It's the *Kama Sutra,* which she says isn't in the library. But Gisela's parents have a copy which they think is hidden away on the top of their shelf. We looked it up there." And the adult to whom she tells this says, "You put that book back where you found it. And don't read any more."[21] In India today, urban, affluent, usually anglophone people might give a copy of the *Kamasutra* (in English translation) as a wedding present to demonstrate their open-mindedness and sophistication, but most people will merely sneak a surreptitious look at it in someone else's house. On the other hand, "a reported two thirds of young adults . . . would have casual, pre-marital sex before an arranged marriage,"[22] and, since 1991, they have been able to buy condoms called *KamaSutra.* Clearly the attempt to transform the *Kamasutra* into what many people, Hindus and non-Hindus alike, mistakenly refer to as the *Karmasutra* (presumably a *sanatana* dharma text about reincarnation) has not succeeded.[23] Vatsya-yana lives.

Today the verdict of obscenity seems more appropriate to certain passages of the *Arthashastra* than of the *Kamasutra*, as the German Indologist Friedrich Wilhelm bitterly re-marked. And indeed, he continues, "The modern world has become more sensitive to the misuse of artha than to anoma-lies of kama."[24] Yet, unlike in the case of the *Kamasutra*, no translation of the *Arthashastra* has ever been subjected to a lawsuit, and the *Arthashastra* has had greater success than the *Kamasutra* in contemporary India. Between 1905 and 1909, Rudrapatna Shamashastry began translating the Sanskrit text of the *Arthashastra* and publishing the work in sections, and the first full English translation was published in 1915. National pride brought new attention to the ancient Indian science of politics, which was far more useful, for nationalist purposes, than the science of erotics. Sunil Khilnani remarked that the ancient manuscript of the *Arthashastra*, newly discovered in 1905, "would help Indian nationalists imagine a realpolitik for an aspiring India of the twentieth century. Here was a self-help manual for a start-up nation."[25] And, indeed, Jawaharlal Nehru kept the *Arthashastra* by his bedside.[26]

Henry Kissinger, in his book *World Order* (2014), praises the *Arthashastra's* "dispassionate clarity" (surely the under-statement of the year) and notes that it is a work of "practical statecraft, not philosophical disputation."[27] Also in 2014, this notice appeared in the *New Indian Express:*

> In an effort to introduce the teachings of the Artha-shastra in Indian security and strategic studies, the Institute for Defence Studies and Analyses has recently published some works on it and iden-

tified Indian and foreign scholars engaged in a
deeper study of the text. National security adviser
Shivshankar Menon has taken part in some discussions. Some enterprising enthusiasts have set up an
institute in Mumbai to teach leadership qualities
to youngsters looking for careers in the corporate
world and politics and written popular books on
the Arthashastra. The text is being introduced in
training courses for soldiers and diplomats. But
there is no systematic effort on the part of the establishment to revive traditions of Indian strategic
thought and answer the ridiculous charge that we
lack a culture of strategic thinking.[28]

The author of this article, Arvind Gupta, was the director
general of the Institute for Defence Studies and Analyses. He
went on to say more:

In popular imagination Kautilya is compared with
Machiavelli for ruthlessness and unethical conduct. The Pakistani military studies Kautilya to
understand the supposedly devious Indian mind.
This is oversimplification and a gross distortion of
Kautilya. The perception must be rectified. . . . The
Arthashastra must be adapted to suit contemporary realities. A new Arthashastra for contemporary geopolitical realties should be evolved.[29]

Does Mr. Gupta actually approve of the methods of the *Arthashastra*? How much "adaptation" would be required for the
book to be used in India today? (Probably very little, though
the tricks with cobra deities underwater might not work so

well.) And does Gupta admire Machiavelli's ruthlessness and regard "Machiavellian" as a compliment?

The accusation that the Pakistanis, too, were studying the *Arthashastra*, not to make use of its suggestions (as Mr. Gupta thinks the Indian government should do) but to find out what the Indians were thinking, might have been inspired by statements such as the following, made by Javid Husain, a retired ambassador and the president of the Lahore Council for World Affairs, as reported in a Lahore newspaper in 2015: "Just a few years ago, a former Indian National Security Adviser praised this book [the *Arthashastra*] as an important guide on strategy. So it should be a matter of interest for us to study it and see what kind of advice it offers to Indian policy makers in the conduct of relations with Pakistan."[30] Kautilya lives.

Science, *Sanatana* Dharma, and Nationalism

The spirit of dissent that was nourished first by the scientific temper of the *Arthashastra* and the *Kamasutra* and then by the Charvaka mythology of skepticism has now come up against a new incarnation of the forces of repressive dharma, now supporting pseudoscientific claims. Once again science, now the sciences of physics, aeronautics, and medicine rather than politics and erotics, has come into direct conflict with authoritarian aspects of dharma.

This, too, began back during the British Raj. By assimilating the same British Protestant judgments that inspired the Hindu reaction against kama, members of Reform Hinduism came to admire both British science (particularly as expressed in technology such as trains) and British moral codes, in essence British ethical and social dharma—progressive in opposition to aspects of Hindu social dharma such as suttee.[31]

They accepted the idea of moral progress as an integral part of scientific progress. But then, in a kind of compensatory reaction against their uncomfortable admiration of their colonizers, many Hindus kept the foreign values but denied that they were foreign. Just as they had reasserted their own "eternal" *sanatana* dharma in response to British moral codes, now they asserted that their own oldest religious document, the Veda, back in 1500 BCE, had already anticipated European science. They claimed that ancient Indian scholars had made major scientific discoveries not only in grammar and mathematics (which they had, though not in the Vedas) but in aeronautics (which they had not, ever). Swami Dayanand Saraswati argued that the incarnate god Krishna and the *Mahabharata*'s human hero Arjuna (Krishna's close friend) had gone to America five thousand years ago, traveling through Siberia and the Bering Straits.[32] And so, others insisted, since the Vedic people had discovered America long before Columbus, he was, therefore, actually right when he called the native Americans "Indians."[33] Confusion here hath made its masterpiece!

Those who made these claims referred to the Vedas for their authority, ignoring the far more scientific *shastras*, for two reasons. First, because it's always easier to argue that something is "in the Vedas" than in a later text, since Vedic language is so archaic (it is to classical Sanskrit what Beowulf is to Shakespeare) that only relatively few priests and scholars know what's in the Vedas well enough to contradict anyone who cites the Vedas as their authority. And second, because the Vedas, being much older than the *shastras* (indeed, even older than the Bible), have more authority—particularly, of course, religious authority.

Hindu Nationalists, working to expel the British from India, therefore advanced a series of two-pronged arguments, not just "You are scientific, but we are spiritual" (though this was often said, too), but, better, "Our religion is wiser than your science—*and* our religious texts contain science much older than yours." And, finally, "We're better than you, in religion *and* science, because our religion is scientific and our science is religious, and we want you to leave."

The complex relationship between science and religion in India continued into the twentieth and twenty-first centuries and took a sharp turn to the right under the impetus of a Nationalist movement known as Hindutva, "Hinduness." This term was invented by the nationalist Vinayak Damodar Savarkar in his 1923 pamphlet entitled *Hindutva: Who Is a Hindu?* Hindutva's members call themselves Hindutva-vadis ("Those who profess Hindutva"), but one can call them, more simply, Hindutvats (on the analogy of bureaucrats). They propound a bowdlerized Hinduism that owes much to the Reform Hinduism of the nineteenth century, a variety of *sanatana* dharma now heavily laced with anti-Muslim and anti-woman sentiments.

The seeds of ambivalent resentment (what Nietzsche would have called *ressentiment*) sown during the Raj found fertile ground after Indian Independence, in 1947. V. S. Naipaul, in 1976, was appalled by "the prickly vanity of many Hindus who asserted that their holy scriptures already contained the discoveries and inventions of Western science."[34] In 1985, a man from Varanasi (which the British had called Benares) accused the nineteenth-century German Indologist Friedrich Max Mueller of having stolen chunks of an ancient Vedic text that "facilitated German scientists' later development of the atom bomb."[35] National pride in India's great progress was shadowed by the realization that it had been accomplished in large part by borrowing technological advances from the West. This science envy is wonderfully captured in a statement by the Vishwa Hindu Parishad's joint general secretary, Swami Vigyananand, referring to the Indus River, whose name is the source of the words "India" and "Hindu": "I am telling you the 'industry' word has come from us—Indus. We were very industrialised . . . that is why [the British] used the word."[36] Meera Nanda spells out the thinking behind the resurgence of the old Raj ambivalence about "Western" science:

> It rankles with us that these impure, beef-eating "materialists," a people lacking in our spiritual refinements, a people whose very claim to civilisation we delight in mocking, managed to beat the best of us when it came to nature-knowledge. So that while we hanker after science and pour enormous resources into becoming a "science superpower," we simultaneously . . . decry its "materialism," its "reductionism" and its "Eurocentrism." We *want* the science of the materialist upstarts from the West but cannot let go of our sense of spiritual superiority.[37]

The solution is obvious: locate the science in the spiritual, which is to say, in the Vedas, and sometimes in the *Ramayana*.

The *Ramayana* tells us that an army of talking monkeys built a bridge or causeway for Rama to cross over from India to the island of Lanka (*not* the same island as the present-day Sri Lanka) to rescue his wife Sita from the ten-headed demon Ravana. The Hindutvats identify that causeway with the stone formations that extend into the channel between India and

Sri Lanka, obstructing the passage of ships there. This mythical causeway was real enough, in September 2007, to inspire
Hindutva protests that put an end to a major government
project to build a much-needed shipping canal through the
area where, the protesters said, Rama's bridge was built. One
scholar, arguing that "modern science had insidiously dated
[the causeway] to be far younger than it actually was," claimed
that he himself had ordered a specimen rock from the underwater rock formation said to be where that causeway was
built: "After validating the authenticity of the rock, by check-
ing whether it floated on water (it did), he conducted his own
research and managed to prove the carbon dating wrong."[38]

The Subversion of Science under Narenda Modi

Mythoscience thrives in the climate that was created after the
BJP (the right-wing Hindu party) took power in 2014 and
Narendra Modi became prime minister.[39] Government allegiance to Hindutva and its "eternal dharma" is now coupled
not only with strong anti-Muslim agendas but also with a
virulent repression of other versions of Hinduism and its history, particularly those that contradict the skewed construction of Hindu history proclaimed by Hindutva.[40] This regime
encourages the by now entrenched bad habit of seeking scientific authenticity in religious rather than scientific texts from
the past. The Modi government has now set up ministries of
yoga and Ayurveda (ancient Hindu homeopathic medicine)
to peddle their versions of these ancient Hindu sciences.[41]
And Modi has commissioned a number of revisions of textbooks (the modern heirs to the ancient *shastras*) mandated as
supplementary reading for all government primary and sec-
ondary schools. Many of these books, including the widely

assigned 125-page book *Tejomay Bharat* (*Brilliant India*), had originally been published in 1999 in Gujarat; Modi had written the forewords to Batra's books when he was chief minister in Gujarat and now reissued the books and wrote new forewords for them.[42]

These revised textbooks include outlandish claims about the history of science in India, often producing weird anachronisms.[43] One maintained not only "that ancient India had the nuclear bomb, it even practised non-proliferation by carefully restricting the number of people who had access to it" (presumably to Brahmins).[44] There have also been books about Vedic physics and Vedic string theory.[45] In 2015, the incumbent minister at the Ministry of Science and Technology and the Ministry of Earth Sciences publicly announced, "We all know we knew 'beej ganit' ["seed-counting," the Indian word for algebra] much before the Arabs, but very selflessly allowed it to be called al-gebra" (a Latin word based on the Arabic *al-jabr*).[46]

Claims have also been made about Vedic quantum mechanics and general relativity:[47]

> Following the Prime Minister's bold lead, the Home Minister Rajnath Singh last week laid out the Varanasi interpretation of quantum theory. Werner Heisenberg, Singh explained, had based his famed Uncertainty Principle on the Vedas. Some of Singh's fellow travelers admitted that Heisenberg hadn't really read the Vedas, but quickly added that he did once have a conversation with Rabindranath Tagore, which was pretty much the same thing. That the Heisenberg-Tagore conversation took place two years after the German physicist had completed his career-defining work was irrelevant,

for time is relative. To understand more, they said,
read Einstein. Or the Vedas.

Girish Shahane, the author of this paragraph, calls this Raving
Loony Hindutva History.[48]

The most notorious of these wildly counterfactual claims
concern ancient airplanes, which "capture the imagination of
this resurgent, neo-Hindu India like nothing else."[49] The argument that ancient India had airplanes is a very old one, as
Hindus long pointed out that characters in the two ancient
Sanskrit epics (the *Mahabharata* and the *Ramayana*) fly about
in flying palaces called *vimanas*. The revised history textbooks
insist that the Vedic Indians knew about airplanes, and the assertion that these *vimanas* were actually very much like our
modern airplanes—motor-driven, aeronautically sound, and
so on—brings the argument directly into the path of science.
The claim that the ancient Indians knew about airplanes was
already included in textbooks that the BJP revised when it
came to power earlier, in 1999.[50]

The 102nd Indian Science Congress in Mumbai in January 2015, a prestigious event that dates back to 1914, included
programs on scientific advances ranging from India's 2013
Mars orbital mission to developments in cancer biology, with
talks by Indian and foreign scientists, among them a number
of Nobel laureates. Prime Minister Modi opened the congress,
and the man he had recently appointed to head the Indian
Council of Historical Research spoke of Vedic aircraft (*vimanas*) capable of interplanetary travel and invisibility, possess-
ing radar systems and mine detectors.[51] An assistant professor
of computational linguistics at the Department of Sanskrit,
University of Delhi, has insisted that the flying chariot on
which Ravana, the demonic villain of the *Ramayana,* flew

through the air ran not on fuel but on mercury. "It's really not that difficult," he added; "if the science can exist today, it could have existed in ancient times as well."[52] The revised textbooks maintain that the Hindu god Rama flew the first airplane.[53] On one occasion, Modi remarked, "If we talk about space science, our ancestors had, at some point, displayed great strengths in space science." Referring to Aryabhata, a great Hindu mathematician and astronomer in the fifth and sixth centuries CE, Modi continued, "What people like Aryabhatt had said centuries ago are being recognised by science today. What I mean to say is that we are the country which had these capabilities. We need to regain these."[54]

According to the new textbooks, the ancient Indians also knew about automobiles: "What we know today as the motorcar existed during the Vedic period. It was called anashva rath [literally, a "horseless chariot"]."[55] And they had television. One of the textbooks states that there was "an even older television [Doordarshan]" created when Hindu sages used magic yogic powers to attain divine sight. "There is no doubt that the invention of television goes back to this."[56] In the *Mahabharata,* a sage uses his divine sight to tell a blind king what is happening on the battlefield many miles away; this was "a live telecast of the battle." One scholar from Punjab University insisted, "The TV has been there since the time of the Mahabharat. Even missiles are not a new invention."[57]

Modi also maintains that stem cell technology was known in ancient India. As the *Guardian* reported: "America wants to take the credit for invention of stem cell research, but the truth is that India's Dr Balkrishna Ganpat Matapurkar has already got a patent for regenerating body parts."[58] And indeed Matapurkar, a surgeon with the Maulana Azad Medical College in New Delhi, did take out such a patent, in 1976. But "this research is not new . . . Dr Matapurkar was inspired by the Mahabharata." For the *Mahabharata* tells us that a queen gave birth prematurely to a hard mass of flesh, which a great sage divided into 100 parts and nourished for two years until 100 kings were born out of it. And so, the revised textbook tells us, "On reading this, he [Matapurkar] realized that stem cell was not his invention. This was found in India thousands of years ago."[59] On another occasion, at a conference organized by the southern chapter of the All India Biotech Association, Matapurkar explained his reasoning: "No woman can give birth to 100 children in her lifetime, that too all males and of the same age."[60]

When inaugurating a hospital on October 28, 2015, Modi added genetic engineering and plastic surgery to the list of ancient Hindu scientific achievements. Referring to the myth in which the god Ganesha was beheaded but then given an elephant's head, Modi said, "Some plastic surgeon must have been around at that time, who by attaching an elephant head to the body of a human started off plastic surgery."[61] Moreover, he said that the statement in the epic *Mahabharata* that the hero Karna "was not born from his mother's womb . . . means that genetic science was present at that time."[62] As a result (Modi continued), "We can feel proud of what our country achieved in medical science at one point of time." The novelist Amit Chaudhuri has an interesting take on Modi's comment about Ganesha's plastic surgery. It "made people shake their heads and laugh, but all Modi was saying was that Hindu my-thology as a domain of poetry, irreverence, humour and sym-bolism . . . made far less sense to him than the Renaissance and Enlightenment realism which, in a weirdly distorted form, has shaped the BJP as well as its secretive cultural-militant wing, the RSS."[63]

In yet another reversion to the Raj mentality, many Hindu Nationalists blame Europe for the suppression of Indian science. One said that in 1895 a Sanskrit scholar named Shivkar Bapuji Talpade had used an ancient Indian treatise on airplanes to build and fly an airplane.[64] The treatise had been forgotten because of "the passage of time, foreign rulers ruling us, and things being stolen from this country," or the cultural amnesia injected into India by foreigners ruling the country. A Hindi news channel claimed that Talpade's design for the first airplane was eventually stolen from him by a British company under the false pretense of helping him and that it was quite likely this design that ended up in the hands of the Wright brothers. British-controlled media then also allegedly edited Talpade's invention out of history.[65]

That argument could also have been generalized to answer this awkward question: If ancient India had all those scientific inventions, what became of them? The final lines of a 1999 book about the Charvakas blames their demise for India's failure to develop the "positive sciences":

> Clearly, and some would say unfortunately, the Charvaka school was snubbed. It is difficult to say what might have happened if it had become mainstream Indian thinking. It is entirely possible that Indian civilization would have degenerated into a pleasure-seeking hedonistic world like ancient Rome, and perished in its insatiate orgies. Or again, the no-nonsense attitudes towards what they regarded as priestly mumble-jumble, and the crass Skepticism of the Charvakas might have saved Indian culture from the myriad superstitions that still plague it. More significantly, the Charvakas might

have sown the seeds for the positive sciences which would have germinated in India rather than in sixteenth century Europe. Who can tell![66]

Amartya Sen, however, attributes to the Charvakas a positive contribution to the positive sciences: "We can argue that the flowering of Indian science and mathematics that began in the Gupta period (led particularly by Aryabhata in the fifth century CE, Varahamihira in the sixth, and Brahmagupta in the seventh) benefited from the tradition of skepticism and questioning which had been flourishing in India at that time."[67] And Sen cites as an example the episode of Jabali in the *Ramayana* that we considered in chapter 6.

Somehow the real history of real science in India has not been entirely swamped by Modi's mythological science. The annual Indian Science Congress includes a session called "Ancient Sciences through Sanskrit" devoted to the considerable technical knowledge in Sanskrit texts, particularly in mathematics, metallurgy, and medicine.[68] On April 25, 2016, the minister of human resource development informed the parliament that the Indian Institutes of Technology should encourage students to learn about aspects of science and technology that are mentioned in Sanskrit texts.[69] This announcement was met with predictable Internet enthusiasm from Hindutvats, to whom "Sanskrit" meant "the Vedas" and compulsory Sanskrit (and Hinduism) in the curriculum. But reasonable people of no particular Hindutva affiliation welcomed the idea that scientists should learn more about genuine ancient Indian science. One simultaneously mocked the old Raj mythology and the Eurocentrism that had originally spawned it, asking, sarcastically, "Don't we know that all science flows from English (why not German or French or Hebrew?), and that we had nothing but vain fancies about flying machines or cosmic weapons?"[70] Another made a valid point about the true scope of Indian science, in the Sanskrit *shastras* rather than the Vedas: "In fields including linguistics, homeopathic medicine, agriculture, water management, construction, statecraft, philosophy, psychology, ethics, environmental conservation, management [and] mathematics . . . Indian accomplishments have retained much relevance and applicability. Astronomy, chemistry, botany, zoology and a few more disciplines also saw brilliant developments which, if no longer relevant today, still need to be studied as they are an important part of the history of ideas."[71] These *shastras,* however, are not the texts cited by the theocrats, who insist on locating ancient Indian science firmly in religion, which is to say, in the Vedas.

The Vedic arguments are causing great embarrassment to Indian scientists, who have strongly objected to what journalists call the Modi-fication of science.[72] An Indian materials scientist affiliated with NASA started an online petition on Change.org against the epidemic of "pseudo-science."[73] The campaign quickly garnered sixteen hundred supporters.[74] Another online petition, signed by more than two hundred scientists, objected to the mixing of mythology with science, citing the example of Modi's reference to Ganesha's plastic surgery.[75] The petition read, "We as a scientific community should be seriously concerned about the infiltration of pseudo-science in science curricula with the backing of influential political parties."[76]

Indian scientists have also protested the government's recent announcement of its intention to prove that the traditional Indian concoction of the "five products of the cow" (*pancha-gavya*—milk, cow urine, cow dung, yogurt, and clarified butter), traditionally used for the reparation of ritual errors and still used to treat various medical problems, has actual scientific value.[77] "The truth is that panchagavya is very strong and very powerful," India's science minister, Harsh Vardhan, told *Science*. The validation effort, he says, will use modern scientific tools "to show to the world the supremacy of Ayurveda."[78] The *pancha-gavya* program—also known as "cowpathy"—will be carried out at the Center for Rural Development and Technology.[79] Chetan Sharma, an animal rights activist with People For Animals, stated at a Hindu conference: "Cow is also the reason for global warming. . . . When she is slaughtered, something called EPW is released, which is directly responsible for global warming. It's what is called emotional pain waves."[80] (This may be a mangled version of the problem of cows farting methane, which really does contribute to global warming, a problem that would be solved by the slaughter rather than the protection of cows, not what the BJP has in mind.)

Mathematics experts said they were not convinced by the view of the Indian minister of science and technology that Indians (more precisely an ancient Vedic sage named Baudhayana) invented the Pythagorean theorem, "but we very sophisticatedly gave its credit to the Greeks."[81] A mathematics professor from Mumbai University, who was clearly trying to keep out of trouble, said, of the minister's Pythagorean claim, "We know Indians have contributed to mathematics to a great extent. However, I was surprised to hear what he said. Maybe the way he thinks about mathematics is different than what we academicians do."[82] The problem of such scientists, though not the motivation for the Hindutva science madness, is reminiscent of that of Soviet scientists under Stalin—or that of American scientists, especially climate scientists, under President Trump.

The deviousness of Modi's politics inspired Javid Husain to compare him with Kautilya: "In view of the commitment of the present Narendra Modi–led BJP government in India to Hindutva, the probability that its strategy in dealing with Pakistan would be deeply influenced, if not governed, by the rules laid down by Kautilya in Arthashastra cannot be totally ruled out."[83] Indeed, if the members of Modi's government were to take to heart the true lesson of the *Arthashastra*—not the alleged "Machiavellian" message but the skepticism and the "dispassionate clarity" that Kissinger praised—it might provide a useful counterweight to the reign of *sanatana* dharma and its false science. Until then, India remains a land in which, after so many centuries in which scientific traditions managed to keep alive a subversive attack on religion, religion now is invoked in the subversion of science.

Notes

1
The Three Human Aims

1. See Olivelle, *Between the Empires.*

2. Thapar, *Early India,* 279.

3. Schoff, *The Periplus of the Erythraean Sea,* 43, paragraph 49.

4. Thapar, *Early India,* 261.

5. Keay, *India: A History,* 125.

6. A great deal has been written about the *shastras.* A good place to begin reading about them would be Anna Libera Dallapiccola, ed., *Śāstric Traditions in Indian Arts,* particularly Sheldon Pollock, "The Idea of Śāstra in Traditional India" and "Playing by the Rules: Śāstra and Sanskrit Literature."

7. The earliest grammatical *shastras* probably date from that time; the most famous, that of the grammarian Panini, is of uncertain date but possibly from as early as the fourth century BCE. In a broader sense, all commentaries on the Veda are *shastras,* and these may be as early as the ninth century BCE. See the various discussions of *shastras* by Sheldon Pollock, particularly in "The Theory of Practice and the Practice of Theory in Indian Intellectual History."

8. Here and throughout, in citing basic texts (Manu, *Arthashastra, Kamasutra, Mahabharata, Ramayana*), I will give the verse or line number in parentheses at the end of the citation rather than in an endnote.

9. See *Kamasutra* 2.2.30 for the acknowledgment that the long list of embraces could be supplemented by others. See also Tieken, "The *Arthaśāstra* as a Fount of Fun," 115–16.

10. See Malamoud, "On the Rhetoric and Semantics of *puruṣārtha,*" and Doniger, "Three (or More) Forms."

11. The best of the enormous literature on dharma is summarized and illuminated in Patrick Olivelle's work, especially his *Dharma: Studies in Its Semantic, Cultural, and Religious History,* and in Alf Hiltebeitel's *Dharma: Its Early History in Law, Religion, and Narrative.*

12. In the *Mahabharata,* Dharma is cursed to be born as a human servant (Vidura, 1.101), and he takes the forms of a water spirit (a Yaksha, 3.297–98) and a dog (17.2–3). For Kama, see Doniger O'Flaherty, *Ascetism and Eroticism in the Mythology of Siva.*

13. For Pururavas and Urvashi, see *Rig Veda* 10.95 (Doniger O'Flaherty, *The Rig Veda: An Anthology,* 253–56) and Doniger, *Splitting the Difference,* 280–81.

14. Sen, *The Argumentative Indian,* 25.

15. It is largely because I believe that the *Kamasutra* is a scientific text that I disagree with Michel Foucault's rather Orientalist categorization of it as an example of (Oriental) *ars erotica* rather than (European) *scientia sexualis* (Foucault, *History of Sexuality,* Vol. 1, 57–58). Yet a very interesting argument in defense of Foucault's take on the *Kamasutra* is advanced by Sanjay K. Gautam in *Foucault and the* Kamasutra, and another, different but also compelling defense is made by Laura Desmond in "The Pleasure Is Mine."

16. My favorite satire on this view of the *Kamasutra* appeared in the *New Yorker* (September 24, 2012) in an article by Farley Katz and Simon Rich, "The Married Kama Sutra," which began: "When the man is loading the dishwasher, and the woman must come over, because he is loading it wrong, it is called 'the dishwasher position.'" It concluded: "When the man lightly kisses the woman's neck, and the woman tenderly strokes the man's chest, and the child runs into the room screaming, because he heard a scary noise, or some other bullshit, it is called 'the interrupted congress.'"

17. See Doniger, "Three (or More) Forms."

18. Derived from the Sanskrit *kūṭila,* "crooked." L. N. Rangarajan (*Kauṭilya: The Arthaśāstra,* 16) suggests that Kautilya was descended from a man named Kutila.

19. Olivelle, "Kauṭilya's *Arthaśāstra,*" 1.

20. Trautmann, *Kauṭilya and the Arthaśāstra,* 184. Trautmann has demonstrated that individual sections of the *Arthashastra* are from different time periods.

21. Trautmann, in *Kauṭilya and the Arthaśāstra,* 185, argues that the *Arthaśāstra* is older than the dharma *smṛtis.* And Patrick Olivelle, in "Manu and the *Arthaśāstra,*" 281, agrees with Kangle that "sections of the *Arthaśāstra* are older than Manu and are the source for some of the passages and vocabulary" in Manu.

22. The *Kamasutra* must have been written after 225 CE because the political situation that Vatsyayana describes shows the Abhiras and the Andhras ruling simultaneously over a region that had been ruled by the Andhras alone until 225. The fact that the text does not mention the Guptas, who ruled North India from the beginning of the fourth century CE, suggests that the text predates that period. The *Kamasutra* is mentioned by name in the *Vāsavadattā* of Subandhu, composed under Chandragupta Vikramaditya, who reigned at the beginning of the fifth century CE. Trautmann, in *Kauṭilya and the Arthaśāstra,* 175, states, "There is little by which the *Kāmasūtra* may be dated, except its reference to king Śatavāhana . . . [in] c. first century BC." And, on 171: "Our conclusion must be, then, that Books 1, 3, 4 and 5 of the *Kāmasūtra* are by a single author, presumably Vātsyāyana, whose name the work bears. This author was not responsible for the style of Books 2 and 6, and probably not for Book 7, which, however, is too short to reach a firm decision; and each of these three books, or at least Books 2 and 7, have distinctive styles." The *Kamasutra* may have been composed in Pataliputra (near the present city of Patna, in Bihar), a town that Vatsyayana refers to by name once (1.1.11) and indirectly on another occasion (2.9.31).

23. It refers to one text about artha as "The Tasks of the Superintendent" (1.2.10), the name of a preexisting source, the *Adhyakṣapracāra,* which may predate the extant text of the *Arthashastra* by a century or more and which forms the bulk of book 2 of that text. Olivelle, "Kauṭilya's *Arthaśāstra*," 1.

24. Nevertheless, Trautmann (in *Kauṭilya and the Arthaśāstra,* 173) asserts that Vatsyayana "certainly knew the *Arthaśāstra* in more or less its present form."

25. Dumont, *Homo Hierarchicus.*

26. King Jr., *Where Do We Go from Here?,* 39. This originated as a speech delivered at the 11th Annual Convention of the SCLC (Southern Christian Leadership Conference).

27. The last compound could also be translated as Olivelle does: "those who are unrighteous (*adharmān*) and those who hate Success." But at 8.3.4–22 Kautilya defines the cause of hatred as anger and argues that anger is even more destructive than kama. So I think he means "hatred," rather than "those who hate," here too. In any case, the parallelism requires a third term as the opposite of kama.

28. In one single verse (3.1.1), Vatsyayana says that if a man wants a legal son, he should marry a woman of his own class; and that is the end of it, as he immediately moves on to other sorts of women.

29. Jean Fezas, in "Remarques sue la forme," 146, points out that the *Kamasutra* is not only for "galants" and courtesans but also for princesses.

30. See also the discussion of this passage by Sheldon Pollock in "The Theory of Practice," 506–7.

31. For vernacularization, see Doniger, *The Hindus*, 4–7, and Pollock, *The Language of the Gods in the World of Men*.

32. This English pun on a Sanskrit pun I blame on David Shulman, who committed it in a class on April 4, 2017, in Chicago.

33. Among the many versions of the story, there is one in the *Kathāsaritsāgara* 1.6.

34. De, "Ancient Indian Erotics," 98.

35. Trautmann, *Kauṭilya and the Arthaśāstra*, 172: "Vātsyāyana mostly quotes these [named] authorities with approval; views attributed to *ācāryāḥ*, *eke* [scholars/teachers, some], etc. are on the other hand more often contradicted." See also Wilhelm, "Das Beziehungen zwischen *Arthaśāstra* und *Kāmasūtra*," 73, n. 3.

36. I use the word "subversion," here and throughout, in the rather limited sense of the first *Oxford English Dictionary* definition: "The action or process of undermining the power and authority of an established system or institution."

37. "Bārhaspatyas" is the word I am translating as "materialists," and the Sanskrit for "how the world works" is *lokāyātra*, lexically closely related to Lokāyata. See chapter 6.

2
The Influence of the *Arthashastra* on the *Kamasutra*

1. Winternitz, *Geschichte der indischen Litteratur*, Vol. 3, 537; *History of Indian Literature*, Vol. 3, 621.

2. I owe all that I know about Machiavelli to my colleague Nathan Tarcov, who knows *all* about Machiavelli, and with whom I was privileged to teach a seminar on Machiavelli (*The Discourses* and *The Prince*) and the *Arthashastra* in autumn 2005 at the University of Chicago.

3. Weber, *Politics as a Vocation*, 25. John Keay, reviewing Sunil Khilnani's *Incarnations: India in Fifty Lives* in the June 10, 2016, *Times Literary Supplement*, referred to this line in describing the *Arthashastra*: "It is a treatise on scruple-free statecraft that might appeal to Vladimir Putin and which makes Machiavelli's *Il principe* seem 'harmless.'"

4. Wilhelm, "Das Beziehungen zwischen *Arthaśāstra* und *Kāmasūtra*," 300. Wilhelm calls him Kauṭalya rather than Kauṭilya, as do many texts.

5. Bhandarkar, "Date of Kauṭalya," 65 ff.; see especially 76 ff.

6. De, "Ancient Indian Erotics," 95.

7. Wilhelm, "Das Beziehungen," 305, 309–10. And in 1978 he remarked that "the *Kāmasūtra* of Vatsyayana contains considerations which reveal the influence of the *Arthaśāstra*." Wilhelm, "The Concept of Dharma," 76.

8. Trautmann, "A Metrical Original for the Kauṭilīya *Arthaśāstra?*," 348; *Kauṭilya and the Arthaśāstra*, 73–75.

9. Fezas, "Remarques sur la forme"; Tieken, "The *Arthaśāstra* as a Fount of Fun," 119.

10. Tieken, "The *Arthaśāstra* as a Fount of Fun," 120; see also Taylor, *The Fall of the Indigo Jackal*.

11. McClish, *Political Brahmanism*, 111, 115, 124, etc.

12. R. P. Kangle's suggestion that the *Arthashastra* is quoting from an original verse version that was then reworked in prose, and that the author of the prose text kept these verse sections "just as he found them in his sources" (Kangle, *The Kauṭilīya Arthaśāstra*, 33), has been successfully disputed by Trautmann, among others (Trautmann, "A Metrical Original," 349).

13. Trautmann, *Kauṭilya and the Arthaśāstra*, 174. "I believe, then, that the various hands we have detected in the *Arthaśāstra* belong to the *pūrvācāryas*, the previous teachers whose works, in condensed form perhaps, were bound into a single work by a compiler who divided the work into chapters, *added the terminal verses* [italics mine], composed the first and last chapters (and possibly one of the three long books), and who may have added other original material but did not rework his sources to the extent that their stylistic features were obscured."

14. Fezas, "Remarques sur la forme," 133.

15. Ibid., 130–32; Trautmann, *Kauṭilya and the Arthaśāstra*, 75.

16. I owe the arguments in this paragraph to Mark McClish, personal communication, February 3, 2017.

17. *Arthashastra* 1.16 and throughout the book; *Kamasutra* 1.5.35–36, 3.4.32–33, 3.5.1–11, 3.5.19–27, 5.4.

18. See Doniger, "Invisibility and Sexual Violence."

19. Wilhelm, "Das Beziehungen," 305. The three fruits are varieties of either myrobalan or nutmeg, areca nut, and clove. See Olivelle, *King, Governance, and Law*, 565.

20. Plato had a similar problem with them in the *Republic*.

21. The Buddhists say that nuns should *not* be go-betweens, so the *Kamasutra* is going against Buddhist law as well as Hindu law in using them.

22. See also *Arthashastra* 7.15.12; 9.2.3–6; 9.3.39; 9.4.8. *Śakti* and *siddhi* are the words here translated as "power" and "success." Herman Tieken, in "The *Arthaśāstra* as a Fount of Fun," 120, sees this as implicitly compared with "a

gathering of specialists in statecraft sitting in conclave discussing possible candidates for the position of trusted courtier."

23. Manu says that there are in fact ten vices of kama: hunting, gambling, sleeping by day, malicious gossip, women, drunkenness, music, singing, dancing, and aimless wandering. But the usual four are the worst, and of them, drinking is the very worst, then gambling, then women, and then hunting (7.47, 50). Kautilya differs slightly: again drinking is the worst, but then come women, gambling, and hunting (8.3.38–63).

24. The Hindus generally formulated a group of three emotions, usually desire, anger, and greed (*Bhavagad Gita* [*Mahabharata* 7].101.14) or, occasionally, desire, anger, and fear. But they often added a fourth, metaphysical, epistemological emotion: delusion (*moha*), corresponding to the fourth sometimes added to the Triad of human aims, *moksha*. *Mahabharata* 18.5.50 has a slightly different quartet: "A man should never abandon dharma because of kama or fear or greed, not even for the sake of his life."

25. Penzer and Bhatt, *Poison-Damsels*.

26. Slander, physical violence, malice, envy, resentment, destruction of property, verbal abuse, and assault are the eight vices born of anger (Manu 7.49).

27. Lorraine Daston, personal communication, September 14, 2014.

28. Vena was an evil king who murdered people and prevented sacrifices until the priests killed him (*Mahabharata* 12.59.99–103). Nahusha, a human king, rose to become another Indra in heaven until he had the audacity to proposition Indra's wife and to harness the Seven Sages to his chariot in place of horses, whereupon he was cursed to become a snake and fell from heaven (*Mahabharata* 5.9–17). Sudas was a great king, with Vishvamitra as his family priest and Vasishtha as his enemy, until he had his men kill Vasishtha's son Shakti, whereupon Vishvamitra abandoned him and he was defeated (*Rig Veda* 7.18, 7.32, with Sayana's commentary); he reappears as Saudasa Kalmasapada in the *Mahabharata* (1.166–68), where he again kills Shakti and Vishvamitra curses him to become an ogre. Sumukha does not seem to appear in the Vedas or Epics. Nimi would not wait for his family priest, Vasishtha, to return before he undertook a great sacrifice; Vasishtha cursed him to lose his body; when he died, the priests churned his body to produce a son, Janaka of Videha (*Mahabharata* 13.91; *Devibhagavata Purana* 6).

29. This line is one that Ludo Rocher, in "The *Kāmasūtra*: Vātsyāyana's Attitude toward Dharma and *Dharmaśāstra*," 527, regards as "one of the best specimens to illustrate the extent to which the *Kāmasūtra* occasionally emulates the 'Machiavellian' tendencies of the *Arthaśāstra*."

30. De, in "Ancient Indian Erotics," 100, remarks, "It is striking that he omits and ignores the Asura [demonic] form in which the bride is purchased by offer of money."

31. Edwardes, *The Rape of India: A Biography of Robert Clive and a Sexual History of the Conquest of Hindustan.*

3
Dharma and Adharma in the *Arthashastra*

1. He uses the term *sarveṣām* in place of *sādhāraṇa.*

2. Doniger, *The Hindus,* 277–303.

3. The Sanskrit for the conflicted authors is *dharmacintakaiḥ* . . . *tattvārthās.*

4. McClish, "Political Brahmanism and the State," 212: "The relatively late appearance in the text of attitudes and prescriptions favorable to Brahmins, the hereditary sacerdotal class of the classical period . . . will contradict the prevailing notion that pro-Brahmanical sentiment and religious bias favoring Brahmins were standard features of state policy in classical South Asia."

5. The idea that Manu himself was this first king is not part of the dharma text attributed to Manu, though there, as well as in the broader mythology of Hinduism, Manu is regarded as the first human being and often, as in the *Mahabharata,* he is the first king.

6. Dumézil, *The Destiny of the Warrior; The Destiny of a King.*

7. See also *Arthashastra* 1.13, 5.1, 7.5, 8.2 and 9.5.

8. Many Sanskrit texts (including Manu 9.66–67) cite the story of the wicked king Vena, who flaunted dharma until he finally went too far and took away the livelihood of the Brahmins, whereupon they killed him. But this is hardly a revolution.

9. And one that was not, incidentally, shared by Buddhists in India, but that is another story.

10. Davis, "What Do Indian Images Really Want?"

11. See also *Arthashastra* 2.2.2; 4.13.32–33.

12. Sen, *The Argumentative Indian,* 25.

13. Ibid., 25.

14. "Some [of the "ascetic" spies] may have been ascetics recruited as the *udāsita,* the apostate renouncer; but at least in some accounts, they appear to be secret agents acting as ascetics, because all the man's disciples are also agents." Personal communication from Patrick Olivelle, February 28, 2012.

15. See White, *Sinister Yogis,* and Doniger O'Flaherty, "The False Ascetic," in Doniger O'Flaherty, *Asceticism and Eroticism,* 64–68.

16. Kautilya does not hold women renouncers in very high regard or figure that their lives are worth much. For example, he recommends a small fine for having sex with a female renouncer (4.13.36), whereas sex with a virgin is punishable by paying "the bride price and twice that much as a fine"

(3.13.12). He regards the woman renouncer as even less valuable than the servant woman.

17. This trick is also attributed to Hero of Alexandria (in the first or second century CE), who made the same sort of machines to trick people; and, in *The Arabian Nights,* a pagan king employs a man to slip inside the idol and give out oracles from within the statue. But here, apparently, unlike the king in the *Arthashastra,* the pagan king does not use the idol to kill the supplicants. Warner, *Stranger Magic,* 55; the 570th night: Dahesh and Solomon.

4

Adharma and Dharma in the *Kamasutra*

1. Keith, *A History of Indian Literature,* 466.

2. Raja, "Dissent in Ancient India."

3. See also De, "Ancient Indian Erotics," 97–98.

4. Elsewhere we learn that a courtesan may sleep with a Brahmin who falls in love with her at first sight, and even bear him a child; *Kamasutra* 6.2.44.

5. Wezler, "Some Remarks on the Final Verses," 337.

6. De, "Ancient Indian Erotics," 100.

7. Wilhelm, "The Concept of Dharma," 72.

8. Surya, the sun god, says this to persuade the young and unmarried Kunti to allow him to impregnate her with Karna.

9. *Brihadaranyaka Upanishad* 6.4.4. See also *Brihadaranyaka Upanishad* 6.2.1–2, 13 (and *Chandogya Upanishad* 5.3.1–4) and also *Chandogya Upanishad* 6.1.1–6.

10. *Chandogya Upanishad* 6.4.10 and *Brihadaranyaka Upanishad* 6.4.3, 7 (as well as *Chandogya Upanishad* 2.13) analogize the Vedic chant to the act of intercourse: when the man asks the woman, it is the introductory praise; when he lies down with the woman, it is the high chant; when he lies upon the woman, it is the response; when he ejaculates, it is the concluding chant; when he withdraws, it is the concluding chant. "He should not hold back from any woman." See also *Brhadaranyaka Upanishad* 6.2.9–16: a woman is a fire; her firewood is her vulva, her smoke is her pubic hair, her flame is her vagina; when one penetrates her, that is her embers; her sparks are the climax. Cf. also *Brihadaranyaka Upanishad* 6.4.2–3 (her vulva is the sacrificial ground, her pubic hair the sacred grass, etc.).

11. He refers to *Chandogya Upanishad* 6.1 ff. Chattopadhyaya first made this claim in an earlier paper, later reprinted as "Materialism in Indian Phi-

losophy," chapter 7 of his *Knowledge and Intervention,* 196 ff. He elaborated the theme in "Uddalaka Aruṇi: The Pioneer of Science."

12. De, "Ancient Indian Erotics," 90.

13. Doniger, *Splitting the Difference.*

14. See Doniger, "The Mythology of Kama," in Doniger, *On Hinduism.*

15. Manu 3.5 insists that the wife must be a virgin.

16. Manu 5.162: "No (legal) progeny are begotten here by another man or in another man's wife; nor is a second husband ever prescribed for virtuous women." And, in 5.163: "A woman who abandons her own inferior husband and lives with a superior man becomes an object of reproach in this world; she is said to be 'previously had by another man.'"

17. Wezler, "Some Remarks on the Final Verses," 337–38.

18. Sometimes Vatsyayana assigns the deviant views to people from bad parts of India, such as Andhra (*Kamasutra* 2.6.22), Bahlika (2.6.45 and 49), Ahichattra, Saketa, and Surasena (2.9.28–34). Similarly, he chides several South Indian kings for their sexual excesses (2.7.28–30).

5
Glossing Adharma with Dharma

1. See, for example, Rocher, "The *Kāmasūtra.*"

2. Manu: "The root of dharma is the entire Veda, and (then) the tradition and customs of those who know (the Veda), the conduct of virtuous people, and *what is satisfactory to oneself*" (2.6). "The Veda, tradition, the conduct of good people, and *what is pleasing to oneself*—they say that this is the four-fold mark of dharma, right before one's eyes" (2.12). "If a woman or a man of lower caste does anything that is better, [a man] should do all of that diligently, and *whatever his mind and heart delight in*" (2.223). "Whatever activity *satisfies him inwardly* when he is doing it should be done zealously; but he should avoid the (activity) that is the opposite" (4.161). "A person should recognize as lucidity *whatever he perceives in his self* as full of joy, something of pure light that seems to be entirely at peace. . . . When he longs with his all to know something and is not ashamed when he does it, and *his self is satisfied by it,* that (act) has the mark of the quality of lucidity" (12.27, 37). Emphasis added to all passages.

3. Ludo Rocher regards the *Kāmasūtra's* goal of "happiness" (*sukha*) as "the basic concept which sets the *Kāmasūtra* apart from the texts on dharma." Rocher, "The *Kāmasūtra,*" 529.

4. Sen, *The Argumentative Indian,* 25.

5. Sattar, *Uttara: The Book of Answers.*

6. Moreover, shortly thereafter Kautilya makes a disparaging remark about the Barhaspatyas, followers of Brihaspati, this time meaning the historical person, the materialist (possibly a mythical character named after the unscrupulous god). This greatly undercuts, or at least blurs, the dharmic authority of the god.

7. De, "Ancient Indian Erotics," 92.

8. See the discussion of this passage in Sheldon Pollock, "The Theory of Practice," 513. Pollock regards it as "most interesting for the intriguing historical patina it bears."

9. There are nine: in addition to the two general editors (Shvetaketu Auddalaki [son of Uddalaka] and Babhravya of Panchala), the individual editors of each of the seven books are Charayana, Suvarnanabha, Ghotakamukha, Gonardiya, Gonikaputra, Dattaka, and Kuchumara. The *Arthashastra* cites founders of five schools: Brihaspati, Ushanas, Manu, Parashara, and Ambhi.

10. More precisely, the *Arthashastra* calls him Bahudantiputra, "Son of Bahudantin."

11. See, on this, the excellent article by Albrecht Wezler, "Some Remarks on the Final Verses of the Kāmasūtra."

12. De, in "Ancient Indian Erotics," 91, translates it well. Here is the first verse: "If he has spoken attractively of things that inflame desire because his subject demands it, he has taken care immediately to censure and prohibit them."

13. De, "Ancient Indian Erotics," 91.

14. Though Sudhir Kakar made a well-educated guess in his novel *The Ascetic of Desire.*

15. "Because I wanted to emit creatures, I generated inner heat that is very hard to produce, and then at the start I emitted the ten great sages, lords of creatures: Marichi, Atri and Angiras, Pulastya, Pulaha, Kratu, Prachetas, Vasishtha, Bhrigu, and Narada."

16. Ali, "Rethinking the History of the 'Kāma' World," 9.

17. De, "Ancient Indian Erotics," 93.

18. Trautmann, *Kauṭilya and the Arthaśāstra,* 171–74.

19. Wilhelm, "The Quotations," 403; "The Concept of Dharma," 68.

20. Wilhelm, "Das Beziehungen zwischen *Kāmasūtra* und *Arthaśāstra,*" 297: "Im *Arthaśāstra* debattieren die Einzelverfasser zumeist in stereotyper Reihe miteinander. Ihre Zitate sind zumindest stilistisch bearbeitet, vielleicht sogar fiktiv. Im *Kāmasūtra* aber sind die Zitate der Einzelverfasser glaubwürdig."

21. Trautmann, *Kauṭilya and the Arthaśāstra,* 172–73.

22. Fezas, "Remarques sur la forme," 146; Wilhelm, "The Quotations," 404.

23. Wilhelm, "The Quotations," 403.

24. He names Bharadvaja, Vishalaksha, Parashara, Pishuna, Kaunapadanta, and Vatavyadhi.

25. Here the same group testifies, one by one, in the same order, with the addition of Bahudantiputra.

26. Trautmann, *Kauṭilya and the Arthaśāstra*, 173.

27. Raja, "Dissent in Ancient India."

28. Doniger, "Why Should a Brahmin Tell You Whom to Marry?"

29. Trautmann, *Kauṭilya and the Arthaśāstra*, 73–74.

30. Sen, *The Argumentative Indian*, 21.

31. This sort of negative quotation is used all the time, not just in India. Steven Marcus, in *The Other Victorians: A Study of Sexuality and Pornography in Mid-Nineteenth-Century England*, actually quoted, in the course of an academic discussion and with apparent disapproval, a number of pornographic texts that could not otherwise have been legally published at that time.

32. *Chandogya Upanishad* 5.11.1–17.

33. *Cāraka Saṃhitā* 1.1.15.3–34; Doniger O'Flaherty, *Textual Sources*, 92–93.

6
Skepticism and Materialism in Ancient India

1. The term *Lokāyatika* occurs in Panini's *ukthagaṇa*. *Laukāyatika* also occurs, and some texts use *Lokāyata* to refer to the people, too.

2. This was the opinion of the Sanskritist Panchanana Tarkaratna on *Kamasutra* 1.2.30, cited by Ramakrishna Bhattacharya in *Studies on the Carvaka/Lokayata*, 133.

3. See the story of Satyakama Jabali's mother, Jabala, who did not know who his father was because she used to "get around" (*char*) at the time when she conceived him; *Chandogya Upanishad* 4.4–9.

4. Franco, "Lokāyata," 634–36. Many citations from the *Bṛhaspatisūtra* are collected in the probably sixth-century CE *Tattvasaṃgraha* of the Buddhist philosopher Śāntarakṣita.

5. *Mahabharata* 12.140.17–18; see also *Maitrāyaṇī Saṃhitā* 7.9 and Doniger O'Flaherty, *Origins of Evil*, 124.

6. *Prabodhachandrodaya* of Krishnamishra, act 2, verse 26. See Kapstein on 2.65–70, with notes on 298 ff.

7. Madhava is traditionally regarded as the author of the *Sarvadarśana-saṃgraha*, though it is not always clear whether by this is meant Madhava Acarya Vidyaranya, who was famous in the Vijayanagar kingdom, or his nephew, also named Madhava, the son of the great Vedic scholar Sayana. Kapstein, in "Interpreting Indian Philosophy," argues that the author of the *Sarvadarśanasaṃgraha* might in fact have been a logician named Cannibhaṭṭa. But that is a fight beyond the arena of our immediate concern.

8. Mādhava, *Sarvadarśanasaṃgraha* 1, near the beginning.

9. Frauwallner, *Geschichte der indischen Philosophie*, vol. 2, 216.

10. Warder, *Outlines of Indian Philosophy*, 39.

11. Kapstein, "Interpreting Indian Philosophy."

12. The other two are Sankhya and Yoga. Ramakrishna Bhattacharya suggests that the sentence in question as a whole could be understood to mean that "the logic-based philosophical system" is comprised of nothing but the two philosophical systems, Sankhya and Yoga, "and the science of disputation called Lokāyata." Bhattacharya, *Studies*, 135.

13. Bronkhorst, *Greater Magadha*, 150–59.

14. He teaches it to Draupadi's brother.

15. www.carvaka4india.com.

16. *Rig Veda* 10.129.1–2, 6–7. Trans. Doniger O'Flaherty, *The Rig Veda: An Anthology*, 25.

17. Sen, *The Argumentative Indian*, 22.

18. Jha, *Ancient India*, 69–70.

19. *Jaiminīya Brāhmaṇa* 2.269–70; Doniger O'Flaherty, *Tales of Sex and Violence*, 105–7. The Brahmin is Yavakri.

20. *Mahabharata* 3.137.1–20; Doniger O'Flaherty, *Tales of Sex and Violence*, 109–11.

21. He actually calls them Laukayātikas, a variant of Lokayātikas.

22. *Abhidhānacintāmaṇi* of Hemacandra 3.862–63.

23. Kapstein, note on the Charvaka, in *The Rise of Wisdom Moon*, 298 (see *Prabodhacandrodaya*). He glosses "hedonist" as "the representative of worldliness and materialism" (xx).

24. Doniger, "The Concept of Heresy."

25. The Greeks are Yavanas, "Ionians"; the "Skull-Bearers" are Kapalikas; and the Tantrics are Kaulas, "Members of the Family," a common term for Tantrics. *Saura Purana* 38.54.

26. Apte, *A Practical Sanskrit-English Dictionary*, s.v. *nāstika*.

27. *Rig Veda* 2.12.5. *utem āhur naiṣo astīty enam.*

28. *Katha Upanishad* 6.12. *astīti bruvato 'nytra kathaṃ tad upalabhyate.*

29. *nāsti paraloka īśvaro veti matir yasya. Śabdakalpadruma*, s.v. *nāstika*.

30. Burton, *Vikram and the Vampire*, 162–63.

31. Heesterman, "On the Origin," 171.

32. Ibid., 180–81. See also *Rig Veda* 5.30.1, 6.18.3, 6.27.3, 8.64.7, 8.100.3, 10.22.1.

33. Heesterman, "On the Origin," 184.

34. *Śukranītisāra* 4.1.97–98.

35. Mādhava, *Sarvadarśanasaṃgraha* 1, near the beginning.

36. *Śabdakalpadruma*. The Buddhist schools are Madhyamikas, Yogacharas, Sautrantikas, and Vaibhashikas. These match the six *darshanas* of the Astika religion, the major philosophies, usually listed as Sankhya, Yoga (of Patanjali), Purva Mimamsa (of Jaimini), Vedanta, Nyaya, and Vaisheshika. The Jains are Digambaras.

37. The Hellenistic skeptics, by contrast, argued that, since we can't know anything for sure, we can't be sure that there *aren't* gods, and we might as well sacrifice. This is a form of Pascal's wager.

38. Though, perhaps significantly, Jabali is the matronymic of the Upanishadic sage Satyakama Jabali, who does not know who his father is because his mother, Jabala, admits that she had numerous sexual partners during the period in which she became pregnant with him. (*Chandogya Upanishad* 4.4–9.) So he comes from what might be described as an adharmic gene pool.

39. Alternative verses inserted after *Ramayana* 2.100.16 [*2241.15–25]. In some editions and translations of this passage, Jabali expresses Buddhist ideas, too.

40. Later Indian traditions, and translations, often identify Jabali as a Charvaka. Pollock (*Ramayana* 2.509–10) says that Jabali presents "the *cārvāka* or *lokāyatika*, 'materialist' or 'realist,' position." He also points out that these lines express sentiments attributed to Charvakas in the *Sarvadaśanasaṃgraha* as well as to Vishnu in *Vishnu Purana* 3.18.28.

41. This is the same problem that Arjuna confronts in the *Bhagavad Gita*.

42. *Veṇīsaṃhāra*, act 6; see Kale edition, 142 ff.

43. Gitomer, "The '*Veṇīsaṃhāra*' of Bhaṭṭa Nārāyaṇa," 401.

44. Johannes Bronkhorst, in *Greater Magadha*, 309–28, sees a Charvaka stance in the text, while he cites Shujun Motegi's argument that Panchashikha *refutes* the Nastikas and is quoting their arguments merely as a *purva paksha*.

45. *Bhagavad Gita* 16.1–24. Trans. Doniger in *Hinduism*, 193–95.

46. Doniger O'Flaherty, *The Origins of Evil*.

47. See, for instance, *Vishnu Purana* 4.9.1–22, and Doniger O'Flaherty, *The Origins of Evil*, 123–26.

48. *Vishnu Purana* 3.17.9–45, 3.18.1–34; Doniger O'Flaherty, *The Origins of Evil*, 189.

49. *Vishnu Purana* 3.18.30. *yuktimadvacanam*.

50. *Kalika Purana* 78.2006.

51. *Skanda Purana* 4.1.36, 43, and 44; Doniger O'Flaherty, *The Origins of Evil*, 193.

52. Jayanta Bhaṭṭa's *Āgamaḍambara*, translated by Csaba Dezső as *Much Ado about Religion*, in the Clay Sanskrit Series (which translation I am citing here). Jayanta Bhaṭṭa also mentions the Charvakas in his *Nyāyamañjarī*.

53. Csaba Dezső's introduction to the Clay volume argues this and gives historical evidence.

54. Kaulas, "Members of the Family," is a common term for Tantrics.

55. See Christian Wedemeyer, *Making Sense of Tantric Buddhism*.

56. *Prabodhacandrodaya* of Kṛṣṇamiśra, act 2, verse 26, 74–77, trans. Kapstein 2.65 ff., notes on 298 ff.

57. *Naiṣadhacarita* of Śri Harṣa 17.13–37, 88–201. For heretics (*pākhaṇḍas*), see Doniger, "The Concept of Heresy," 39.

58. Mādhava, *Sarvadarśanasaṃgraha*. Kapstein, in "Interpreting Indian Philosophy," translates it as "The Compendium of All Viewpoints."

59. He lists Buddhists, Jains, and Vedantins as well as Shaivas and followers of Panini, Sankhya, Patanjali, etc.

60. Ramakrishna Bhattacharya has pointed out the problems that this raises: "[*The Anthology of All Philosophies*] rarely quotes any Cārvāka aphorism that can be taken as genuine. . . . Nor does he mention the name of a single Cārvāka work, text or commentary (which he does profusely while dealing with other philosophical systems in the same work). So it may be admitted that all Cārvāka works had disappeared from India even before [Mādhava's] time." Bhattacharya, *Studies on the Cārvāka/Lokāyata*, 72.

61. Bronkhorst, *Greater Magadha*, 157.

62. Mādhava, *Sarvadarśanasaṃgraha* 1.26–28, Cowell's translation. See also *Prabodhacandrodaya*, act 2, verse 26.

63. Kapstein, "Interpreting Indian Philosophy."

64. See Doniger, "Sacrifice and Substitution," "Indra as the Stallion's Wife," and "The Mythology of Horses," all in *On Hinduism*.

65. Kapstein, "Interpreting Indian Philosophy."

66. Sen, *The Argumentative Indian*, 24.

67. *Śaṅkaradigvijaya*. Maitra, "The Construction of Religious Authority in the *Śaṅkaradigvijaya*."

68. "Left-Hand Worshippers" translates Vamacharas.

69. *Śaṅkaradigvijaya* of Ānandagiri, chaps. 23–24.

70. Maitra, "The Construction of Religious Authority."

71. Śaṅkaradigvijaya 9–10.

72. Maitra, "The Construction of Religious Authority."

73. Payasi Suttanta 1–2. Translated by T. W. Rhys Davids in Sacred Books of the Buddhists, Vol. 3, and Dialogues of the Buddha, Vol. 2, 346–74. See also Frauwallner, Geschichte der indischen Philosophie, Vol. 2, 216; Franco, "Lokāyata," 634.

74. Vidāynandin, Satyaśāsasanaparīkṣā. Borgland, Investigation into the True Teaching, 202–28.

75. Monier-Williams, s.v. vitaṇḍaśāstra.

76. Collins, Selfless Persons, 88; Franco, "Lokāyata," 633–34.

77. Rhys-Davids, Dialogues of the Buddha, 194; Ten Suttas from the Digha Nikaya, 83.

78. Kosambi, The Culture and Civilisation of Ancient India.

79. K. N. Jayatilleke explains the anomalies in the following way: "The Buddhists identified all the known materialist views with Ajita, who symbolizes the philosophy of Materialism, inconsistently putting together the tenets of mutually opposed schools since they both (or all) happened to be in some sense (metaphysical or pragmatic) materialists." Jayatilleke, Early Buddhist Theory of Knowledge, 95.

80. Samañña-phala-sutta 35 ("The fruits of the life of an ascetic"), the second sutta in the Digha Nikaya.

81. Franco, "Lokāyata," 640.

82. Tattvopaplavasiṃha. Amartya Sen, in The Argumentative Indian, 24, calls him not Jayarashi (Jayarāśi, "Abundance of Victory") but Jayarishi ("Holy Man of Victory"). The title may also be translated as "The Lion That Devours All Categories" or "The Lion That Upsets All Principles."

83. Franco, Perception, Knowledge and Disbelief, 7, citing Tattvopaplavasiṃha, 125, 13–18.

84. Franco, Perception, Knowledge and Disbelief, 3.

85. Bhattacharya, Studies on the Cārvāka/Lokāyata, 76, n. 43.

86. Franco, Perception, Knowledge and Disbelief, 3.

87. Ibid., 9. In glossing Franco, I am calling the Naiyayikas "logicians" and the Mimamsakas "Vedic scholars" while translating paśus as "beasts" and śrutilalāsa as "fanatics of the revealed texts."

88. Werner, review of Eli Franco, Perception, Knowledge and Disbelief.

89. Franco, Perception, Knowledge and Disbelief, 14–15.

90. Ernst Steinkellner argued that earlier scholars "appear to have composed commentaries on heterodox Skeptic (Cārvāka) works." Steinkellner, "Die Literatur des Alteren Nyāya," 153 ff.

91. Saletore, "Historical Notices of the Lokāyatas," 391. One such inscription, from 1085 CE, praises the Brahmins of Beguru as being acquainted with the tenets of the Nyaya, Vaisheshika, Lokayata, Sankhya, Bauddha, Mimansa, "and other systems of logic." Another, from 1103, lists the Lokayata system with the Sankhya, Mimansa, and Nyaya (Saletore, 392). An inscription from 1415 CE praises a man for having overcome the Sankhyas, Yaugas, Charvakas, Bauddhas, Bhattas, and Prabhakaras. In 1036 CE a teacher is praised "for cutting down the Lokāyata great tree." An inscription from 1163 CE praises a teacher who was "a submarine fire to the ocean of the maintainers of the Cārvāka system" (Saletore, 395).

92. Dakshinaranjan Shastri is said to have published sixty verses attributed to Charvakas, in 1928, and fifty-four selected verses of the so-called *Bārhaspatya sūtram*, in 1959. Ramakrishna Bhattacharya, in "Cārvāka Fragments: A New Collection," published in 2002, attempted a new reconstruction of sixty-eight fragments. Commentaries are attributed to Aviddhakarna, Udbhata Bhatta, Kambalashvatara, Purandara, and Bhavivikta.

93. Kapstein, "Interpreting Indian Philosophy."

94. Franco, "Lokāyata," 642.

95. Kapstein, "Interpreting Indian Philosophy."

96. Ibid.

97. Ibid.

98. Conversation with Bruce Lincoln, May 2014.

99. Doniger, *The Hindus*, 4–7.

100. *Akbarnama*, Vol. 3, trans. Beveridge, 365. He spells it "Charbakas."

101. Jarrett translates this sentence differently. He writes: "*Chárváka*, after whom this school is named, was an unenlightened Bráhman. Its followers are called by the Bráhmans, *Nástikas* or Nihilists." The word that Jarrett translates as "unenlightened" ("*nāshināsā*") can mean that, but also "unrecognized," which seems more appropriate here. I have corrected the whole passage with the help of Muzaffar Alam. See *The A'in-i Akbari [by] Abu'l-Fazl 'Allami.*

102. Abu'l Fazl, *The A'in-i Akbari*, Vol. 3, 217–18.

103. Ibid.

104. Roger, *La porte ouverte*, 23–24.

105. Raghavan, *Vimuktiḥ*, 150–51; autocommentary, viii. I am indebted to Charles Preston for his analysis of this play.

106. Sen, *The Argumentative Indian*, 23: "There are . . . a great many controversies between defenders of religiosity on one side, and advocates of general skepticism on the other. The doubts sometimes take the form of agnosticism, sometimes that of atheism. . . . The Lokayata philosophy of

skepticism and materialism flourished from the first millennium BCE, possibly even in Buddha's own time. . . . Atheism and materialism continued to attract adherents and advocates over many centuries, and were increasingly associated with the exposition of the intellectually combative Charvakas."

7
Epilogue

1. Manu is far better known than the other two; over the course of the centuries, Manu's text attracted nine complete commentaries, attesting to its crucial significance within the tradition, and it is cited in other ancient Indian texts far more frequently than any other *dharma-shastra*.

2. Wilhelm, "Das Beziehungen zwischen *Arthaśāstra* und *Kāmasūtra*," 310.

3. *Ratirahasya* 13.9, cited by Wilhelm in "The Concept of Dharma," 76.

4. Ali, "Rethinking the History of the 'Kāma' World in Early India," 9.

5. Ali, "Padmaśrī's 'Nāgarasarvasva' and the World of Medieval Kāmaśāstra," 50.

6. De, "Ancient Indian Erotics," 95.

7. Ali, "Rethinking the History of the 'Kāma' World," 10–11.

8. Herman Tieken points this out for Hala's *Sattasai*; see Tieken, "The *Arthaśāstra* as a Fount of Fun," 116–17.

9. Trautmann, "A Metrical Original for the Kauṭilīya *Arthaśāstra?*," 348.

10. Doniger, *Redeeming the Kamasutra*, 50.

11. A great deal has been written on this subject, which I have drawn upon for my brief summary. In particular, see Gyan Prakash, *Another Reason: Science and the Imagination of Modern India*, and Ashish Nandy, *The Intimate Enemy: Loss and Recovery of Self under Colonialism* and *Science, Hegemony and Violence: A Requiem for Modernity*.

12. Doniger, *The Hindus*, 596–97.

13. Wilhelm, "The Concept of Dharma," 77.

14. Nussbaum, "A Law against Dignity." She continues: "This is strikingly similar to the experience in Britain itself, where neither Victoria's son the Prince of Wales, nor the scullery maid, felt the need to pretend that they weren't having fun in the bedroom."

15. Srinivas, *Social Change in Modern India*.

16. McConnachie, *The Book of Love*, 197–98.

17. Ibid., 55, 57.

18. Naipaul, *Half a Life*, 110.

19. McConnachie, *The Book of Love*, 197–98.

20. Pankaj Mishra, "Modi's Idea of India," *New York Times*, October 24, 2014, op ed page.

21. Chandra, *Love and Longing in Bombay*, 126.

22. McConnachie, *The Book of Love*, 229.

23. Doniger, "From Kama to Karma."

24. Wilhelm, "The Concept of Dharma," 77.

25. Khilnani, *Incarnations*, 31.

26. Ibid., 338.

27. Kissinger, *World Order*, 3.

28. Gupta, "Need for a Modern Arthashastra."

29. Ibid.

30. Javid Husain, "Kautilya's Arthashastra and Pakistan," *The Nation*, Lahore, under "Pakistan Defence," March 17, 2015, pakistantimesusa.net/epaper/2015/19-11-2015.

31. Doniger, *The Hindus*, 596–97.

32. Dayanand's story is cited by Helena Petrovna Blavatsky in *From the Caves and Jungles of Hindostan*, 63–64. He based his argument on the *Mahabharata* episode in which Arjuna visits *patala*, the usual Sanskrit word for a subterranean watery hell; Dayanand said *patala* designated America. See also Ricardo Palleres, "Who Discovered America?," http://archaeologyonline.net/artifacts/who-discovered-america, January 2012, and Chaman Lal, "Who Discovered America?," *Hindu Forum*, January 31, 2016.

33. Girish Shahane, "A Short History of How Modi and Rajnath Came to Believe That Mythology Is Science," *Scroll In*, November 20, 2014.

34. Cited by Pankaj Mishra in "Modi's Idea of India."

35. Pinney, "Epistemo-patrimony." The text was the *Sama Veda*.

36. *Scroll* Staff, "The word 'industry' comes from Indus, says VJP joint general secretary," *Scroll In*, May 22, 2016. They cite an article in the *Times of India*. Vigyananand made the statement at a summit in Bengaluru organized by the World Hindu Economic Forum, which he heads.

37. Nanda, "Hindutva's Science Envy."

38. Shoaib Daniyal, "Rewriting the Past," *Scroll In*, October 2, 2015.

39. BJP stands for Bharatiya Janata Party (Party of the People of India). Its militant branch is the RSS (Rashtriya Swayamsevak Sangh, or Society for the Self-Service of the Nation).

40. See Ellen Barry, "'A Censor Is Seated Inside Me Now': Hometown Wrath Tests a Novelist," *New York Times*, August 22, 2016, and Doniger, "Banned in Bangalore" and "India: Censorship by the Batra Brigade."

41. "PM Modi Now Has a Minister for Yoga, Ayurveda," NDTV, November 10, 2014.

42. See "PM Modi Takes Leaf from Batra Book: Mahabharat Genetics, Lord Ganesha Surgery," *Indian Express,* October 28, 2014; Ritu Sharma, "Man Who Got Wendy Doniger Pulped Is Made 'Must Reading' in Gujarat Schools," *Indian Express,* July 25, 2014; and Maseeh Rahman, "Indian Prime Minister Claims Genetic Science Existed in Ancient Times," *The Guardian,* Delhi, October 28, 2014. See also these more recent reports: Ashutosh Bhardwaj, "Dina Nath Batra Again: He Wants Tagore, Urdu Words Off School Texts," *India Express,* July 24, 2017, http://indianexpress.com/article/india/dina-nath-batra-again-he-wants-tagore-urdu-words-off-school-texts-4764094/, and "Remove Riots, English and Urdu Words, and Praise of Mughals from Textbooks: Dinanath Batra," *The Wire,* July 24, 2017, https://thewire.in/160977/dinanath-batra-textbooks-ncert/.

43. Mridula Mukherjee and Aditya Mukherjee, "Communilisation of Education: The History Textbook Controversy; An Overview," 10, citing Sarsanchalak K. S. Sudershan. Vedic sages not only described the construction of airplanes but discussed details such as "what types of aeroplanes would fly at what height, what kind of problems they might encounter, how to overcome these problems, etc."

44. Subir Roy, "What Is History?," *Business Standard,* November 28, 2001. The man who made these changes was Rajendra Singh.

45. Raja Ram Mohan Roy, *Vedic Physics: Scientific Origin of Hinduism,* and Bhakta, *Vedic String Theory.*

46. Vinamrata Borwankar, "Pythagoras's Theorem Actually an Indian Discovery: Harsh Vardhan," *Times of India,* January 4, 2015.

47. Varma, *Vedic Physics.*

48. Girish Shahane, "A Short History of How Modi and Rajnath Came to Believe That Mythology Is Science."

49. Deb, "Those Mythological Men."

50. Mukherjee and Mukherjee, "Communilisation of Education."

51. Deb, "Those Mythological Men." The man was Y. Sudershan Rao.

52. Shoaib Daniyal, "Rewriting the Past," *Scroll In,* October 2, 2015.

53. Maseeh Rahman, "Indian Prime Minister Claims Genetic Science Existed in Ancient Times," *The Guardian,* Delhi, October 28, 2014.

54. "PM Modi Takes Leaf from Batra Book," *Indian Express,* October 28, 2014.

55. *Tejomay Bharat,* 60, cited by Pankti Dalal in "Gujarat Model of Using Epics as Facts in Education," *DNA,* July 27, 2014.

56. Ritu Sharma, "Science Lesson from Gujarat: Stem Cells in *Mahabharata,* Cars in Veda: *Tejomay Bharat* Is to Be Distributed along with Eight Books Written by Dina Nath Batra," *Indian Express,* Ahmedabad, updated July 27, 2014, 1:35 p.m.

57. Janamejaya describes much of the *Mahabharata* to the blind king Dhritarashtra. See *Tejomay Bharat,* 64, cited in Dalal, "Gujarat Model," and Daniyal, "Rewriting the Past." The scholar from Punjab University was Vikram Viveki.

58. Rahman, "Indian Prime Minister Claims Genetic Science Existed in Ancient Times."

59. *Tejomay Bharat,* 92–93, cited in Dalal, "Gujarat Model"; Ritu Sharma, "Science Lesson from Gujarat."

60. "Kauravas Were Cloned, Says Scientist," *Times of India,* May 4, 2002.

61. Deb, "Those Mythological Men."

62. Maseeh Rahman, "Indian Prime Minister Claims Genetic Science Existed in Ancient Times." See also Nanda, "Genetics, Plastic Surgery and Other Wonders of Ancient Indian Medicine," in *Science in Saffron,* 93–126.

63. Amit Chaudhuri, "Diary: Modi's Science."

64. Talpade allegedly flew an unmanned heavier-than-air machine on a beach in Bombay. Apparently he built the aircraft on the basis of Vedic texts, powering his machine with mercury and solar energy and getting it to rise to 1,500 feet before it crashed. One Hindi news channel claimed that Talpade's machine was not just the modern world's first airplane but, since it had been operated with a remote control, could also rightfully be described as the world's first drone. There are no contemporaneous accounts of the flight. Deb, "Those Mythological Men."

65. Deb, "Those Mythological Men."

66. Randreas, *Charvaka Caritra,* 382.

67. Sen, *The Argumentative Indian,* 26.

68. Deb, "Those Mythological Men."

69. Rhema Mukti Baxter, "How to Say Thermodynamics in Sanskrit? Smriti Irani's New Plan for the IITs Sparks Mirth," *Scroll In,* April 26, 2016.

70. Michel Danino, "The Public Ignoramus," www.mydigitalfc.com, May 2, 2016.

71. Ibid.

72. Deb, "Those Mythological Men."

73. The scientist was Ramprasad Gandhiraman.

74. Deb, "Those Mythological Men."

75. Yogita Rao, "Heard at Science Meet: Ancient Indian Planes Flew to Planets," *Times of India,* January 5, 2015.

76. Rao, "Heard at Science Meet."

77. Pushpa Mittra Bhargava, a biologist and former director of the Centre for Cellular and Molecular Biology in Hyderabad, India; Suvrat Raju, a physicist at the International Centre for Theoretical Sciences in Bengaluru,

India; Gauhar Raza, former chief scientist with the National Institute of Science; Madabusi Santanam Raghunathan, a mathematician at the Indian Institute of Technology in Mumbai; and others led the protests. Kumar, "Critics Assail India's Attempt to 'Validate' Folk Remedy."

78. Kumar, "Critics Assail India's Attempt to 'Validate' Folk Remedy."

79. R. Ramachandra, "India's Premier Science Bodies Moot National Programme to Study Concoctions of Cow Excreta," *The Wire,* May 16, 2017.

80. Smita Nair, "All India Hindu Conclave: At Goa Event, Gaumutra Drives Purification Ride," *Indian Express,* June 18, 2017.

81. Actually, there is considerable basis for the Indian claim, though it is here swallowed up in *ressentiment* toward the ancient Greeks. Āpastamba (*śulbasūtra* 1.4; Baudhāyana *śulbasūtra* 48) reads: *dīrghacatursyākṣṇayā rajjuḥ pārśvamānī tiryaṇmānī ca yat pṛthagbhūte kurutas tad ubhayaṃ karoti.* This provides a geometric statement of the general claim (without proof) if we read it like this: "The diagonal of a rectangle produces by itself both the areas which the two sides of the rectangle produce separately." The concept of "areas" does duty for squaring. I am grateful to Sonam Kacchru and John Nemec for supplying me with these passages. See also Nanda, "Who Discovered the Pythagorean Theorem?," in *Science in Saffron,* 19–48.

82. Vinamrata Borwankar, "Pythagoras's Theorem Actually an Indian Discovery: Harsh Vardhan," *Times of India,* January 4, 2015.

83. Husain, "Kautilya's Arthashastra and Pakistan."

Bibliography

Primary Texts in Sanskrit, Listed by Title

Abhidhānacintāmaṇi of Hemacandra. Ed. Pandit Shivadatta and Kashinatha Pandurang Parab. *Abhidhānasaṅgraha,* nos. 6–11. Bombay: Nirnaya Sagara, 1896.

Āgamaḍambara of Jayanta Bhaṭṭa. Ed. and trans. Csaba Dezsö as *Much Ado about Religion.* Clay Sanskrit Series. New York: New York University Press, 2005.

Arthaśāstra of Kauṭilya (critical edition). Ed. R. P. Kangle. Bombay: University of Bombay, 1960.

———. Trans. Patrick Olivelle as *King, Governance, and Law in Ancient India: Kauṭilya's Arthaśāstra.* New York: Oxford University Press, 2013.

Bhāgavad Gītā. Book 7 of the *Mahābhārata,* s.v.

Bṛhadāraṇyaka Upaniṣad. See *Upanishads.*

Cāraka Saṃhitā. Ed. and trans. Jayadeva Vidyālankara. 2 vols. Delhi: Motilal Banarsidass, 1963.

Chāndogya Upaniṣad. See *Upanishads.*

Devībhāgavata Purāṇa. Benares: Pandita Pustakalaya, 1960.

Digha Nikāya. Trans. T. W. Rhys-Davids as *Ten Suttas From the Digha Nikaya.* Sarnath, Varanasi: Central Institute of Higher Tibetan Studies, 1987.

Kālikā Purāṇa. Ed. Sri Biswanarayan Sastri. Varanasi: Chowkhamba Sanskrit Series Office, 1972.

Kāmasūtra of Vātsyāyana, with the commentary of Yaśodhara. Edited with the Hindi "Jaya" commentary by Devadatta Shastri. Kashi Sanskrit Series 29. Varanasi: Chaukhambha Sanskrit Sansthan, 1964.

———. Trans. Wendy Doniger and Sudhir Kakar. Oxford and New York: Oxford University Press, 2002.

Kathāsaritsāgara (The Ocean of the Rivers of Story) of Somadeva. Bombay: Nirnaya Sagara, 1930.

Kaṭha Upaniṣad. See *Upanishads.*

Mahābhārata. Ed. V. S. Sukthankar et al. Poona: Bhandarkar Oriental Research Institute, 1933–69.

Maitrāyaṇī Saṃhitā. Ed. L. von Schroeder. Wiesbaden: R. Steiner, 1970–72. First published 1881.

Mānavadharmaśāstra. Ed. Harikrishna Jayantakrishna Dave. Bombay: Bharatiya Vidya Series, Vol. 29 ff., 1972–78.

———. Trans. Wendy Doniger with Brian K. Smith as *The Laws of Manu.* Harmondsworth: Penguin, 1991.

Naiṣadhacarita of Śri Harṣa. Ed. Jivananda Vidyasagara. Bombay: Nirnaya Sagara, 1986.

Prabodhacandrodaya of Kṛṣṇamiśra. Ed. and trans. Matthew Kapstein as *The Rise of Wisdom Moon.* Clay Sanskrit Library. New York: New York University Press, 2009.

Rāmāyaṇa of Vālmīki. Baroda: Oriental Institute, 1960–75.

———. Volume 2. Trans. Sheldon Pollock. New York: New York University Press, 2008.

Rayapaseniyasutta (Paesikahanayam), in *Payasi Suttanta,* ed. Tripathi (DN, II: 23), trans. T. W. Rhys-Davids. London: H. Frowde, 1910.

Śabdakalpadruma of Raja Sir Radhakant Deb Bahadur. Calcutta, 1886; Delhi, 1961.

Śaṅkaradigvijaya of Mādhava (Vidyāraṇya). Ed. Mahadeva Apte. Pune: Anandasrama, 1891.

Śaṅkaravijaya of Ānandagiri. Ed. J. Tarkapancanana. Calcutta: Bibliotheca Indica, 1868.

Sarvadarśanasaṅgraha. By Mādhava Ācārya. Ed. Pandita Iswarachandra Vidyasagara. Calcutta: Bibliotheca Indica [Nos. 63 and 142], 1858.

———. By Madhava Acharya. Trans. E. B. Cowell and A. E. Gough as *The Sarva-Darśana-Samgraha, or, Review of the Different Systems of Hindu Philosophy.* London: Trubner, 1882.

———. By Sayana. Ed. Vasudev Abhayankar. Poona: Bhandarkar Oriental Research Institute, 1978.

Śatapatha Brāhmaṇa. Chowkhamba Sanskrit Series. Varanasi: Chowkhamba Sanskrit Series Office, 1964.

Saura Purāṇa. Calcutta: Bangabasi, 1910.

Skanda Purāṇa. Bombay: Shree Venkateshvara, 1867.

Śukranitisāra. Edited with commentary by Pandit Jibananda Vidyasagara Bhattacaryya. Calcutta: Saraswati, 1882.

Tattvasaṃgraha of Śantarakṣita, with the Pañjika Commentary of Kama-laśila. Ed. Swami Dwarikadas Shastri. Varanasi: Bauddha Bharati, 1968. Vol. 2: "Lokāyataparīkṣṣā," 633–70.

Tattvopaplavasiṃha of Jayarāśi Bhaṭṭa. Ed. Sukhlalji Sanghavi and R. Parikh. Baroda: GOS 87, 1940.

Upanishads: One Hundred and Eight Upanishads. Bombay: Nirnaya Sagara, 1913.

———. Ed. and trans. Patrick Olivelle as *Early Upanishads*. New York: Oxford University Press, 1998.

Veṇīsaṃhāra of Bhaṭṭa Nārāyaṇa. Ed. Moreshwar Ramchandra Kale. Delhi: Motilal Banarsidass, 2011.

Viṣṇu Purāṇa. Calcutta: Sanatana Shastra, 1972.

Secondary Sources, Listed by Author

Abu'l Fazl. *A'in-i Akbari*. Delhi: Matba' Isma'ili, 1855; reprinted Sir Syed Academy, Aligarh Muslim University, Aligarh, 2005.

———. *The A'in-i Akbari [by] Abu'l-Fazl 'Allami*. Ed. H. Blochmann. Vol. 3, trans. Henry Sullivan Jarrett. Calcutta: Asiatic Society of Bengali, 1891.

———. *Akbarnama*. Vol. 3, trans. Henry Beveridge. London: Royal Asiatic Society, 1902–39.

———. *The History of Akbar*. Ed. and trans. Wheeler M. Thackston. Murty Classical Library of India. Cambridge, MA: Harvard University Press, 2015.

Ali, Daud. "Padmaśrī's 'Nāgarasarvasva' and the World of Medieval Kāmaśāstra." *Journal of Indian Philosophy*, vol. 39, No. 1 (February 2011), 416–22.

———. "Rethinking the History of the 'Kāma' World in Early India." *Journal of Indian Philosophy*, Vol. 39, No. 1 (February 2011), 1–13.

Apte, V. S. *The Practical Sanskrit-English Dictionary*. 3 vols. Revised and enlarged edition. Poona: Prasad Prakashan, 1957–59.

Bhakta, M. Anant. *Vedic String Theory*. North Charleston, SC: BookSurge, 2006.

Bhandarkar, D. R. "Date of Kautalya." *Annals of the Bhandarkar Oriental Research Institute 7* (1926), 65–84.

Bhattacharya, Ramakrishna. "Cārvāka Fragments: A New Collection." *Journal of Indian Philosophy*, Vol. 30, No. 6 (December 2002), 597–640. Reprinted as a chapter of *Studies on the Cārvāka/Lokāyata*.

———. "History of Indian Materialism." *Carvaka 4 India*, Tuesday, December 20, 2011.

———. *Studies on the Cārvāka/Lokāyata*. London, New York, Delhi: Anthem, 2011.

———. "What the Cārvākas Originally Meant." *Journal of Indian Philosophy*, Vol. 38, No. 6 (December 2010), 529–42.

Blavatsky, Helena Petrovna. *From the Caves and Jungles of Hindostan: H. P. Blavatsky Collected Writings*. Wheaton, IL: Quest, 1975.

Borgland, Jens W. *Investigation into the True Teaching: An Annotated Translation and Investigation of the Digambara Philosopher Vidyanandin's Sanskrit Text Satyasasanapariksa*. Wiesbaden: Otto Harrassowitz, 2016.

Bronkhorst, Johannes. *Greater Magadha: Studies in the Culture of Early India*. Delhi: Motilal Banarsidass, 2007.

Burton, Sir Richard Francis. *The Kama Sutra of Vatsyayana: The Classic Hindu Treatise on Love and Social Conduct*. Intro. by John W. Spellman. New York: E. P. Dutton, 1962.

———. *Vikram and the Vampire, or Tales of Hindu Devilry*. London: Tylston and Edwards, 1893; reprinted New York: Dover Publications, 1969.

Chandra, Vikram. *Love and Longing in Bombay*. Boston: Little, Brown, 1997.

Chatterjee, Satischandra, and Dhirendramohan Datta. *An Introduction to Indian Philosophy*. 8th reprint edition. Calcutta: University of Calcutta, 1984.

Chattopadhyaya, Debiprasad. *In Defence of Materialism in Ancient India: A Study in Cārvāka/Lokāyata*. Calcutta: Peoples' Publishing, 1988.

———. *Indian Philosophy*. New Delhi: People's Publishing, 1964; 7th edition, 1993.

———. *Knowledge and Intervention*. Calcutta: K. L. Mukhopadhyaya, 1985.

———. "Uddalaka Aruṇi: The Pioneer of Science." Zakir Husain Memorial Lecture, New Delhi, August 2, 1988; *IHR*, Vol. 13, Nos. 1–2 (1988), 37–57.

Chattopadhyaya, Debiprasad, and M. K. Gangopadhyaya, eds. *Carvaka/Lokayata: An Anthology of Source Materials and Some Recent Studies*. New Delhi: Indian Council of Philosophical Research, 1990.

Chaudhuri, Amit. "Diary: Modi's Hinduism." *London Review of Books*, Vol. 37, No. 24 (December 7, 2015).

Collins, Steven. *Selfless Persons: Imagery and Thought in Theravada Buddhism*. Cambridge: Cambridge University Press, 1990.

Dakshinaranjan Shastri. *Charvaka Philosophy*. Calcutta: Purogami Prakashan, 1967.

———. *A Short History of Indian Materialism, Sensationalism, and Hedonism*. Calcutta: Bookland Private, 1957.

Dallapiccola, Anna Libera. *Śāstric Traditions in Indian Arts*. Wiesbaden: Steiner, 1989.

Dasgupta, Surendranath. *History of Indian Philosophy*. 5 vols. Cambridge: Cambridge University Press, 1932–55; reprinted Delhi: Motilal Banarsidass, 1975.

Daston, Lorraine. *Rules: A Short History of What We Live By*. Princeton, NJ: Princeton University Press, forthcoming.

Davis, Richard. *Lives of Indian Images*. Princeton, NJ: Princeton University Press, 1999.

———. "What Do Indian Images Really Want? A Biographical Approach." In *Sacred Objects in Secular Spaces: Exhibiting Asian Religions in Museums*, ed. Bruce M. Sullivan. London: Bloomsbury Academic, 2015, 92–95.

De, Sushil Kumar. "Ancient Indian Erotics." In *Ancient Indian Erotics and Erotic Literature*. Calcutta: K. L. Mukhopadhyay, 1959.

Deb, Siddhartha. "Those Mythological Men and Their Sacred, Supersonic Flying Temples: What Tales of Ancient Vedic Aircraft Tell Us about India's Place in the Modern World." *New Republic*, May 14, 2015.

Derrett, J. Duncan M.. *Dharmasastra and Juridical Literature*. Wiesbaden: Otto Harrassowitz, 1973.

Desmond, Laura. "The Pleasure Is Mine: The Changing Subject of Erotic Science." *Journal of Indian Philosophy*, Vol. 39 (2011), 153–59.

Doniger, Wendy. "Banned in Bangalore." *New York Times*, March 5, 2014, op ed page.

———. "The Concept of Heresy in Hindu Mythology." In Doniger, *On Hinduism*, 36–69.

———. "From Kama to Karma: The Resurgence of Puritanism in Contemporary India." In Doniger, *On Hinduism*, 396–408.

———, ed. *Hinduism*. Vol. 1 of *The Norton Anthology of World Religions*, ed. Jack Miles. New York: Norton, 2014.

———. *The Hindus: An Alternative History*. New York: Penguin, 2009.

———. "India: Censorship by the Batra Brigade." *New York Review of Books*, May 8, 2014, 515–23.

———. "Indra as the Stallion's Wife." In Doniger, *On Hindusim*, 473–88.

———. "Invisibility and Sexual Violence in Indo-European Mythology." *Social Research. Invisibility*, Vol. 83, No. 4 (Winter 2016), 849–79.

———. See *Kāmasūtra* .

———. "The Kautilyan *Kamasutra*, or, The Legacy of the *Arthashastra*." In Doniger, *The Mare's Trap*, 175–81.

———. *The Laws of Manu*. With Brian K. Smith. Harmondsworth: Penguin, 1991.

———. *The Mare's Trap: Nature and Culture in the* Kamasutra. Delhi: Speaking Tiger, 2015. US edition retitled *Redeeming the* Kamasutra. New York: Oxford University Press, 2016.

——. "The Mythology of Horses." In Doniger, *On Hinduism*, 438–51.

——. "The Mythology of the *Kamasutra*." In Doniger, *On Hinduism*, 381–95.

——. *On Hinduism*. Delhi: Aleph, 2013; 2nd edition, New York: Oxford University Press, 2014.

——. *Redeeming the Kamasutra*. New York: Oxford University Press, 2016.

——. *The Ring of Truth and Other Myths of Sex and Jewelry*. New York: Oxford University Press, 2017.

——. "Sacrifice and Substitution." In Doniger, *On Hinduism*, 207–32.

——. *Splitting the Difference: Gender and Myth in Ancient Greece and India*. Chicago: University of Chicago Press; London: University of London Press, 1999.

——. "Three (or More) Forms of the Three (or More)-Fold Path." In Doniger, *On Hinduism*, 21–35.

——. "Why Hindu Nationalists Insist That Ancient Indians Had Nuclear Weapons." Paper presented at the conference Fetishizing Science at the Einstein Forum, Potsdam, June 9–11, 2016.

——. "Why Should a Brahmin Tell You Whom to Marry? A Deconstruction of the *Laws of Manu*." In Doniger, *On Hinduism*, 259–68.

——. "You Can't Make an Omelette." In *Fightin' Words: 25 Years of Provocative Poetry and Prose from 'The Blue-Collar' PEN*. Ed. Judith Cody, Kim McMillon, and Claire Ortaldo. Berkeley, CA: Heyday, 2014.

Doniger O'Flaherty, Wendy. *Asceticism and Eroticism in the Mythology of Siva*. Oxford, UK: Oxford University Press, 1973.

——. *Karma and Rebirth in Classical Indian Traditions*. Berkeley: University of California Press, 1980.

——. "The Origin of Heresy in Hindu Mythology." In *History of Religions*, Vol. 10, No. 4 (May 1971), 271–333.

——. *The Origins of Evil in Hindu Mythology*. Berkeley: University of California Press, 1976.

——. *The Rig Veda: An Anthology; 108 Hymns Translated from the Sanskrit*. Harmondsworth: Penguin Classics, 1981.

——. *Tales of Sex and Violence: Folklore, Sacrifice, and Danger in the Jaiminiya Brahmana*. Chicago: University of Chicago Press, 1985.

——. *Textual Sources for the Study of Hinduism*. Chicago: University of Chicago Press, 1990.

——. *Women, Androgynes, and Other Mythical Beasts*. Chicago: University of Chicago Press, 1980.

Doniger (O'Flaherty), Wendy, and J. Duncan M. Derett, eds. *The Concept of Duty in South Asia*. New Delhi: Vikas, 1978.

Dumézil, Georges. *The Destiny of a King*. Chicago: University of Chicago Press, 1973.

————. *The Destiny of the Warrior*. Chicago: University of Chicago Press, 1970.

Dumont, Louis. *Homo Hierarchicus: The Caste System and Its Implications*, trans. Mark Saisbury, Louis Dumont, and Basia Gulati. Paris, 1967; Chicago: University of Chicago Press, 1980.

Edwardes, Allen. *The Rape of India: A Biography of Robert Clive and a Sexual History of the Conquest of Hindustan*. London: Julian, 1966.

Fezas, Jean. "Remarques sur la forme de deux traités de l'Inde Ancienne: L'*Arthaśāstra* et le *Kāmasūtra*." In *Genres Litteraires en Inde*, ed. Nalini Balbir. Paris: Presses de la Sorbonne Nouvelle, 1994, 123–50.

Foucault, Michel. *The History of Sexuality*, Vol. 1: *An Introduction*. New York: Vintage, 1990.

Franco, Eli. "Lokāyata." In *Brill's Encyclopedia of Hinduism*, ed. Knut A. Jacobsen (Leiden: Brill, 2011), Vol. 3, 629–42.

————. *Perception, Knowledge, and Disbelief: A Study of Jayarāśi's Scepticism*. Stuttgart and Wiesbaden: Franz Steiner, 1987.

Frauwallner, Erich. *Geschichte der indischen Philosophie*, Vol. 2. Salzburg: Otto Mueller, 1956. Trans. as *History of Indian Philosophy*, Vol. 2. Delhi: Motilal Banarsidass, 1973.

Gautam, Sanjay. *Foucault and the Kamasutra*. Chicago: University of Chicago Press, 2016.

Gitomer, David Laurence. "The *Veṇīsaṃhāra* of Bhaṭṭa Nārāyaṇa: The Great Epic as Drama." PhD dissertation, Columbia University, New York, 1988.

Gupta, Arvind. "Need for a Modern Arthashastra." *New Indian Express*, April 14, 2014.

Heesterman, Jan C. *The Inner Conflict of Tradition: Essays in Ritual, Kinship, and Society*. Chicago: University of Chicago Press, 1985.

————. "On the Origin of the Nastika." *Beitrage zur Geistesgeschichte Indiens: Festschrift für Erich Frauwallner, Wiener Zeitschrift zur Kunde des Sud- und Ostasiens*, 1968–69, 171–85.

Hiltebeitel, Alf. *Dharma: Its Early History in Law, Religion, and Narrative*. Oxford, UK: Oxford University Press, 2011.

Jayatilleke, K. N. *Early Buddhist Theory of Knowledge*. London: George Allen and Unwin, 1963; Delhi: Motilal Banarsidass, 1980.

Jha, D. N. *Ancient India*. New Delhi: Manohar, 1977; revised 1998.

Kakar, Sudhir. *The Ascetic of Desire: A Novel of the Kamasutra*. London: Penguin, 1999.

Kangle, R. P. *The Kauṭilīya Arthaśāstra*. Vol. 1: Text; Vol. 2: An English Translation with Critical and Explanatory Notes. Delhi: Motilal Banarsidass, 1963.

Kapstein, Matthew. "Interpreting Indian Philosophy: Three Parables, III: Who Were the Cārvākas?" In *The Oxford Handbook of Indian Philosophy*, ed. Jonardon Ganeri, 2014. Available at www.oxfordhandbooks.com/view/10.1093/oxfordhb/9780199314621.001.0001/oxfordhb-97801993 14621-e-44_. Accessed July 17, 2017.

———. See also *Prabodhacandrodaya*.

Keay, John. *India: A History*. New York: Grove, 2000.

Keith, Arthur Berriedale. *A History of Indian Literature*. London: Oxford University Press, 1920.

Khilnani, Sunil. *Incarnations: A History of India in Fifty Lives*. New York: Farrar, Straus, and Giroux, 2016.

King, Martin Luther Jr. *Where Do We Go from Here: Chaos or Community?* Boston: Beacon, 2010.

Kissinger, Henry. *World Order*. New York: Penguin, 2014.

Kosambi, D. D. *The Culture and Civilisation of Ancient India in Historical Outline*. London: Routledge and Kegan Paul, 1965.

Kumar, Sanjay. "Critics Assail India's Attempt to 'Validate' Folk Remedy." *Science*, Vol. 355, No. 6328 (March 3, 2017), 898.

Maitra, Nabanjan. "The Construction of Religious Authority in the *Śankaradigvijaya*." Unpublished essay, 2016.

Malamoud, Charles. "On the Rhetoric and Semantics of puruṣārtha." In *Way of Life: King, Householder, Renouncer: Essays in Honour of Louis Dumont*, ed. T. N. Madan. Delhi: Vikas, 1982, 33–54.

Marcus, Steven. *The Other Victorians: A Study of Sexuality and Pornography in Mid-Nineteenth-Century England*. New York: Basic, 1974.

McClish, Mark Richard. "The Dependence of Manu's Seventh Chapter on Kauṭilya's *Arthaśāstra*." *Journal of the American Oriental Society* (2014), 241–62.

———. "Political Brahmanism and the State: A Compositional History of the *Arthaśastra*." PhD dissertation, University of Texas at Austin, 2009.

McConnaichie, James. *The Book of Love: In Search of the Kamasutra*. London: Atlantic, 2007.

Mishra, Pankaj. "Modi's Idea of India." *New York Times*, October 24, 2014, op ed page.

Monier-Williams, Sir Monier. *A Sanskrit-English Dictionary*. Revised edition. Oxford, UK: Oxford University Press, 1992.

Mukherjee, Mridula, and Aditya Mukherjee. "Communilisation of Education: The History Textbook Controversy; An Overview." Delhi Historians' Group, Delhi, August 5, 2001. Available at http://indiancultural forum.in/2017/01/14/history-textbooks-controversy/. Accessed July 17, 2017.

Naipaul, V. S. *Half a Life*. New York: Vintage, 2002.

Nanda, Meera. "Hindutva's Science Envy." *Frontline*, PBS, August 31, 2016.

———. *Science in Saffron: Skeptical Essays on History of Science.* Gurgaon: Three Essays Collective, 2016.

Nandy, Ashish. *The Intimate Enemy: Loss and Recovery of Self under Colonialism.* Delhi: Oxford University Press, 1987.

——— ed., *Science, Hegemony, and Violence: A Requiem for Modernity.* Delhi: Oxford University Press, 1987.

Nussbaum, Martha. "A Law against Dignity." *Indian Express,* December 27, 2013. Available at www.indianexpress.com/news/a-law-against-dignity/1212167/0. Accessed January 6, 2014.

Olivelle, Patrick. *Dharma: Studies in Its Semantic, Cultural, and Religious History.* Delhi: Motilal Banarsidass, 2009.

———. *A Dharma Reader: Classical Indian Law.* Trans. and ed. Patrick Olivelle. Historical Sourcebooks in Classical Indian Thought. New York: Columbia University Press, 2017.

———. *Dharmasūtras: The Law Codes of Ancient India.* Trans. Patrick Olivelle. New York: Oxford University Press, 1999.

———. "Kauṭilya's *Arthaśāstra*: A Very Short History." Unpublished essay, 2015.

———. *King, Governance, and Law in Ancient India: Kauṭilya's Arthaśāstra.* Trans. Patrick Olivelle. New York: Oxford University Press, 2013.

———. "Manu and the *Arthaśāstra*: A Study in Śāstric Intertextuality." *Journal of Indian Philosophy,* Vol. 32, No. 2/3 (June 2004), 2812–91.

———, ed. *Between the Empires: Society in India 300 BCE to 400 CE.* New York: Oxford University Press, 2006.

Penzer, Norman Mosley, and Somadeva Bhatt. *Poison-Damsels: Folklore of the World.* Manchester, NH: Ayer, 1980.

Pinney, Christopher. "Epistemo-patrimony: Speaking and Owning in the Indian Diaspora." *Journal of the Royal Anthropological Institute* (2001), 193–206.

Pollock, Sheldon. "The Idea of *Śāstra* in Traditional India." In *Śāstric Traditions in Indian Arts,* ed. Anna Libera Dallapiccola. Wiesbaden: Steiner, 1989, 17–26.

———. *The Language of the Gods in the World of Men: Sanskrit, Culture, and Power in Premodern India.* Berkeley: University of California Press, 2006.

———. "Playing by the Rules: *Śāstra* and Sanskrit Literature." In *Śāstric Traditions in Indian Arts,* ed. Anna Libera Dallapiccola. Wiesbaden: Steiner, 1989, 301–12.

———. See *Rāmāyaṇa.*

———. "The Theory of Practice and the Practice of Theory in Indian Intellectual History." *Journal of the American Orientalist Society,* Vol. 105 (1985), 499–591.

Prakash, Gyan. *Another Reason: Science and the Imagination of Modern India*. Princeton, NJ: Princeton University Press, 1999.

Raghavan, V. *Vimuktiḥ: A Two-Act Philosophical Farce with a Sanskrit Commentary*. Madras: Punarvasu (author's imprint), 1968. Originally published as "*Vimukti Prahasanam*," *Saṃskṛta Pratibhā*, Vol. 4, No. 2 (1964), 127–60.

Raja, Sharath. "Dissent in Ancient India." Unpublished essay, March 2014.

Randreas, Manga. *Charvaka Caritra: Tale of a Hindu Hedonist/Skeptic*. Bryn Mawr, PA: iUniverse, 1999.

Rangarajan, L. N. *Kauṭilya: The Arthaśāstra*. Trans. L. N. Rangarajan. New Delhi: Penguin, 1992.

Rhys-Davids, T. W. *Dialogues of the Buddha*. Vol. 2 of *The Sacred Books of the Buddhists*. London: H. Frowde, 1899.

———. *Ten Suttas from the Digha Nikaya*. Sarnath, Varanasi: Central Institute of Higher Tibetan Studies, 1987.

Rocher, Ludo. "The *Kāmasūtra*: Vātsyāyana's Attitude toward Dharma and Dharmaśāstra." *Journal of the American Oriental Society*, Vol. 105, No. 3 (July–September 1985, *Indological Studies Dedicated to Daniel H. H. Ingalls*), 521–29.

Roger, Abraham. *La porte ouverte, pour parvenir a la connaissance du paganisme caché*. Amsterdam: Jean Schipper, 1670.

Roy, Raja Ram Mohan. *Vedic Physics: Scientific Origin of Hinduism*. United States: Mount Meru, 1999, 2015.

Ruben, Walter. "Der Minister Jabali in Valmīki's *Rāmāyaṇa*." *Acta Antiqua Academiae Scientiarum Hungaricae*, Vol. 4 (1956), 355–63.

Saletore, Bhaskar Anand. "Historical Notices of the Lokāyatas." *Annals of the Bhandarkar Oriental Research Institute*, Vol. 23 (1942), 386–97.

Sarasvati, Dayanand. *The Light of Truth*. English translation of Svami Dayanand's *Satyārtha prakāśa*, with Sanskrit text and transliteration by Ganga Prasad Upadhyaya. Delhi: Govindram Hasanand, 2008.

Sattar, Arshia. *Uttara: The Book of Answers*. Delhi: Penguin Books, 2016.

Schmidt, Richard. *Das Kamasutram: Die indische Ars Amatoria; Nebst dem vollständigen Commentare (Jayamangala) des Yasodhara*. Aus dem Sanskrit übersetzt und hrsg. von Richard Schmidt. Leipzig: Wilhelm Friedrich, 1900.

Schoff, Wilfred H., trans. and ed. *The Periplus of the Erythraean Sea: Travel and Trade in the Indian Ocean by a Merchant of the First Century*. New Delhi: Munshi Ram Manohar Lal, 1974.

Scott, James A. *Domination and the Arts of Resistance: Hidden Transcripts*. New Haven, CT: Yale University Press, 1990.

———. *Weapons of the Weak: Everyday Forms of Peasant Resistance*. New Haven, CT: Yale University Press, 1985.

Sen, Amartya. *The Argumentative Indian: Writings on Indian History, Culture, and Identity.* New York: Farrar, Straus and Giroux, 2005.

Sharma, Ritu. "Science Lesson from Gujarat: Stem Cells in Mahabharata, Cars in Veda; *Tejomay Bharat* Is to Be Distributed along with Eight Books Written by Dina Nath Batra." *Indian Express* (Ahmedabad), updated July 27, 2014, 1:35 pm.

Srinivas, M. N. *Social Change in Modern India.* Berkeley: University of California Press, 1966.

Steinkellner, Ernst. "Die Literatur des Alteren Nyaya." *Wiener Zeitschrift* (1961), 149–62.

Taylor, McComas. *The Fall of the Indigo Jackal: The Discourse of Division and Pūrṇabhandra's Pañcatantra.* Albany: State University of New York Press, 2007.

Thapar, Romila. *Early India: From the Origins to 1300.* London: Penguin, 2002; Berkeley: University of California Press, 2004.

Thomas, F. W. *Brihaspati Sutra.* Lahore: The Punjab Sanskrit Book Depot, 1916; reprinted 1921.

Tieken, Herman. "The *Arthaśāstra* as a Fount of Fun." *Journal of the Rashtriya Sanskrit Sansthan. Sanskrit Vimarsha,* Vol. 6: World Sanskrit Conference Special, 2012, 113–20.

Trautmann, Thomas R. *Kauṭilya and the Arthaśāstra: A Statistical Investigation of the Authorship and Evolution of the Text.* Leiden: Brill, 1971.

———. "A Metrical Original for the Kauṭilīya *Arthaśāstra?,*" *Journal of the American Oriental Society,* Vol. 88, No. 2 (April–June, 1968), 347–49.

Varma, Keshav Dev. *Vedic Physics: Toward Unification of Quantum Mechanics and General Relativity.* Delhi: Motilal Banarsidass, 2015.

Warder, A. K. *Outlines of Indian Philosophy.* Delhi: Motilal Banarsidass, 1971.

Warner, Marina. *Stranger Magic: Charmed States and the Arabian Nights.* New York: Belknap, 2012.

Weber, Max. *Politics as a Vocation.* Munich: Duncker and Humboldt, 1919.

Wedemeyer, Christian. *Making Sense of Tantric Buddhism: History, Semiology, and Transgression in the Indian Traditions.* New York: Columbia University Press, 2014.

Werner, Karel. Review of Eli Franco, *Perception, Knowledge and Disbelief. Bulletin of the School of Oriental and African Studies,* University of London, Vol. 58, No. 3 (1995), 578.

Wezler, Albrecht. "Some Remarks on the Final Verses of the Kāmasūtra." In *Indian Linguistic Studies: Festschrift in Honor of George Cardona,* ed. Madhav M. Deshpande and Peter E. Cook. Delhi: Motilal Banarsidass, 2002, 315–43.

White, David. *Sinister Yogis.* Chicago: University of Chicago Press, 2009.

Wilhelm, Friedrich. "The Concept of Dharma in Artha and Kama Literature."
    In *The Concept of Duty in South Asia,* ed. Wendy Doniger (O'Flaherty)
    and J. Duncan Derett. New Delhi: Vikas, 1978, 66–79.

——. "Das Beziehungen zwischen *Kāmasūtra* und *Arthaśāstra.*" *Zeitschrift
    der Deutschen Morgenländischen Gesellschaft,* Vol. 116 (1966), 291–310.

——. *Politische Polemiken im Staatslehrbuch des Kauṭalya.* Wiesbaden:
    Otto Harrassowitz, 1960.

——. "The Quotations in the *Kāmasūtra* of Vātsyāyana." In the *L. Stern-
    bach Felicitation,* Vol. 1: *Indologica Taurinensia* 7, 1979, 401–12.

Winternitz, Moriz. *Geschichte der indischen Litteratur,* Vol. 3. Leipzig: Ame-
    lang, 1920.

——. *History of Indian Literature,* Vol. 3, trans. Subhadra Jha. Delhi: Moti-
    lal Banarsidass, 1967.

Yaśodhara. See *Kāmasūtra.*

Index